ALEXANDER MASTERS' first book, *Stuart: A Life Backwards*, won the Guardian First Book Award, the Hawthornden Prize and was shortlisted for the Samuel Johnson Prize and the Costa Biography Prize. Eighteen different newspapers and popular magazines chose it as Book of the Year. It was turned into a BBC film starring Tom Hardy and Benedict Cumberbatch. His second book, *The Genius in my Basement*, received rave reviews that compared his work to Kurt Vonnegut and Italo Calvino, and his third, *A Life Discarded: 148 Diaries Found in a Skip*, was compared to Paul Auster, Alan Bennett and Barbara Pym. Alexander lives in Sussex.

By the same author

The Genius in My Basement
A Life Discarded: 148 Diaries Found in a Skip

St Helens College

Library

Water Street, St. Helens, Merseyside, WA10 1PP

TEL: 01744 623 256

This book is due for return on or before the last date shown below.

4th Estate
An imprint of HarperCollins*Publishers*
1 London Bridge Street
London SE1 9GF
www.4thEstate.co.uk

This 4th Estate Matchbook Classics edition published 2019
1

First published in Great Britain by 4th Estate in 2005
Published in paperback by HarperPerennial in 2006 and
4th Estate in 2011

Copyright © Alexander Masters 2005

All drawings (except p. 111) by the author

Alexander Masters asserts the moral right to
be identified as the author of this work

A catalogue record for this book
is available from the British Library

ISBN 978-0-00-832972-3

Printed by ScandBook in EU

MIX
Paper from
responsible sources
FSC® C021394

This book is produced from independently certified FSC® paper
to ensure responsible forest management.

For more information visit: www.harpercollins.co.uk/green

For my father, Dexter Masters

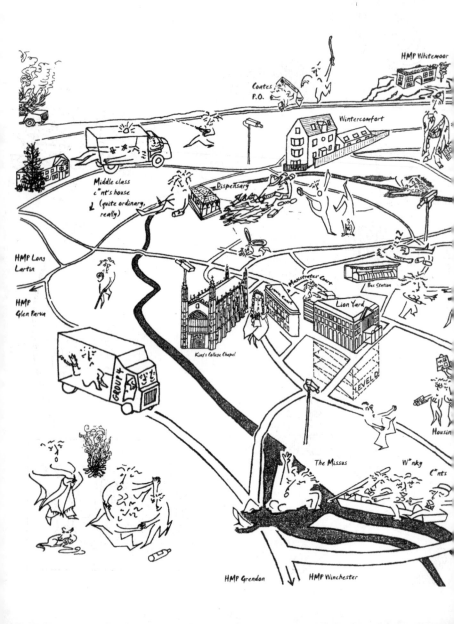

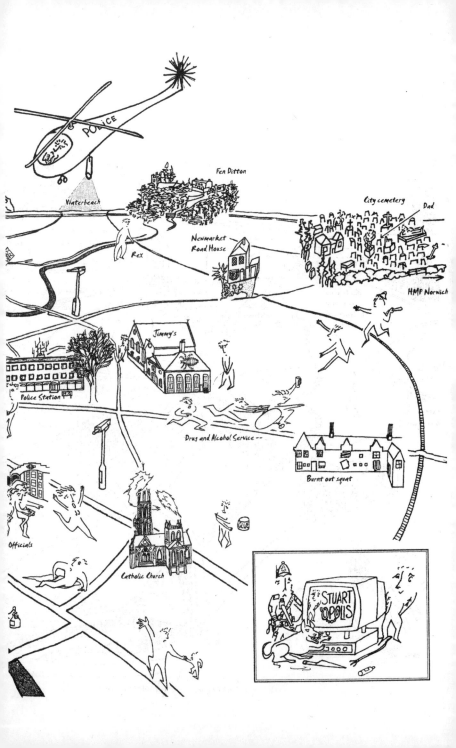

'Alexander, sort it out – you're the writer.
I just done the living.'

Stuart Shorter

0

Stuart does not like the manuscript.

Through the pale Tesco stripes of his supermarket bag I can see the wedge of my papers. Two years' worth of interviews and literary effort.

'What's the matter with it?'

'It's bollocks boring.'

He fumbles in the lumpy bulges of his pockets, looking for roll-up papers, then drops into my armchair and pushes his face forward, surveying the drab collection of twigs and dead summertime experiments on my balcony. One arm remains, as it landed, squeezed in beside his thigh. Outside, it is getting dark; the trees in the garden have started to grow in size and lose their untended shapes.

'I don't mean to be rude. I know you put a lot of work in,' Stuart offers.

Put briefly, his objection is this: I drone on.

He wants jokes, yarns, humour. He doesn't admire 'academic quotes' and background research. 'Nah, Alexander, you gotta start again. You gotta do better than this.'

He's after a bestseller, 'like what Tom Clancy writes'.

'But you are not an assassin trying to frazzle the president with anthrax bombs,' I point out. You are an ex-homeless, ex-junkie psychopath, I do not add.

Stuart phrases it another way, then: 'Something what people will *read*.'

There are numerous types of homeless person:

There are those who were doing all right beforehand, but have suffered a temporary setback because their wife has run off with another man (or, surprisingly often, another woman). Their business may have collapsed. Their daughter has been killed in a car crash. Or both. Self-confidence is their main problem and, if the professionals can get hold of them in the first few months, they'll be back at work or at least in settled, long-term accommodation within a year or two.

Men outnumber women ten to one on the streets. For women, it is usually sex or battering or madness that has brought them to this condition. They are better at coping with financial failure and betrayal, or their expectations are more self-effacing.

Then there are the ones who suffer from chronic poverty, brought on by illiteracy or social ineptness or what are politely called 'learning disabilities'. Perhaps they are dyslexic, autistic, shy to the point of inanity, never went to school. They may be just ill or blind or deaf or dumb. They move from garden shed to bedsit, shelter to hostel to garage to friend's sitting-room floor, to the wheelie bins at the side of King's College. They are never quite able to rise above their circumstances.

The youngsters who have fallen out with their parents, or have come out of care and don't know what to do next or even how to make their own breakfast: they're a third homeless category. If they haven't, within six months, found a job or a room or a girlfriend to put them to rights, there's a good chance they'll be on the streets instead.

Ex-convicts and ex-army – take away the format of their lives and all they can do is crumple downwards. This is just the beginning.

Right at the bottom of this abnormal heap are the people such as Stuart, the 'chaotic' homeless. The chaotic ('kai-yo-ic', as Stuart calls them, drawing out the syllables around his tongue like chewing gum) are beyond repair. When Stuart was first discovered, Kaspar Hauser-like, crouched on the lowest subterranean floor of a multi-storey car park, the regular homeless

One arm remains, as it landed, squeezed in beside his thigh.

wanted nothing to do with him. They called him 'Knife Man Dan' and 'that mad bastard on Level D'.

The chaotic have usually been to prison, but they are not career criminals. Stuart's conviction sheet is twenty pages thick, but he has only once stolen to make himself rich and on that ridiculous occasion he scooped (after taking overheads into account) £500, or £100 for each year he spent behind bars as a result. Among the few staples in a chaotic person's life are heroin and alcohol. For some their habit is what has brought them low, while for others addiction is like a hobby taken up since arriving. The chaotic are not always poor, even if they are on the streets. During the three years I have known Stuart, my income has rarely exceeded his from the state. An unemployed man with a physical or mental disability, or alcohol or drugs dependence, can qualify for up to £180 a week from social services. On top of this, housing benefit pays the rent.

What unites the chaotic is the confusion of their days. Cause and effect are not connected in the usual way. Beyond their own governance, let alone within grasp of ours, they are constantly on the brink of raring up or breaking down. Charity staff fuss especially hard over these people because they are the worst face of homelessness and, when not the most hateful, the most pitiable extremity of street life.

Two years ago, Stuart was living out of skips. When the city outreach workers discovered him, he was a polydrug-addicted, alcoholic, 'Jekyll and Hyde' personality with delusional paranoia and a fondness for what he called 'little strips of silver' – knives, to you and me.

He still is.

But something remarkable has happened since then: he is not quite so much of a drug-addicted nightmare. No one can understand it. It is highly unusual, suspicious even. All chaotic people have good and bad periods, but Stuart genuinely appears to have turned over a new leaf. He has separated himself from the street community, got himself on to the council housing

list, started a methadone programme to get off heroin, renegoti-
ated his court fines and begun paying fortnightly instalments,
bought himself a discount computer. None of this is normal.
Many of Stuart's old friends would rather die than take a shower
and pay debts, and quite a few do: overdoses, liver or kidney
failure or both, hypothermia. Rough sleepers have a life expect-
ancy of forty-two years. They are thirty-five times more likely
to commit suicide than the rest of the population. In the great
bureaucracy of the police and social support services, everyone
is patting their backs at Stuart's extraordinary return from this
medieval existence towards respectability and secretly waiting
for him to grab the nearest meat hook and run amok.

Furthermore, not only has Stuart enough undestroyed brain
cells left to describe what such a life is like, but he can pinpoint,
almost to the hour – between 4 and 5 p.m., one weekday in early
summer, when he was twelve – the symbolic moment when he
made the change from (in his mother's words) a 'real happy-go-
lucky little boy', always 'the considerate, very considerate' one
of her two children, into the nightmare *Clockwork Orange* figure
of the last two decades. If his own life were not still so dis-
ordered, he could make good money explaining to parents what
makes children turn into authority-despising delinquents.

'This is what I don't like, Alexander,' observes Stuart, interrupting my thoughts and picking out a page from the dog-eared
manuscript that he has now tipped on the floor. 'Joyriding.' It
concerns his adolescence, when he used to sneak around streets
at night smashing the windows of Ford Cortinas. I have opined:

> Technically, joyriding does not involve stealing a car,
> because the person who takes the vehicle doesn't intend to
> keep it: he 'twocs' it. It's an acronym that comes from the
> charge: *t*aking a vehicle *w*ithout the *o*wner's *c*onsent. In the
> *Juvenile Joyrider*,* Jeff Briggs proposes, in addition to theft

* Jeff Briggs, 'A Profile of the Juvenile Joyrider, and a consideration of the efficacy
of motor vehicle projects as a diversionary strategy', extract of MA Thesis, University of Durham, 1991.

of a car's contents, five different categories of car crime: a) 'twocking for profit', b) 'long-term twocking', c) 'twocking for the purposes of joyriding', d) 'twocking for use in other crimes' and e) 'utilitarian twocking'. To date, Stuart has been guilty of c), d) and e).

'Uty-*what*?' Stuart sucks in his cheeks for a final attempt. '"Uty-lity-aryan twocking." What's that when it's at home?'

I cut the passage.

The accompanying flow chart, entitled 'Dr Kirkpatrick's Joyrider-Progression Schematic', he dismisses with: 'Looks like an Airfix kit.'

He knows about Airfix toy-aeroplane kits: he used to sniff the tubes of glue from them.

'*Kilpatrick hypothesises that joyriding guides children into delinquency for the sake of interest, then delinquency for the sake of profit, and then adult crime,*' I see that I have written. '*It is one of the conduits of corruption, from innocence to criminality.*'

Stuart does not bother to comment on this one.

'And another thing . . .' he says.

'Yes?' I sigh.

'Do it the other way round. Make it more like a murder mystery. What murdered the boy I was? See? Write it backwards.'

So here it is, my second attempt at the story of Stuart Shorter, thief, hostage taker, psycho and sociopathic street raconteur, my spy on how the British chaotic underclass spend their troubled days at the beginning of the twenty-first century: a man with an important life.

I wish I could have done it more quickly. I wish I could have presented it to Stuart before he stepped in front of the 11.15 London to King's Lynn train.

1

'It was cutting me throat what got me this flat.'

Stuart pushes open the second reinforced door into his corridor, turns off the blasting intercom that honks like a foghorn whenever a visitor presses his front bell, and bumps into his kitchen to sniff the milk. 'Tea or coffee, Alexander?'

He is a short man, in his early thirties, and props himself against the sink to arch up his head and show me the damage. The scar extends like a squashed worm from beneath the tattoos on one ear to above his Adam's apple.

The kettle lead is discovered beneath a pack of sodden fish fingers. 'How about a sarnie? Yes?'

Stuart stretches his hand to the other end of the kitchen, extracts a double pack of discount economy bacon from the fridge and submerges six slices in chip-frying oil. 'Cooked or incinerated?'

It is a cramped, dank little apartment. One room, ground floor. The window looks across a scrappy patch of grass to a hostel for disturbed women.

'One of the few times I've been happy happy, the day I got this flat,' Stuart smiles at me. 'That's why I want you to write a book. It's me way of telling the people what it was like down there. I want to thank them what got me out, like Linda and Denis and John and Ruth and Wynn, and me mum, me sister and me dad, well, I call him me dad, but he's me stepdad, if truth be told.'

The bread starts to burn. Stuart pumps the toaster release and the slices fly high into the air.

'Cos there's so much misunderstanding,' he concludes angrily. 'It's killing people. Your fucking nine to fives! Someone needs to tell them! Literally, every day, deaths! Each one of them deaths is somebody's son or daughter! Somebody needs to tell them, tell them like it *is*!'

I move into the main room. There is a single bed in the corner, a chest of drawers, a desk – sparse, cheap furniture, bought with the help of a government loan. Also, a comfy chair. I drop into it. It is not comfortable at all. I flop on to the sofa instead. A 1950s veneer side cabinet, with bottles and pill cases on top, is against the inside wall, and in the corner a big-screen TV standing on an Argos antique-style support.

Stuart likes his TV. He has thrown it at the wall twice and it still works.

In return for a crate of Foster's, Stuart explains from the kitchen, 'the bloke upstairs has promised to make me a James Bond mattress base that folds up against the wall, which will give me more room. It'll have big springs on either side what does the moving, and latches on the floor, because otherwise, it's boing, boing, whoosh.'

'Boing, boing, whoosh?'

'Well, a bird's not going to be too happy if she suddenly finds her face squeezed against the plaster, is she?'

Another friend is going to put up shelves, partition off the kitchen and repaint the walls gold, instead of green on the bottom half, cream above, as they are at the moment, like a mental institution.

The man in the bedsit above is a cyclist – a short, bespectacled Scotsman whose legs hardly touch the pedals; next to him a mute woman who beats out chart tunes on the floor with her shoe heel; and on the other side of the entrance lobby, Sankey, son of an RAF pilot – he sleeps with an aluminium baseball bat beside his bed.

The only problem Stuart has in his desirable new home is mould. It prickles up the bathroom wall and creeps across the ceiling in speckled clumps, so that he has to stand on a chair and scrub it back once a month as though he were stripping paint. Now and then it floats down the hall to his bed side and his clothes; he smells like a garden shed on those days.

'By the way,' he calls out, 'I'm thinking of sticking a reflective sheet over that window. What d'you reckon?'

'It's dark enough in here as it is – why make it even darker?'

'It's to stop them spying on me.'

'Don't be silly. No one's spying on you. Who's them?'

'I've seen them but not seen them, if you know what I mean. Red sauce or brown?'

He is also going to block up the air vent above the freezer because there could be microphones secreted between the slats. 'Not being funny, you got to think about these things when you're redecorating.'

Stuart has also had a 'brilliant' idea for a job. If it works, it will be the first honest work he's been able to hold down in his life. New flat, new job, new Stuart. Already he has signed himself up for an IT course.

'Think about it, right? For the foreign businessman what hasn't got time to waste, what's he need? An office! In a van! It's lateral thinking, isn't it? Gets off the plane at Stansted, straight in the back of me van and I drive him to meetings. No time wasted, see? It'll have everythink, this van. Good-looking bird – one what can do shorthand – fax, Internet, mobile phone. His own office, just for the journey. Wires all over the fucking gaff. Brilliant!'

In the centre of Stuart's table is a brown folder with his purple handwriting on it:

THEORY DriViNG
QueSTiOn'S & PRATCIL HELP

A moment later, Stuart is at the desk himself. He has remembered an important engagement with an Internet-savvy friend, and now has his diary out of its home-made plastic wallet and pressed against the table.

In order to keep track of his newly busy life, Stuart has devised a special colour-coding for this book: green highlighter for family, yellow for social, orange for duty. His handwriting is not excellent. Even when there's only one word to be got down, he sometimes begins his gigantic letters too far across the line and has to pack the end into a pea-size, as if the letters had bunched up in fright at the thought of dropping off the page. At other times the phrases are neat and slow. His spelling is part phonetic, part cap-doffing guesswork: 'Monday: ADDanBRocK's.' 'Tuesday: QuiSt going to Vist VoLanteR service's. ASK for NAME & ADReSS For AwarD organation.'

March: SAT'S LOTTO 5 10 17 20 44 48
7.30 Cam. 2 meeting Bath House if not Brambram.

April: Phone to DR P——. CAnCell if in court.
2OCLOCK go TO ALEXDER'S BooK must go ScriPt PicK ~~200~~ 100.

May: MuSic FesTervile.
STUART LOOK ——▶ SET ALRAM.
MAKE SURE ALRaM
Button is up not Down. When WeaK up is needed.

'I still don't know me alphabet,' he calls out blithely. 'First place I get stuck is N. I only remember the S, T, U bit because it's me name, Stu.'

Pages stiff with Tipp-Ex in his diary indicate appointments made too far ahead, subsequently cancelled, because events take place with startling swiftness in Stuart's life and he can never be certain that, though happy and full of plans on Monday, he won't be in prison, or in hospital, by Friday.

'ADDanBRocK's' is Addenbrooke's, the hospital complex of beds, smoke stacks and research departments on the edge of Cambridge; it looks over the wheat fields and the train line to London, like a crematorium. 'Brambram' is Babraham, a village three miles outside Cambridge. You'd think he could get at least that one right: he's been a local boy all his life. 'When WeaK up is needed'? Who knows what that means. 'ScriPt PicK 200 100' refers to his methadone prescription. 100 ml is high. Between 60 and 80 ml is the average for street addicts. 200? In his dreams.

'ALEXDER'. That's me. In speech, Stuart is careful to give my name its full four syllables. But in writing, he always drops the third syllable: not Alex, but Alexder.

Stuart's backwards inspiration has turned out to be excellent. At a swoop, it has solved the major problem of writing a biography of a man who is not famous. Even with a well-known person it can be boring work to spend the first fifty pages reading facts and guesses about Grandpa, Granny, Mum, Dad, subject aged one, two, three, seven, eight. But introduce Stuart to readers as he is now, a fully-fledged gawd-help-us, and he may just grab their interest straight away. By the time they reach his childhood, it is a matter of genuine interest how he turned into the person that he is. So we'll move backwards, in stages, tacking like a sailboat against the wind. Familiar time flow – out the window. Homogeneous mood of reflectiveness – up in smoke. This way, an air of disruption from the start.

Will it work? Can a person's history be broken up? Isn't a life the sum of its pasts? Perhaps Stuart's approach is possible only with Stuart, whose sense of existence is already broken into fragments.

At long last, the sarnies arrive, drippling marge and ketchup, the top slice of bread moulded into the shape of Stuart's palm.

Stuart Clive Shorter – the first time I saw him, in 1998, he was pressed in a doorway next to the discount picture-framing shop, round the corner from Sidney Sussex College in Cambridge. He had an oddly twisted way of sitting on his square of cardboard, as if his limbs were half made of rubber. Pasty skin, green bomber jacket, broken gym shoes, hair cropped to the scalp and a week's worth of stubble; his face, the left side livelier than the right, was almost mongoloid. Several of his teeth were missing; his mouth was a sluice.

I had to get down on my knees to hear him speak.

'As soon as I get the opportunity I'm going to top meself,' he whispered.

He picked at the sole of his gym shoes. The tattoos on his hands were home-made. A huge 'FUCK' began on his bicep, right arm, and ended just above his cuff.

'Yeah, I'm gonna top meself and it's got to seem like someone else done it. Look, if you're not going to give me money, do you mind moving on?'

The legs of Christmas shoppers and delayed businessmen hurried beside us. Clip, clop, clip, clop – a pair of high heels rushed past, sounding like a horse. It was, it struck me, comforting to be at this level: a two-foot-high world, shared with dogs and children. Adult noises dropped down with the context of the conversation missing and sibilants exaggerated. The smell of street grime, the wind and hot underwear of passers-by, was not unpleasant, rather like salami. Someone stooped and dropped a coin; another person threw across a box of matches. A third declared he would buy a sandwich, but 'I won't donate money. You'll only spend it on drink and drugs.' Stuart opted for bacon and cheese.

On Christmas Eve a beggar can earn £70–120 in Cambridge.

'But how are you going to make suicide look like murder?' I asked.

'I'll taunt all the drunk fellas coming out the pub until they have to kill me if they want a bit of peace.' He slurred; it was

I had to get down on my knees to hear him speak.

as if the words had got entangled in his lips. 'Me brother killed himself in May. I couldn't put me mum through that again. She wouldn't mind murder so much.'

2

'Gotta have shuume tea! Buncha cunts! I'll fuuughck-ing do you all in! Gimme me fuuughcking tea!'

Among the odds and ends of jobs I did during that year, after I first met Stuart begging by Sidney Sussex, was part-time fund-raising assistant at Wintercomfort, a rough sleepers' day centre in Cambridge. My brief was to find benefactors, make trust applications, write the lesser press releases and produce an erratic newsletter. This was not an altruistic job for me: I did it for the money. (£9 an hour, more than I have earned ever since.) I worked in an attic room, out of reach of the beer-sloshing rabble three floors below and, with a bit of luck, if I arrived early enough I could get through the gate, past the art group's paintings of hallucinogenic mushrooms, and up the stairs to my office without encountering a single one of the 'clients'.

On this day, however, something was wrong.

'Fuuuccking tosshhers, open up!' burbled the blotchy-faced drunk toppled against the front door. His face came attached to a grizzled beard; a finger jabbed at the reinforced glass. 'What you fuccchking cloasshh-ed for? Gimme me fuucchhking tea!'

I slipped in the staff entrance and stared through to the dining hall. The man had a point. At this time of day it should have been open and full of fifty fellow smackheads, crackheads, psychotics, epileptics, schizophrenics, self-harmers, beggars, buskers, car thieves, sherry pushers, ciderheads, just-released-that-morning convicts, ex-army, ex-married-men-with-young-children-who'd-discovered-their-wife-in-bed-with-two-members-of-the-university-rowing-team-*at-the-same-time*. Out in the courtyard would be the merry sound of baying knee-high dogs with names like PayDay and Giro and Dregs.

Instead, the hall was empty. Blotchy was abusing a deserted room. I daringly let myself in and looked through to the blue glow of the kitchen; not even Sue, the indomitable cook, was at work. The industrial fridge and fly-killer tubes droned gently, like ship engines. The only human sound was the new secretary from North Dakota, tapping away in one of the upstairs rooms.

Wintercomfort was a good organisation. Set up in 1989 by a local businessman horrified at the number of people he saw sleeping in doorways when he walked back home from work, it was fresh and crusading and full of pep. Wintercomfort excelled at the job no one else wanted to do – acting as a last safety net for the worst street cases, calming the most violent, soothing the suicidal, comforting those about to be sectioned in the desolate wards of 'Hospital Town', encouraging the hopeful and the full-of-plans and cleaning up Cambridge. By giving the homeless a supportive place to go during the day, it meant they were less frustrated, less bored, less desperate and hence less often blocking up the pavement and less anti-social.

But today everyone had vanished. I crept out of the dining hall as if I were the thief, and the intruder, and the pariah, and up the stairs.

The secretary, pale and shaken, not yet one month into the job, explained what had happened. Yesterday, the police had raided. Six cars and vans had banged to a stop on the pavement outside; six car- and vanloads of men and women in uniforms and crackling radios had shouldered their way in, spreading out through the dining hall, arresting left and right, then surging up to the admin and outreach and funding departments, separating staff into empty rooms, refusing to answer questions, demanding statements. Even she, with the breeze of North Dakota still in her hair, had had to give one.

That afternoon, the police had arrested the director, Ruth Wyner, on suspicion of 'knowingly allowing' the supply of heroin.

A week later, they would take in her deputy John Brock as well.

For the last five months, among the roof tiles of Christ's College boathouse across the road – halfway down, and three feet in – a tiny surveillance camera poking through the tiles had been filming the charity premises. In the Wintercomfort forecourts, eight people had been clearly recorded selling each other £10 bags of heroin.

Downstairs, I could hear the drunk running out of steam. 'Fuuaarkeeeen tttsssseeeee. Yoouh, fuuaarkeen gimmuuheee!' His lips slid up and down the glass in a smear of spittle, but he perked up when he saw me approaching. 'Bout fuccking time! Where you been? It's me fucking right to have me tea! I exschpect you to stay open later now, to fucking make up for it!'

I wrenched open the door. Ruth and John were kind, good, thoughtful people, passionately concerned about the welfare of the impoverished and the disenfranchised.

'Fuck off, pisshead!' I said.

The charity held an open meeting: wine in stemmed glasses, colourful things on crackers called – in the playful, roundy typeface of the poster – 'nibbles'. The charity governors, the charity's friends, the volunteers, neighbours. Everyone tinkled around the homeless dining hall.

A former Labour Cambridge mayor, a no-nonsense political bruiser, called the gathering to silence. 'Order, order, ORDER! WILL YOU *PLEASE* BE QUIET!'

She then began the process that would end up taking the next year of my life: she started to turn us into a protest movement. I felt, everyone in that room of pretty wine glasses

felt, appalled and personally affronted. The arrests of Ruth and
John were no longer just a matter of helping the less fortunate.
They had been an attack on Us. This was the closest most of
us had come to feeling what it was like to be treated with public
loathing. With shock, we realised we now had something in
common with the homeless. How dare the police, the Crown
Prosecution Service, the Home Office.

Indeed, their anti-drugs policy was regarded by many as a
model of good practice. The judge himself, at the trial, had
admitted there was no suggestion that Ruth or John or any
other member of the Wintercomfort staff had in any way been
involved in the deals that had been filmed. There was also no
evidence to show that either Ruth or John had ever seen any
deal and not immediately done something to stop it. In fact,
when Ruth or John rang the police to get them to remove a
suspected dealer from the premises, the police had often not
even bothered to show up. They also did not turn up, though
invited, to charity drugs policy meetings.

Ruth and John's crime was, in effect, twofold: first, that their
anti-drugs policy had not been successful; second, that they had
disagreed with the police about the best way to make it better.
The second aspect centred around their policy of confidentiality towards their clients, a policy regarded as essential to getting these peculiar, suspicious and often violent people's trust
so that they could be encouraged to face their addiction, take
advantage of public services and come *off* drugs, *stop* begging,
give up the streets and leave the rest of us law-abiders alone.
Ruth and John – but particularly Ruth, as boss – had refused
to give to the police the names of people they had banned from
the premises for suspected drug use, which was often based
on little more than an overheard conversation or a suspicious
gesture near the downstairs toilets. This, the judge and jury,
who never visited Wintercomfort, had dismissed as being nothing more than a deliberate scam to prevent police getting in-
criminating evidence.

The open meeting was being held today because yesterday Ruth and John had been sentenced.

John had been given four years in prison; Ruth, five.

A hundred wonderful ideas swirled around that meeting hall: demonstrations, vigils, international tribunals, questions for Parliament, a banner on Canary Wharf, a picket of homeless people outside the House of Commons, endless letters to *The Times*. Relieved by the purity of our purpose, we let rip.

'Everyone running homeless charities must present themselves to the police and demand to be arrested,' announced one humorous man, who ran such a charity himself. 'If Ruth and John are guilty then so is everyone else. It is a crime for us to remain free!'

'That's elitist!' snapped back a Socialist Worker, dressed in solid black. 'Why should you be allowed to get arrested when the rest of us can't?'

My two favourite ideas were sinking the Cambridge boat at the Oxford–Cambridge boat race and a march of homeless people on Number 10 (the big trouble with this, I realised, would be to keep the marchers from ambling off down irrelevant side streets, falling in the Thames, etc., but I figured you could probably coax them into a reasonable line by driving a vanload of Special Brew cans in front, just out of reach).

A lady with a silk headscarf observed wisely that as the undercover operation had also depended on two officers dressing up as tramps and buying heroin from dealers during lunch – a subsidised meal of spaghetti and meatballs, which, in order to lend verisimilitude to their plot, the officers had shared – the police could be sued for defrauding the charity.

The bursar of St John's College – lawyer, mathematician, former Conservative mayor of the city – wondered about sending writing paper to Ruth and John: was it better to put it in

the post sealed, in bundles of three pads, or unsealed, in single
sheets?

Another lady suggested throwing stones at the judge's windows. But each idea ended in the discovery that words are just words and jail bars are made of metal.

Everyone agreed that we must send Ruth and John dozens of books to keep them occupied until we got them out – as we *surely* would.

It was at this point that a soft voice, vaguely familiar to me, butted in from the front row.

'Excuse me, but that won't work.'

The green bomber jacket struck a chord, too.

'Why not?' demanded our chairwoman.

'They won't fit in the box.'

'Box?'

'For the inmate's belongings. Alright, in Whitemoor and Long Lartin, in them top-security jails, you're also allowed a piece of carpet, what don't fit in the box, and a budgie or a canary, and obviously the cage ain't going to fit in the box. Books won't fit in the box. The screws'll chuck 'em out.'

It was Psycho. Knife Man Dan. Stuart Shorter. Wearing the same clothes as when I'd first seen him round the corner from Sainsbury's, a year before.

'So each inmate has a box?' someone asked.

'Two boxes. One in possession and one in reception. I'm not being funny, but you should know about boxes if you're going to have a campaign.'

The most important thing we could do, he persevered, was write letters, send stamps, and not expect to get replies. Letters go missing. Depression comes.

Stuart stood as he was talking. The chairwoman demanded it, and it appeared to cause him a little trouble to find his balance. He was about five foot six, bow-legged and anaemic. His hands he kept shoved in his jacket pockets like a man on the sidelines during a cold football match. He raised his voice for a few words when people at the back called out 'Louder!' 'Speak up!' then forgot himself and lapsed back into his regular murmur. But he would not stop talking. It was as though, having tasted at last what lack of diffidence was like, he was determined not to lose a single second of the pleasure.

'Don't expect the visits to go well, neither. See, because visits is only two hours every two weeks, when you're a prisoner you build yourself up to such a pitch that when the visit comes it can't go right. It's not –' directing himself at John's wife – 'that he don't love you, it's just that visits is all what you live for when you're inside.'

'Because if most men are true,' he observed a moment later, 'when they go back to their cells that's when you know the loneliness. You can't take it. You know the loss.'

And about the stone throwing, Stuart was adamant. 'I understand the old dear there is feeling rageous, but prison is all about having privileges and taking them away. If you break the judge's windows it's Ruth and John what will suffer.'

'How can they suffer more?' an indignant man called out. 'They've taken away their freedom and their dignity, what else is left?'

'Their wages,' replied Stuart.

A silence.

Then a bemused female voice from the other side of the room: 'Prisoners get *wages*?'

3

In the top drawer of Stuart's large office desk are his legal drugs.

'Yeah, feel free,' he calls out from the kitchen, where he's dumped the sarnie plates into the sink among the tea mugs and is battling with a six-pack of Stella.

I hold up a grey plastic tube. All the substances he takes appear to cause him problems.

'Chlorpromazine. Cabbages you. It's also called Largactil. Heard of it? No? The liquid cosh? Well, they gave it me a lot in the kids' homes. Used to put me in a wheelchair in them days.'

'Why do you take it at all?' I wonder and place the tube back in his collection.

'Nah – it's just another anti-psychotic. The side effects are that it leaves a nasty taste in your mouth.'

Stuart reels off the names of his medications like a classics scholar. 'Ophenidrine. A mate of mine what was looking on the Internet said he found Saddam Hussein used it for tactical military weapons. Zopiclone, what calms you; I've also been on drugs like Melarill, what are banned now, amitriptyline, pain-killer, which *gives* you muscle spasms. Mad, in'it? At the minute I'm only on diazepam, which is Valium. It's a well-known fact that alcohol and diazepam don't mix, and they know I drink.'

'They' is shorthand for doctors, social workers, drug advisers and policemen, although in this case it is balanced against one doctor in particular whom he is convinced is out to ignore his interests. One of the things that intrigues me about Stuart is his categorisation of his enemies. The biggest foe is 'the System', the amorphous body of government-funded institutions that has chased him about like a bad rain cloud ever since he was twelve years old. All homeless people hate the System, even though many of its organisations – housing benefit, social security, the rough sleepers unit, dozens of charities – have been set up especially to make their lives easier. To Stuart these supportive bodies prove the essential duplicity of the System. What the person with a house might consider to be an admirable carrot-and-stick approach to making the homeless return to 'mainstream' society (the encouragement of welfare payments, back-to-work schemes, subsidised housing, backed up, for those who don't cooperate, by the threat of the police and prison time) is looked at quite differently by Stuart. It is an approach that patronises you at one end and swipes you raw at the other. For many homeless, the reason they've ended up on the streets is precisely because this carrot-and-stick tactic has, in their case, got into a jumble. The government network of organisations that offers them dole cheques, a free health service and endless numbers of worried social workers, also puts them into a home with rampant paedophiles (unwittingly, maybe, but what does that signify when you're fourteen years old with 'a grown man's dick down your throat'?) and then beats them up under the guise of 'tough love' in quasi-military youth detention centres whenever they do something wrong themselves.

The System is to Stuart a bit like the Market is to economists: unpredictable, unreliable, ruthless, operating in a haze of sanctimonious self-justification, and almost human.

The closest Stuart gets to giving the System a face is through the doctors, drug advisers, housing support officers and outreach workers with whom he deals directly. Although he is generally friendly to this little army of helpers, he respects almost none of them. When they are good, he talks about them as possible friends; when they are disappointing (which is frequently, because they are, after all, just people), they become another piece of evidence against the System. Even one or two of the police he likes now and then.

At the moment Stuart is banging on about doctors. 'Last Monday, my sister and me girlfriend were really worried because I'd gone doolally. Lost it. But my GP refused to even speak to them. They went up to him and said, "Look we're really concerned about his safety. He's got something tied round his neck, I'm not sure what it is, and he's got knives all over the bed." But he refused to see me. I thought that was really fucking rude!'

Recently, I asked Linda Bendall, one of the homelessness workers who helped Stuart when he was sleeping outside, 'Why Stuart? Why did he make it off the streets when so many others have tried and failed?'

'He is one of the rare ones. When I first met him he was completely, totally beaten up, unrecognisable. He wasn't someone who wanted to live inside, because he felt he deserved to be out and deserved a hard time of it. But, ultimately, he had a belief in himself and he knew his limitations. If I offered him a room somewhere he would say, "I'm not going to cope with that now, I'm just going to go in and fail, I'd rather stay on the street." His temper was like a devil on his back. He was scared of it. "I don't dare go there, to that accommodation, because I don't trust myself. I don't care how freezing it is out here." He knew that he had to avoid the hostel cycle: get in a room, get involved in drugs, get thrown out, go in again, get in a row with one of the staff or one of the residents, get thrown out, and on and on and on and on. But he is a deep thinker. He's got everything weighed up, in a way. You tend to find that most people on the streets have a lot of time on their hands but, as a way of coping, either they fall into a mindset that will perpetuate homelessness or they don't like to think too far because they reach painful things that have to be dealt with in order to move on. But Stuart was somebody who said, "Bring it on, bring the pain on, I want to face it." '

The surface of the desk is covered with envelopes, pens and a pile of posters:

FREE
The Cambridge Two

Ruth Wyner
imprisoned for 5 years

John Brock
imprisoned for 4 years

On December 17th 1999 Ruth Wyner, the Director of Wintercomfort for the homeless, and John Brock, the Day Centre Manager, were sent to prison because some of the people they were helping were secretly exchanging drugs on the charity premises.

•

"I see no purpose in the conviction or the sentence,"
said Anne Campbell, MP for Cambridge.
The sentences are "outrageous".

"I have grave concerns about the events leading
to their conviction and I am astonished at the
subsequent sentences," said James Paice,
MP for South East Cambridgeshire.

Peter Bottomley, MP for Worthing, has called for a pardon for
these two dedicated charity workers.

Not for Flyposting

Stuart tells me that he has changed since he began working

on the campaign. People have got friendlier. They've taken seriously what he has to say. When the open meeting at Wintercomfort was over he had asked for a role, and was immediately given one. 'I was really surprised, to be honest,' he says. 'I thought middle-class people had something wrong with them. But they're just ordinary. I was a bit shocked, to tell the truth.'

Stuart and I have given nine or ten talks together about the campaign since we began working together: in Birmingham, London, Oxford, in villages around Cambridge, to a hall full of university students at Anglia Polytechnic. We are the only people on the campaign who have the time to do it and we have developed a good pattern. I speak first, for twenty minutes, about the details of the case and push the petition or protest letter to the local MP or the forthcoming march in London, then Stuart gets up and knocks the audience out of its seat with a story of his life.

'I am the sort of person these two dedicated charity workers were trying to help,' he says, in effect. 'Do you see what a nightmare I was? Do you see how difficult it would have been to govern a person like me? Do you see now why we should have awarded Ruth and John medals for what they were doing rather than sending them to prison for what they could not control?'

Sometimes in his talk a stray 'fuck' or 'cunt' will slip past and then he'll blush or laugh, put a hand to his mouth in an unexpectedly girlish fashion and apologise for 'me French'. He often ends by suggesting that the government kick out their current homelessness 'tsar' and employ Ruth instead. 'I really do honestly believe that.'

Clap! Clap! Clap!

More often than not, a standing ovation.

This speech and tactic are entirely Stuart's ideas. He does

two things for the campaign: he folds letters and he exposes his soul.

'Here, Alexander, you've missed the bus,' exclaims Stuart. He has startled me from my ruminations. 'There isn't one for another two hours. Do you want to stay for supper?'

My heart sinks. More palm-shaped sarnies?

'Me favourite – curry.'

I go out to the local shop and return with supplies. Bulgarian white for me; eight cans more of lager and a packet of tobacco for him.

'What's that you're having? Wine? Ppwaaah!' Stuart sniffs the bottle. 'Smells like sick. Have a Stella.'

Curry is 'Convict Curry'. His mother's recipe. On very special occasions, he used to try to make it in the inmates' kitchen in HMP Littlehey, where he was serving five years for robbing £1,000 and a fistful of cheques from a post office.

'Mushrooms?' A tin of buttons; Stuart tips the little foetuses in.

Then he opens a packet of no-label, super-economy frozen chicken quarters. Pallid and pockmarked, they look like bits of frosted chin, as if he did over a fat Eskimo last week. He extracts an onion from behind the toaster and begins hacking at it with one of his knives.

I finish my survey of his bedsit room.

The picture on the wall is of a place with mountains and a lazy blue lake. The plaster it covers is gashed down to the brickwork from one of his periodic bouts of 'losing it', when he gets into a sort of maelstrom of fury and – highly private occasions, these, he does not like to think about them – takes it out on the furniture and fittings. On the floor beside the desk is an empty carton of Shake n' Vac, decorated in pink flowers.

'Good stuff, that. Use it for anything. Like, see round the bed there? There should be a huge stain because I overdosed there last week. But just put Shake n' Vac down. All the spilt

cans and vomit – cleaned it up really well. Leave it for a week
first though, before you hoover.'

The bills on the bedside cabinet are red.

No, Stuart does not mind if I rifle through them.

Cable: he has five extra channels, none of them sport, and no telephone. The reason homeless people use mobiles is because they're much cheaper than ordinary phones if you take only incoming calls. In fact, with pay as you go, they cost nothing. It's when the homeless start hanging around the public pay-phones that they're doing what ordinary people suspect them of doing on their mobiles: ringing their dealers. Stuart never uses anything but public phones for that sort of call.

Water: Stuart receives a hardship grant from his water company, and has a number of slow-paying arrangements that are taken off his dole cheque at source. As with Latinate medical names, he is an expert at these pathetic calculations – much more in control of them than I am of mine. They are part of what is unpleasantly termed 'life skills'. Not unreasonably, a person sleeping rough must display 'life skills' to his support workers if he is to be found a flat, otherwise he'll simply fall into arrears, annoy everybody and get evicted.

'On the street you get the same money as you get on housing, but now it's half-grant, half-loan to furnish your flat,' he explains, and gives the curry an encouraging prod. 'You could be £15 a fortnight down paying back the loan. So, instead of £102, it's now about £85. The water was fucking £26 a month before they remitted all me fines when I had the meter put in. And that was without electric and the gas and my TV licence. So out of £85 a fortnight I was paying £9 TV licence, £20 in electric because it was winter, £14 food minimum. Then you've got all your toiletries. I was making £49 outgoings go into £42.50. Even on pay day, your money don't do the bills because as soon as you cash your giro you just want to go out. So first thing you do if you've been on the street is fuck the bills. The only thing I made sure is that I had leccy. Spices?'

'How can you live on that, even without the bills?'

'That's the point. I don't.'

Stuart rattles through the shelves above his draining board: economy tomatoes, economy baked beans, economy corn flakes – everything, except the beer, in white packaging with blue lines. Economy raisins, economy powdered milk, economy spaghetti; finally, at the back, Sharwood's high-expense, in-a-glass-jar, multicoloured-label Five Spice, essential for Chinese cookery. He empties in all of it.

Court fines – imposed for drunkenness, driving offences and refusal to pay previous fines – he disregards. 'Just go back and get resentenced, won't I? Do three/four months inside to wipe them off. At the minute, me head's that off-key, I could actually do with going away for a bit.'

Stuart also has the ex-con's mathematical knack of immediately calculating release dates. 'Alright, Ruth got a five,' he says, dipping his finger in the sauce and licking thoughtfully, 'but it's John what I feel really sorry for because he got a four. Anything under four years and you only got to serve half before you automatically get released. If the judge had made it one day shorter – three years, 364 days – John could be out in two years. The extra day is the next bit up. It means he's only up for parole. He could get the full two-thirds: two years and ten months. Look, Alexander, if you want to do something useful, why don't you wash up some plates?'

His kitchen is a bombsite. Environmental health should close it down. I am committing an offence by not reporting it. The slats suspected of containing microphones are above the sink. The sink is invisible. Its rough location is marked by a swarm of dishes trying to escape down the plughole. Disgusting.

The purple sauce burps and splatters. Stuart does not like hot food himself. The first time in his life he ever sat in a restaurant was when he and I and another campaigner, Cathy Hembry, went to Leeds to berate Keith Hellawell, the Labour Party's 'Drugs Tsar'. Stuart ordered a chicken tikka masala,

The purple sauce burps and splatters.

which, he claimed, pushing the plate away and fanning his mouth, was 'kuu-aaah, un*eat*able!' That night in Leeds, he also stayed at his first ever hotel. Since then he has become an expert on Indian restaurants in Cambridge (non-spicy dishes only).

The Convict Curry is served late in the evening. Rich, hot, oily, profound, and infused with powerful flavour when cooked by a master – even if the accompanying rice tastes like builder's slurry – the cheapo-chicken-shaped Eskimo chins become tender, beautifully moist and pull back reassuringly from the bone.

Stuart picks up his plate and drops himself in his chair in front of the television. 'There, where's the remote?' He takes a bite of mushroom and chews breathily.

The Dukes of Hazzard, Starsky and Hutch, Knight Rider – these are his favourite programmes: anything with muted 1980s colour, an atrocious plotline and car chases.

We watch *The A-team* for five minutes. Another car crash. George Peppard dropping watermelons from a helicopter on to

Bad Guy's windscreen, which promptly smashes, sending Bad Guy soaring off the side of the road. In the next shot – car mid-air, heading towards disaster – the windscreen is intact again. Stuart bursts out laughing. 'That's why I love it. It's brilliant.' The car flops into a shallow lake.

'Let's go, partner,' mimics Stuart happily.

A moment later he flicks through the channels again and finds what he really wants. 'This is the best.'

We settle down to watch a programme about archaeology.

The last bus into Cambridge is the 11.10.

'We'll do some book tomorrow, yeah?' says Stuart. 'Get to see what your gaff is like, can't I? Give it the third degree like you just done to mine.' He pokes out his tongue in concentration and squashes his diary over his knee.

In the dark alley out of the estate on to the main road, I discover that I have forgotten to bring enough cash for the bus driver. Stuart pushes a fiver into my hand.

I protest and shove it back. I know that he's been saving this money for a visit to a lock-up pub after I'm gone. 'I can't take your drink money. I'll get a taxi and stop at the bank on the way.'

'No, honestly, Alexander.' Stuart forces it on me a second time. 'I've had enough. You'll be doing me a favour to stop me having any more. You'll be doing society a favour.'

Convict Curry – Recipe

To feed four

7 × economy chicken quarters. ('There's always someone what won't want two.')

4 × onions.

1 × jar of curry paste, 'whatever sort they've got'.

2 × 'cheap and cheering' tins of tomatoes – Aldi, Sainsbury's or Tesco.

Mushrooms, sweetcorn, 'anything like that'.

Mixed spice.

Ground cumin.

Fry the onions and the jar of curry paste together 'until you feel satisfied'. Throw in your two tins of tomatoes, mushrooms, sweetcorn and chicken. Rinse out the curry jar and add the water, sprinkle in the mixed spice and cumin, stir, bring to a splattering boil and simmer for two and a half hours.

4

'When and how did you become . . .'

'This horrible little cunt?'

'No.'

'Sorry.'

'We'll get to that later.'

'Sorry.'

I check the tape recorder and discover I have to begin again anyway because I've forgotten to release the 'pause' button.

'When and how . . .'

Again we have to stop. This time my landlord interrupts. Stuart has come to my rooms today and sits, squashed between the arms of my comfy chair, his legs curved and folded like a cross between a cowboy and a grandmother. Landlord stomps up from downstairs and pokes his head around the door.

'Hullo,' he says, blankly.

'Hello. Me name's Stuart. Pleased to meet you.'

'Hullo.'

Twice winner of a Mathematics Olympiad Gold Medal, co-author of *The Atlas of Finite Groups*, my landlord is a generous, mild man, as brilliant as the sun, but a fraction odd. Women have a habit of shrieking when they come upon him unexpectedly, waxen and quiet, standing on the other side of a door. His hair is wild, his trousers, torn. But one of Stuart's most personable (and most annoying) qualities is his refusal to judge strangers until he knows them, especially if they're peculiar.

Even people who are positively half-witted, open to obvious snap assessments, he will refuse to summarise, suspecting that hidden behind their veneer of idiocy is some pathetic, convoluted tale of grief.

Landlord stomps back downstairs again, tearing at his morning's post.

I reach out again to the tape recorder.

'When and how . . .'

'You ain't got a hot drink, have you, Alexander?'

Unwilling to leave Stuart alone in my room, I dash up to the kitchen, suppressing frustration. 'Thank you,' he calls. 'Four sugars with tea or coffee, please, don't matter which.'

'Thank you,' he shouts again when I yell down to find out if he wants milk.

Although Stuart and I have met dozens of times now, this is his first visit to my house and I am worried. His wild life and humorous criminal anecdotes suddenly seem a little alarming. Perhaps he cannot help himself. Perhaps even now he is squeezing all my possessions into his enormous pockets. At his mother's pub – in the village where he grew up, on the other side of Cambridge – Stuart says the women 'blatantly' hide their handbags when he comes into the lounge bar.

'Which I don't understand,' he likes to observe. 'I don't do bag-snatching. Don't approve of it.'

What about wall decorations – does he 'do' them? My beautifully framed and glazed pink ostrich feather fan? Or the floral teacups on top of the piano? The Volterol (50 mg) in the bathroom medicine cabinet?

I hurl slop out of mugs, plunge for a spoon in the washing-up bowl, swoop through cupboards in search of tea bags, and dart back down the stairs splashing hot water on the carpet.

'Thank you,' he says a third time as I step into the room again.

There is no evidence that he has moved. Nothing appears disturbed. The only noticeable change is the brown blanket that has slipped off the back of the chair and fallen over his ear. A ponderous length of ash drops off his roll-up.

'These books,' he says, nodding at the shelves above my desk. 'Have you read them all?'

'No.'

'Half?'

'Not exactly.'

He notes with surprise one on the floor near his chair: '*The Hunting Wasp* – a whole book just about them little summer things?'

Leaning forward, he picks out another. 'This one, *Mauve*: what's that about?'

'The colour, mauve.'

Stuart slowly shakes his head as he sits back again. 'How'd he fucking get away with it?'

'Right, ready? Right, you done? You're doing me head in with that machine, Alexander. What's that first question again, then?'

'When and how did you become . . .' I begin.

But yet again there is a delay. How difficult can it be to get started on a person's life? Stuart has accidentally knocked the microphone off its perch. I replace it on his knee.

'And you're sure that red light means it's working?' he checks, 'Cos I know what you're like, Alexander, with technology. It shouldn't be green?'

'Stuart, it's a tape recorder, not a traffic light.'

'Just checking. No offence. Bit nervous, I think. Me fucking life, you know. By the way, I've been thinking of a title. *On the Edge of Madness*. What do you think?'

'I think it stinks.'

'Right.'

James Cormick, a linguist friend of mine, describes Stuart's voice as 'a light tenor with a slightly "old" timbre that makes him sound in some way tired or prematurely aged'. Ironically, the weakness in his voice is his strength as a speaker, which is why he does so well on our talks together. He is not a bully boy bragging about his exploits. He comes across as a bit of a weakling – a flimsy article, in fact, if you were to hear him only on tape – who has somehow survived, scoring points by timing and intelligence rather than noise. 'He can describe things with absolute brutality,' says Denis Hayes, the second of the two homelessness workers who most helped Stuart to get off the streets. 'No matter how appalling whatever it was, he has this deadpan delivery. It's disconcerting because the words coming out from this gently spoken person need Peter Cushing to be reading it. It is completely the wrong voice.'

I rewind the tape a fraction and replay a few seconds:

'. . . *Bit nervous, I think. Me fucking life, you know . . .*'

Stuart says 'fucking' frequently, but rarely plain 'fuck' or 'what the fuck' or 'fuck that'. Sex is 'a shag', not 'a fuck'. 'Cunt', his only other swear word, is also never used sexually. A 'cunt' can be a nasty or an ordinary person, or a thing, such as a toilet brush. There's usually no aggression in these terms and they are not there because he's too stupid to think of a more appropriate one. 'Fucking' and 'cunt' are just part of the flicker of his speech.

In this excerpt he's talking about what happens when he gets 'rageous':

> You know, we're not talking kitchen knives, we're talking, like, fuck-off-cunt knives. So, like, obviously me stepdad's a bit fearful. He's a big fella but he's not getting any younger. With ten years he would have fucking thrown me all over the gaff. Now, the family don't know who's going to get hurt, or whether I'm going to end up getting locked up, or is me mother going to end up losing her husband? How do they deal with it? It's hard on them, because this fucking cunt gets scary. It can get scary for the person who does it, because there's no control. It's not until sometimes months afterwards that you can sort of really reflect and see it for what it was, because you're living in this different

world at the time when it happens, because your head's not like on a normal cloud.

Stuart's vowels often turn into diphthongs, as if he has pressed the sound out against the roof and walls of his mouth: not 'of', but '*u*-uhv'; 'you know' becomes 'you knah-ow'.

'Oh, noooo, is that what I sound like? Oh, fucking . . . Don't ever do that to me.' He winces, shakes his head as if caught by a bitter taste, laughs.

'Right, again.'

'When and how did you become homeless?'

Stuart checks his tea by dabbing his finger in it, then sinks half the mug.

'Well, each time is different, Alexander . . .'

5

'Homelessness – it's not about not having a home.
It's about something being seriously fucking wrong.'

2 Laurel Lane:
Aged 29

'I *put* meself on the streets this last time,' Stuart says firmly. '29 years of age. Just come out of prison: robbery, a post office. Done four and a half years out of the five-stretch because I'd been a bit of a bad boy, got this day job at a vehicle recovery company. It was legal, did a lot of police work, but you couldn't help learn a few useful bits and pieces. Like, an XR3i? A Ford XR3i? At the yard, I learnt all you had to do was get the screwdriver, take the two screws out gently from the side indicator, take out the plastic bit, take the light bulb out, get a piece of tinfoil, put it in, put the light bulb back in, shake the car to set the alarm, and it'd fuse it. End of alarm. I really did actually find me job interesting.

'Slide-sticking – that's another one. Sliding a stick down the window to pop the lock? Well, the AA and the RAC had a memo out at that time because in America someone had locked their keys in and they'd put the stick in and the door had a side impact bag. The bag went off and the stick shot up and killed the bloke. Went under his chin and right into his brain. That's why I liked it there. There was always something different. Never got bored.

'Trouble was, money. Too much of it. It's a funny thing about money, in't it? A lot of people, it's not being skint what gets you, it's having your pockets too full. Where, when I had money, I'd come home from work and wouldn't go get a shower some nights. I'd just sit there Monday, Tuesday, Wednesday,

Thursday, drinking. I started to get a bit lairy, agitated on drink. But on the Friday I'd go to Huntingdon and smoke smack. Literally, within three months, a £70 a day habit. A gram a day!'

'Why?' I ask, irritated by the speed at which Stuart's life is turning to waste.

'Well, that's what the book is about, in't it?'

'It's going to be that miserable?'

'Nah, that's the point: heroin isn't miserable, not at first. It makes you feel good. It don't matter if you got lots of troubles or no troubles, it takes them all away. All you people think is nasty, dirty needles because of the adverts, which I think is fucking wrong and dangerous because when you're on the smack, at the start, you don't feel like a dirty, nasty, scummy person so you know the adverts are lying. You feel happy. You like everyone. It's peaceful. Like that feeling you get when you wake up in the morning, feeling really, really tired, and know you don't have to get up.'

'But –'

'Alexander, if we're going to get on, you'll have to learn to stop interrupting. Anyway, like I says – the machine still on? – right, the drink and the drugs were ruling my life. So I started having to go out and thieve at weekends to pay for it. Opportunistic. If I was walking along the street and saw a car with a briefcase in or a laptop, I'd pop the window. Then use the money for drugs, not riches, if you know what I mean. Or I'd take special orders. If someone wanted a new pair of wheels, I'd take them off the scrap heap from work. Not if I knew the boss needed them – of course not. Stuff he was throwing away anyway. Lights, indicators, mirrors, handles. Down the pub. Here you are, mate. Nice one. Off to Huntingdon. Spend the money what I'd got to pay for the habit what was so large because of the money I'd got. Fucking stupid! Fucking Stupid: it is me middle name!'

Stuart plunges his hands into his pockets and takes his

annoyance out on a pouch of Old Holborn – biff, biff, tumble,
squash – then rubs a worm of tobacco into a Rizla.

'If I was a bank I'd have been liquidated years ago.'

Stuart's whole attitude to gaspers could suggest a disdain for my carpet if I didn't know him better. Once lit, not only does he let the burning end go untapped until there is half an inch of ash quivering in the draught, but when it does fall he ignores ashtrays: he tries to catch the powder in his hand. This process continues until the butt has become smaller than a splinter, then he stubs his fag out in the ash pile he is holding, flips his palm and rubs everything that he hasn't dropped on to my floor into his trousers.

'Then one day I'd had enough. So I did what a lot of people who end up on the streets do. I fucked it up – deliberate. Told the manager to stuff the job, stole a packet of money off me mum, took the bus into town and, like I told you, put meself on the streets.'

Recently released prisoners often end up sleeping rough. Institutionalised, broke, addicted to drugs and hated by their old friends – after a month or two of free life under these conditions, giving up your house and responsibilities to sit on the pavement with a bunch of like-minded ex-burglars doesn't look so bad.

Stuart's case was slightly different: his family was supportive; his friends were not disloyal; he was able to get a good job even though he'd just been in for a violent offence and his prison behaviour had been diabolical.

So, 'Why mess it up?'

'I don't know, Alexander, sometimes it gets so bad you can't think of nothing better to do than make it worse.'

'Two old boys called Scouser Tom and Asterix, in the park behind the bus station, them's the first ones I got talking to when I got off the bus.'

'No one on the bus?'

'Wasn't in the mood for talking on the bus, was I? That was the old world still, weren't it?'

'How did you meet Tom and Asterix, then?'

'They were just sitting there.'

'What were your first words?'

'Can't remember.'

'What sort of thing?'

'Haven't a clue. What's it matter?'

A great deal, I think to myself in frustration. The moment of transition is one of the great mysteries of homelessness. At what point does a person change from being inside his house to being outside all houses? When does he go from being one of us to one of them? I can imagine being desperate; I can see being up against the wall, bills dropping through the letter box, wife in bed with the bailiff, bottles piling up on the kitchen floor, closing my own door behind me, walking down the hill with my bag, getting on the bus – what I can't see is the point at which I think to myself, 'Bother! Homeless!' and genuinely believe it. Do I look in a panic through my wallet as the bus pulls out of the station (no credit cards, no chequebook), beat my pockets (no keys, no addresses, no letter from parents with gruesome invitation to return to the room I used to have as a boy), and wonder how I'm going to work up the nerve to start begging? Then suddenly it hits me: Jesus Christ! No bed! No home!

Caitlin Thomas – in the last words of her autobiography, after Dylan's death in New York – says she could make out only two phrases in the sound of the train wheels banging over the rails as she travelled back to Wales: 'No Dylan, no home, no Dylan, no home, no Dylan, no home.' Is this what real homelessness is like? Not just a particular set of roof and walls gone, but a sense of the death of companionship? Is this why outreach workers say it is so important to catch new home-less people within a few weeks of ending up on the streets, maximum, because otherwise they will start to build up a new sense of belonging, to the street community, because they are human and must have companionship, and thereafter it is a hundred times harder to get them back where they started, among the rest of us?

A third possibility: it is a gradual disillusionment. The homeless person is playing at the start. It is almost fun to sleep rough. He is like the waiter in Sartre's *Words*: acting the role of waiter – a waiter in bad faith – until one day he looks around and finds all his friends are rough sleepers, the girl he fancies is a rough sleeper, the things he looks forward to doing each evening are rough-sleeper things, like getting plastered on Tennant's Super behind the Zion Baptist Church; his whole community, no longer with any irony, is made up of rough sleepers, and now, at last, he is among them.

For a person like me, who knows I would never let myself get into this stupid, degrading situation, it is hard to find a good metaphor for this moment of transition. That is why every word of the opening conversation with Asterix and Scouser Tom matters.

'So you just saw these two people,' I try again, 'and said, "Hello, I'm Stuart, I'm homeless," and started a conversation?'

'No, of course not – I didn't say "I'm Stuart, I'm homeless" did I? Why would I do that? I'd known them two cunts for years.'

They sat together behind the bus shelter and drank for three days.

Stuart's night address was 2 Laurel Lane, Christ's Pieces. Set in three acres of mature park, with *en suite* toilets, six tennis courts and a bowling green, he slept soundly. When he woke, he crawled out, covered in old cigarette boxes and polystyrene cups, and bought coffee and a slab of shortbread from the gazebo stall. Christ's Pieces is the public green at the back of

Christ's College. Number 2 is the second shrub from the left – the one with the biggest cavity in the middle. Stuart did not brush his teeth. He did not wash. Between beers with Nick and Paul he puffed away at the heroin he'd bought with the money he'd stolen from his mother. It made Stuart laugh that the police walked by thinking that all he had was an ordinary roll-up.

On his fourth day in the park he met Smudger, a man with a home, and moved on to his floor. Smudger had himself been living on the streets a week earlier. This new tenancy of his was move-on accommodation, provided by the city council, which sets aside a handful of properties every year to be handed out to the homeless. Smudger had a lot of friends: they hurried off the streets to congratulate him on his good luck, drank his coffee, brewed up his tea, stole his chewy muesli bars, tinfoil, spoons, matches, then jacked up on the floor and got bored.

To liven up the evening they went on the rampage (Stuart not included, he insists) and barricaded an eighty-year-old neighbour into her flat with flowerpots.

Another man living in the same block of flats got all his windows shot out with an 'Uzi'. The bullets made a curve on the opposite wall, like this:

Smudger was evicted for non-payment of rent and having atrocious friends.

'But that's just life's story, in't it? Everybody expected everything for nothing not realising that he had bills to pay.'

Stuart moved back into the open. To keep costs down, he

started injecting heroin instead of smoking it. 'I almost overdosed, the buzz was that strong. And I thought, "Ah brilliant,
I've cut me habit from seventy quid to a tenner a day." A
month later I was doing £70 a day in me arm.'

'Can we leave it at that?' says Stuart.

'What? Stop recording? But we've only been doing it half an
hour.'

Stuart shuffles in my armchair. 'Got a busy day,' he complains.

I reach out to click off the tape recorder, think twice, and sit
back. 'OK, but five more minutes. Let's just recap. You were
in prison, yes?'

'That's right, for –'

'We'll get to that, that's for later. Then you came out, messed
up your life for six months and ended up on the streets?'

'Exactly, like I just explained it all. I was thirty at the time,
and I stayed on the streets from June until December.'

'Which is just after I first saw you, round the corner from
Sainsbury's, correct?'

He nods in exasperation and starts struggling with his puffy
jacket.

Busy? What's a benefit bum like him got to do?

'Look, I'll tell you what's bothering me. Why didn't you just
go straight to one of the homeless agencies and get yourself
booked into a hostel? They could have got you on a job programme, into a shared house, or in a private tenancy and
arranged to sort out your deposit. That's why these hostels cost
so much, because the money is used to fund twenty-four-hour
support staff: they're there, specially employed by what you
please to call the System, to help you. In other words, you
didn't have to live outside in parks. If you did, it was because
you insisted on it. Why?'

For a moment Stuart looks at me as if I am beyond hope.

His shoulders slump in disbelief. 'Nah, Alexander, keep your tape recorder on. You fucking nine-to-fives believe everything you read in the bloody newspaper or watch on the telly, when the reality of it is so fucking different, it's unreal.'

Show a tiny element of responsibility, don't assault anyone or openly take drugs, and the staff at Wintercomfort Day Centre will connect you to the outreach team, who will get you into a hostel, usually an English Churches Housing property. Willow Walk hostel for rough sleepers, or Willow Walk's big sister, 222 Victoria Road, are the ones. They have small private rooms with settled accommodation. At 222, there are seventy-four beds. A Dantesque institution with an innocuous pale brick façade not far from where I live, I pass by it on my way to the local supermarket. Occasionally there are ambulances or a police car outside: somebody has overdosed, been beaten up, been beating someone else up or smashed the window of a nearby off-licence and come stumbling back with an armful of chilled beers. It is run by a friend of mine, a conscientious, highly intelligent, imaginative woman who, with her staff, performs something of a miracle to keep this place going every day.

There is a constant air of watchfulness in places like 222 (especially) and Willow Walk (to a much lesser extent). Long periods of quiet are followed by short tempests of violence in which it seems people are 'kicking off' on every wing and the housing officers rush from one incident to the next, clatter along the corridors with fingers on walkie-talkie buttons wondering if the full moon has snagged on the nearby traffic lights.

This is why Stuart hates hostels. 'Because in them places you've got little kids trying to be bully boys and they see someone small and skinny like me, and with a limp, and to people like that I'm an easy target. So I have to deal with them in a severe way, if they take a liberty, to get the message, then I end up in nick again. Well, I can't condemn them because I used to be the same. But if the person killed me, I wouldn't like him to end up having to do even three years in prison. I wouldn't wish it on nobody.'

'You didn't mind the idea of getting three drunks from the pub to kill you, risking their imprisonment,' I remind him.

'Yeah – but they weren't homeless.'

Hostels are not right for most people. They become (as the pun goes) hostiles. Or, worse, a sense of contentment creeps up on the residents. After six months, outrageous incidents are no longer reasons for threatening staff with letters of complaint to the chief executive or promising to tip off the *Cambridge Evening News* – they are gossip. Street life is testimony to man's self-defeating powers of adaptation. The same thing applies in prison: people get used to the outrage of the new circumstances – they give up trying to fight back. John Brock, the former Wintercomfort manager that Stuart and I are campaigning for, is a good example. After a few months inside, he writes to his wife that prison has started to feel right. He likes it when the warden closes the cell door on him. He is beginning to feel that it is easier to be guilty.

Hostels, despite all their best efforts, encourage drug addiction and alcoholism. The main reason why Stuart demanded that the council give him a flat five miles outside of Cambridge was to get away from the city's drug and petty crime set. Putting a man trying to get off heroin and burglaries in a homeless hostel, no matter how dedicated the support staff, is like putting a paedophile in a kindergarten. Temptation is everywhere. The only place that has more drugs in it than a homeless centre is prison.

At 222, Stuart got beaten up and didn't squeal; got beaten up again and still kept his mouth shut; got beaten up a third time, head-butted one of the bullies, 'split all his eye open', had a knife fight with another and had to leave.

He wouldn't go in Jimmy's, either, in the basement of the Zion Baptist Church on the other side of town. Technically,

Jimmy's is a 'shelter' rather than a 'hostel': people do not have rooms there, just the possibility of a bed in a dormitory, which must be arranged night by night. No alcohol, body searches at the door and no sin bins in which to deposit your needles safely.

'There's some nice people who go down Jimmy's, but you get a lot of the mentally ill and the drunks down there. And they chuck you out the door at nine o'clock in the morning. They get a good whack of money for you staying there but they put you out on the street at nine o'clock in the morning till half seven at night.'

Jimmy's, named after a charismatic dosser, another of the homeless now-dead, is something of a throwback to George Orwell flophouses, though a good example of one. It can be a stabilising place for people who would otherwise spend all night on the beer and brown. But it's useless for someone who likes privacy, or is easily bullied, or has a persecution complex, or likes to sleep in a dress, or snores so loudly that the other residents gang up and stuff a sock in his mouth.

Whatever service you provide, no matter how welcoming, tolerant, well staffed and decorated with pretty pot plants, there will always be homeless people it doesn't suit.

'Because that's the point of them, in't it?' explains Stuart. 'The homeless are what's left over after all the usual things what keep people straight and narrow – yes sir, no sir, three bags full sir – like family, career, the army, have been taken out.'

For a year while writing this book I worked at the Willow Walk hostel, the best hostel in the city: twenty-two beds, single rooms, twenty-four-hour staff sitting in an office by the door. Rent: £279 a week per person. (The homeless don't pay that, of course. They pay around £6.50. The rest comes through housing benefit, from you and me.) It is run by Ruth's husband, a kind, relaxed and thoughtful man.

The residents at Willow Walk are in general pleasant, although some individuals have their moments. (The list of people banned from the premises, for example, includes one with six convictions for attempted murder and another for trying to kill a hostel worker.) They are essentially a cautious, edgy crowd who, when they 'lose it', are raging against their own losses more than against anyone else. Some of them have experienced things that would make you throw up if you knew the details, but they don't become serial killers, arsonists, letter bombers. They doubt, they grizzle, they stamp about their little cubicle rooms, they suspect everything is their fault (or they think nothing is their fault and therefore think they have no control over their existence), they cut themselves, they watch the days and months slip by, they get smashed out of their skulls. Some are hilarious, some are very talented, many are kindly, many are boring, a few were once rich, a good number are to some degree insane. Some are so apologetic it is unsettling. They might have been a bit rude to you the day before, called you a 'twat' (frequently with some justice) or just stumbled about for a while, being merry and foolish. But they apologise at the soonest sober opportunity, even when the person listening to these sorries hasn't the foggiest idea what they're on about any longer. It is impossible to be precise in characterising the people who live in such places. In my own estimate, about a quarter of them you could pass on the street and not have the faintest reason to think they are anything other than successful (the best-dressed man in Cambridge at the moment is a man living in Jimmy's). But alongside these are the usual stereotype figures so beloved by people who write about low-life: the crackheads, the dope fiends, the Irish drunks, the nonces, the whores (but don't read that word in a Raymond Chandler voice – think instead of pallid girls with fungal infections, and grandmothers who'll let you feel their varicose veins in return for a mouthful of half-digested beer), the burglars, the shoplifters, the ambitionless, the self-disgusted, the weak of will and, very rarely, the just plain poor.

The final step on the ladder of opportunity – after Winter-comfort, Jimmy's, 222 Victoria Road, the young persons' project in Haverhill, Willow Walk, Emmaus, temporary shared housing with organisations such as the Cyrenians – is to be put into a bedsit or flat of your own.

If this rehabilitation process works well, you can be off the streets, in accommodation of your own and looking for a new job within half a year, though even that is not quick enough. On average, it takes nine years for a person, after the event that has unsettled them (abuse, bankruptcy, marriage break-up, etc.), to become homeless. It then takes four weeks to become 'entrenched', i.e. to settle into street life and begin to adapt irrevocably.*

But the ladder hardly ever works well – at least, not with 'chaotic' rough sleepers. Stuart's sort do not live under the stars and endure piles and hypothermia simply because they've run out of luck and 'self-esteem'. Therefore, it's not just a matter of providing encouragement, vocational training and money to put them back on their feet. To them, every day is a hum of casual outrages. In the worst cases such a person is hardly human at all, but like the shell of a man walking around crammed with minced ego. It is as though some piece of their soul is missing. The way he is and the manner in which he lives are symptoms of a mental disruption – maybe even a full-blown incurable illness – and it is as good to tell him to apply for one of the fifty warehouse packing jobs advertised in the employment office as it is to tell a man with half a leg to drop his crutches and run home.

'See, the homeless culture is a weird culture,' explains Stuart. 'One minute they're all fighting against each other, but then there's days we all stick together through thick and thin, all different little groups. Like, once, I sat there begging with a fellow, and he just jumped up and started kicking me in the face. He don't know why neither.'

* Statistics from Shelter.

At one point, in an effort to get away from this mayhem hostel and street life, Stuart bought a caravan for £25 and had it towed down to the river, but something came a cropper there too. Other people took it over. He let the wrong friends sleep on the floor. They set light to it. It exploded.

Another time, Stuart got into an argument with Frank the Tank, and Frank the Tank walloped him in the park behind the bus shelter. Result: bus shelter out of bounds.

'Even if you get a job, you're caught in a catch-22, because the only time you can get work is if you're living at one of the hostels, because no one gives you work if you haven't got an address. But if you get a job when you're staying there, the staff immediately raise the rent. They got to, because them rooms cost fucking £200–300 a week and benefits won't pay the full whack any more if you got a job, will they? It might go up to £60–70 a week, overnight, from the first fucking day you get work! Fucking frightening to someone who was paying a fiver a week the day before. But this is the stupid bit: legal jobs don't pay except in arrears. Two weeks, a month in arrears, that's when you get the first pay cheque. How can you pay the new fucking ridiculous rent them first four weeks? It isn't possible. Where's the money going to come from? Get a job and what happens? Get kicked out of your accommodation for non-payment of rent.'

I do know about this. I have myself advised homeless people not to get work, especially if they have just arrived on the streets (the benefits situation improves slightly if you've been down and out for six months, although by that time the sense of community with the homeless, and sence of homelessness not being that bad really, has set in) because if they do they will lose their hostel accommodation, and hence their job, too, for exactly the reason Stuart describes.

In short, at every step up the ladder, the chaotic homeless person will stumble. He throws a tantrum, loses his nerve, drinks himself to the brink of oblivion, ends up in the police cells and three weeks later has to be restarted on the bottom rung by people who grow increasingly tired of seeing his mottled face.

This is why Stuart, sicker than most, within a few weeks of leaving Smudger's flat, fell off the ladder and sank like a stone.

Much of what happened over the next four months before the outreach team found him is, even to himself, a blank.

6

'Tying the bastard to the back of a car and dragging him down the road,' growls Stuart. It is three weeks after Stuart's visit to my rooms when we began recording his life. We are walking along the verge of the A10, outside Cambridge, kicking our way through the flowering coltsfoot, towards the Emmaus Homeless Project, which runs a furniture shop. 'Tying him up on a lump of wood like the Japs did, burying him up to his neck in a pool of slurry, and then dragging him up and splitting him, cutting him slightly in places and putting him in so he all got infected and died a painful death. Or just sit there playing darts with him. Slow and suffer. I just wanted him to know what fucking suffering was about.'

Stuart wants a display cabinet. It is to go alongside the Boing, Boing, Whoosh bed. It is for his stereo, his *Teach Yourself Driving* books and his bong. The air blast of a passing pallet lorry makes his legs sway.

Stuart leans out into the A10 and eyes the traffic.

Another HGV appears round the corner half a mile away and Stuart steps quickly back.

'Something's coming – I can feel it. It's not all gone.'

'What's not all gone?'

'The anger and bitter twistedness. I'm not finished. I'm going to be not very clever again. Somebody's going to get hurt, that's what scares me.'

'When is this going to happen? In a week?' The juggernaut

thunders past. 'In the next ten seconds?' I add, humorously.

'Don't know when this thing will come, Alexander,' says Stuart, stopping again and looking up and down the road. 'It's me black mist. It *will* come.'

'Who is this man you want to torture?'

'He knows. I let him know. I've phoned him up a couple of times since I got out of jail, telling him that his time was coming. I've let him know. But anyone can do it over the phone. And then one night before I become homeless it got to the stage where me head was telling me I had to go, his time was now, and I've gone to his house and kicked his door in.'

There was nobody there.

Next, Stuart tried the bedroom door, and it was locked. So he kicked that in, too.

'And there was this girl in there screaming. So I've left her, gone round and there's another door upstairs locked and I just kept head-butting it and punching it until it just fell away, I went through the middle of it, and nobody was in there. I've gone in another room and I'm undoing wardrobes and fucking punching them as I'm undoing them, and I seen this other woman, weeping on the floor, so I picked her up, let her know that I ain't coming to hurt her, but she's seen it as threatening and she's run off. So I've gone out his front door there and that's when I seen all the police. And there he was, sitting on one of their cars. "Ha, ha, you didn't get me, didya?"

'He's laughed at me! Then he's run off down into his garden, shouting to the two coppers with the dog, "He's got a knife, he's got a knife, he's got a knife!" So they set the dog on me, and the dog took the arm clean off my jacket and bit me straight through the arm, even though I didn't have no knife. And the coppers jumped on me, and I started saying to them "What you doing protecting a fucking kiddy-fiddler? What are you doing defending a fucking child molester scum cunt nonce?"

'So, like I say, the boss got a right arsehole with me for going and getting meself involved with the police, cos he'd given me a chance and he has police work. He was unhappy about it.'

'You surprise me.'

Stuart shrugs. 'Up until two years ago, I used to mentally burn out before I'd physically burn out. So if I went on one, I'd mentally burn out and then there'd be a right lull. All the anger would be gone and I'd be physically fucking knackered. Where . . .' Stuart pauses. He often begins sentences with this word, 'Where', as if literally lifting the thought out from a back room in his brain, like a box, and placing it in front of the listener. 'Where, in the last two years there's been so many curious instances, back to back, that I think it is because I don't peak. I physically get exhausted before I do mentally.'

He gives the road in front of us another suspicious up-and-down glance, then indicates a collection of pitched roofs beyond a line of bushes on the other side of the road: Emmaus, the homeless community. It is half a mile from the nearest village, cut off from the rest of human habitation like an Amish settlement.

A Fiesta appears far away, heading from Cambridge – and God's Gift to Road Safety waits for that to pass too.

Then we cross in a hurry. 'Fucking maniacs,' he says.

Set up in Paris in 1949 by a French cleric, Abbé Pierre, the Emmaus communities put homeless people to work repairing and selling cheap household goods in return for an income so small that the wind blows it away before they can clench their fingers on it. Drink is banned. Any hint of drug taking: immediate eviction. The idea has so much right with it that is wrong with hostels: it makes the homeless work to regain their 'self-respect'; it takes them out of the street community that's holding them down; it breaks the cycle of dependency on the welfare state, and because it works them on slave wages they can't afford to splash out on a three-week sherry binge even when they do manage to escape back to the city on their one free day a week. 'Like a detox programme for being homeless,' grumbles Stuart.

'Through here, Alexander.' We duck into a hedge gap, down a little ditch, another hole and finally into a farm courtyard.

An ancient urchin with a face like sucked parchment lifts his screwdriver hand to Stuart, grins, and goes back to staring at the bedside cabinet slumped between his legs.

From another direction, beside a tractor, a black beard nods at us.

'Watcher, Alan!' Stuart calls.

'Stuart,' it returns.

The twenty men and women who live here are happy. The work they do is important. Further up the road they have allotments and greenhouses and keep chickens.

The dens of Emmaus are ordered in mountain ranges. One big room is filled with cabinets and tables and squishy chairs; two smaller ones with Hoovers, fans and sound systems; a side den full of music; then there is a book room, a knick-knack lobby and a cafeteria with a little toothless man sitting outside looking up donated LPs in a book of record values the size of a six-pack.

'Why aren't there Emmauses in every town?' I quiz. Stuart looks around theatrically, shrugs, then plunges among the vaults of junk on the other side of the main entrance. 'Isn't the answer obvious?' his gesture has said. 'Because homeless people don't all want to spend their time mending cheap furniture with Olde English doorknobs for £35 a week. They don't fancy living with two dozen ex-alcoholics and failed bankers five miles away from the nearest pretty girls. Excellent for some, the regime might be. For others it reminds them of prison or Eton.'

Stuart soon discovers something he likes. A glossy 'ebony' display case with leaded windows and a dainty writing surface to pound your head against in disgust. 'That's good that.' He pats one of the glossy shelves. 'Lovely bit of workmanship.'

The price is on a cardboard star stuck to one of the leaded windows. 'Sixty-five quid? Now that's value!'

People sometimes ask me if I am ever frightened of Stuart. Never, not for a second, not in the smallest way. Why not? I don't know. Perhaps it is because his anger has a purpose. It is focused against diffuse but determinable enemies for understandable reasons, i.e. everything associated with care homes and paedophiles and prison and the police. I am not part of those worlds. To be honest, I find his remarks a little silly.

But he has attacked his half-brother, trashed his parents' pub, once threatened his own mother with a knife, people point out. Why should *I* be safe?

I don't know. He just does not frighten me. None of the people I know, who, like me, have become friends with him during the campaign, are frightened by him. Even his addiction counsellor isn't scared and he's thrown a chair at her.

Working at a hostel, one gets used to bold comments about violence and self-destruction from the homeless. The first three or four times they alarm you. By the fifth or sixth, they're becoming old hat. You learn to try to change the subject, tell a joke, treat the person like a petulant schoolboy: 'Now, Tom, I don't think it's really a good idea for you to pick a fight with Jenny this morning. She's already beaten you up three times, and that's quite enough for one day.' Or, 'No, Adam, if you slit your wrists with that razor it will not be "all my fault". It will be your fault, because they're *your* wrists and *you're* the one who's spent the last ten minutes breaking the blade out of your Bic shaver.'

Little clarifications like this are important in hostel life.

'And remember to slit along the vein, not across it,' you sometimes feel like adding.

Even so, a niggling concern remains. One has heard that suicides and violent men frequently need to work themselves up. Big boasts, little trial runs – like sprinters doing exercises in the last minutes before the start gun bangs.

'But I'm still confused on this point,' I say, changing the subject as we return down the A10, along a narrow little lane beneath the rowans, back towards his housing estate. 'Why did you put yourself on the streets?'

'I told you. I was already stealing money off me mum to pay for me smack at the time. So one night, after I lost me job cos of the kiddy-fiddler I took a lot more money and come to Cambridge.'

'But why put yourself on the streets?'

'Alexander! Why, why, why!'

'But it's important. I want to understand.'

'I dunno – because I'm part Romany, I wanted to live like my roots. I liked the Romany, independent lifestyle.'

'But that's what I'm getting at. That's exactly what you weren't doing. You just slept on the pavements of the nearest city and never moved.'

7

'Stop asking why, Alexander. I don't know why. I was so off-key, half the time me mind had a head of its own.'

. . . Psycho!
Aged 29

Lion Yard Car Park is a boat of a place. Its cargo hold, nine concrete storeys of smog and tyre burns, is topped by the glass-covered, centrally heated magistrates' court – the galley, so to speak. The prow of the boat – an eighth of a mile further south, under the Holiday Inn – thrusts towards the university museums of geology and anthropology.

Stuart aged 29 fetched up in this car park after leaving his mother's pub, meeting Asterix and Scouser Tom, being kicked out of Smudger's flat and messing up his chances at Jimmy's and the day centre. He'd been told that ten to fifteen people 'skippered' there every night, but wherever he looked he couldn't find a single one of them. He took his blankets and rags and walked up the circular staircase to the top storey, just under the magistrates' court, where the pigeons sleep. It took him four days to find the place for people.

Between the magistrates' court end and the Holiday Inn end of the building are ramps and an aerial walkway, plus a mezzanine basement dug, it seems, into pure concrete. HUMANS NOT ALLOWED indicates an accompanying sign. Another notice reads TO LEVELS A-B-C-D. A little stick man with a ping-pong head marches behind the letters in an encouraging manner, guiding you along a narrow pavement. Grey drops of chewing gum splatter the way, congesting towards a stair door and lift door at the other end. Then Ping-Pong Head pops up again, on a sign hurrying back towards TOILETS. The pillars supporting the ceiling here (we are now under the Holiday Inn) are stencilled with the letter A. IS THIS $\boxed{A}$RT MUMMY? someone has scrawled around one.

By the lift other signs fight for attention. A bewildering list of charges. More funny round-headed stick figures explaining how to stand in a lift. 'Get into your car or get a move on,' they appear to say. 'Stop being such an uncertain quantity.' A dulled brass honorarium:

To Commemorate the Opening

of the

Lion Yard Car Park Extension

by

The Right Worshipful the Mayor

COUNCILLOR DR GEORGE REID

on

Friday 10 August 1990

Dr Reid, the main university force in our campaign to release Ruth and John: a fine humanitarian, conservative to the ends of his toes (which have gout).

The lift is boarded up. Recently, a student leant against these doors, they opened accidentally and he plunged into the dark down the shaft.

'PLEASE BE AWARE,' declares a bill on the door by the stairs, 'if approached in this car park by someone claiming to need money for petrol or to replace a broken car key please do not give them any money and immediately contact a member of staff at the exit.'

On the other side of the door is the concrete staircase: cinder grey, regular. The banister is red. The smell is dust and disinfectant. Go down two flights. The walls still show the grain of the plywood moulds that once held them when they were poured. If you peer hard through the dark perspex window in the door of this floor – Level B – you can often spot something interesting. Couples kissing passionately in the front seats, couples in the back seats, couples shouting. Depth, in this building, quickly gives a conviction of privacy. Down two more flights and Level C begins to show the strain. The walls are laterally cracked, like an exposed vein of a leaf. Occasionally, the smell loses its warm chemical hint and a waft of urine insinuates itself instead. There are still currents of air.

Down the final two staircases, forty feet under ground, to the lowest subterranean floor. You could take off all your clothes and do handstands down here and you'd be safe any time between 9 a.m. and 9 p.m.

BEWARE
CHILDREN
OF THE
ACID MONKEY

The cleaners have been at this piece of graffiti with their scrubbing brushes many times. Six inches to the right, beneath a picture of a falling bomb, some more:

ha, ha, ha, he, he ...
Love ya,
woof

Above you, the noises could be of people just leaving the staircase at the top; or, equally, stomping across the floor directly above. Sound is impossible to place.

Push through this door, out of the stairwell into Level D, and you will see in front of you 15,000 square feet of car park that is completely empty.

This is where the homeless sleep.

''Ere, Jonny, stop pissing on that bloke, he's trying to snooze.'

'Can I have another sarnie, pl*eaaa*se? I've only 'ad three . . .'

'Coffee with five sugars, love, ta.'

'Jonny! Get over here and tell Linda . . .'

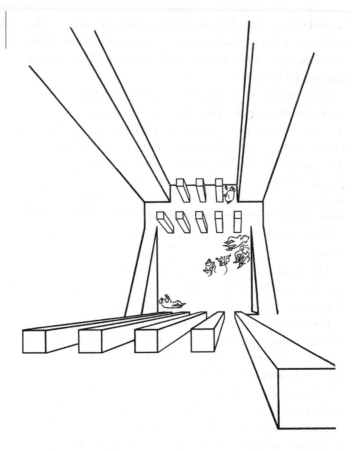

This is where the homeless sleep.

'Aww, that's not fair. *Penny's* had six. *And* she's nicked a burger and chips from that geezer outside Gardenia. Gooo on, jus' *one* more . . .'

'Is that five? You sure? Put another one in, just in case, pet.'

'JONNY! He don't want ketchup poured over him neither! He's not a frigging hot dog! Come here, it's important, tell Linda about Psycho. Honest, Linda, not joking, he's a nutter –

he's taking over Level D. A danger to everyone. Giving us a bad name. Like, we don't even dare go down to Level D no more. You don't know him? Where have you been the last five months? JONNY!'

Linda was one of the two members of the Cambridge Homeless Outreach Team in those days. Her job was to walk round the city streets in the evenings talking to anyone who looked homeless: i.e. anyone selling the *Big Issue* or three months away from a bath or stationed in public spaces at lower than a standing position. On Tuesdays and Thursdays she ran the soup kitchen in the market square. This service is gone now, but in the late 1990s it was not only a charitable provider of food and hot drinks to rough sleepers, it was the best way to learn street gossip.

That evening, after the soup kitchen was locked away, Linda met up with her work colleague, Denis Hayes, an ex-film cameraman, and went to seek out Psycho.

For outreach workers, the best way down to Level D is by the car ramps, because it brings each floor gradually into view – allows them to assess the situation slowly and not to pounce in on it through small yellow stairway doors at one end.

'I always think if I wanted to do a film again, the scene that night would be the opening shot,' remembers Denis. 'I'll never forget that image. It was, like, coooold. Me and Linda go right down until we get to the last bit, Level D, and that would be how I'd start. Coming down the ramp from Level C above, panning slowly across this eerie, vast space. Empty car park. Left to right: not a car, not a car, not a car, nothing, nothing, and then . . . *Psycho!*

What he reminded me of was an IRA hunger striker. Skeletal, in his cell, all his things around him. He was like that man in *Birdie*, crouched on the end of his bed. Nobody could make him up to look how he did at that moment. Angry as hell. Hated me. Hated Linda. Hated everything from the fucking dust upwards.'

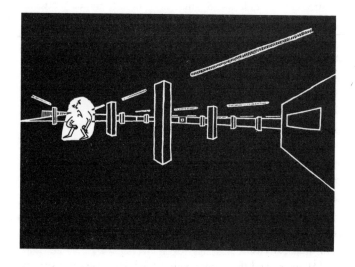

Psycho!

8

Stuart says it is a 'blinding' idea.

He is in my study again, standing by the piano, swiping the air with his arm in excitement. He and I and half a dozen street homeless smackheads and drinkers will sleep rough on the concrete pavement outside the Home Office, corner the Home Secretary when he arrives for work on Monday morning and *force* him to release Ruth and John. That's Stuart's inspiration.

Always the first to discourage unnecessary illegality, Stuart points out that we will have to warn the police about what we are going to do, but not tell them until after 4 p.m. on the previous day, 'because that way the courts will be shut and it'll be too late to get an injunction what can stop us. Then there's the security cameras.'

I look quizzical.

'All over. And that's not counting the ones you can't see,' he adds darkly.

'It's better than that nutter Brandon's idea, in'it?' Stuart enthuses. Professor David Brandon is the ex-director of another charity for the homeless; it was his suggestion that he and half a dozen other homelessness workers present themselves to the police and demand to be arrested. If Ruth and John are guilty of 'knowingly allowing' drugs in their day centre, then they are all guilty of it, since other homeless charities are run according to the same rules. I disagree with Stuart. I think that is a gem of a stunt, too.

'Fucking stupid. Asking to get arrested! Then who's going to get *him* out? Expect his missus will be wanting a go next.'

'But that's the whole trick, isn't it? They can't put him in prison too. He's known all around the country – there'd be an outcry. Cambridge Police Gone Mad!'

Stuart shakes his head, his mood suddenly dampened. 'Fella goes to the Old Bill and asks to be banged up, and they don't do it? Don't make sense.'

I return to typing the campaign newsletter.

'All of us in fucking nick and no one fucking left to get us out. Just a load more work all round, that's what I think,' Stuart rumbles on. 'See, you got all your nine-to-fives saying what drugs is about and they don't know the first fucking thing. Like piss-testing prisoners. Everybody thought that was a good idea cos drugs leave traces in your urine, so with piss-testing you couldn't get away with it any more. More tests, less drugs. Right? Wrong. It's because of them tests that there's a heroin epidemic in prison. Why? Because the drug of choice used to be cannabis, but cannabis lasts up to three weeks in your system, so if the screws do the random tests at weekends, like they do, you've got three chances of getting caught. Where, heroin lasts only three days. Result: everyone starts switching to smack. Your nine-to-fives think they've done something useful, where in fact they've just made the fucking problem worse.'

For a few moments longer Stuart falls back to brooding on the wickedness of ignorance and people who disorder the world by asking to be put in jail. To cheer him up I return to his Blinding Idea. I really do like it. Exciting, freakish, bound to get publicity. The more I think of it, the more it sounds a corker.

'What else should we plan for?' I enquire enthusiastically.

'The brass.'

'Top brass? Policemen, you mean?'

'Alexander, what are you like? In London, the pavement isn't all public: some of it belongs to them and some of it belongs to us. The brass bits is little bits put in outside of all government buildings in London what lets you know the difference – there's brass bits all over London. If we sleep on the bit what belongs to them, they do us.'

'So, we're OK if we sleep on the other bit?'

Stuart shakes his head. 'Nah. If we sleep on the bit that belongs to us they still do us, only it's not the same.'

'The main place you get them is around your bollocks.'

It is six in the morning, six weeks later. We are flicking beneath the motorway lights in convoy, in one friend's beat-upsmellymobile and another friend's smooth new Volvo estate, down towards the doomed Home Secretary and the Home Office in London. The boots are filled with posters, badges, T-shirts, petitions and pale Tupperware boxes containing sandwich-shaped objects beneath the lids. In the back of the seedy conveyance, Stuart and I are squished up with Deaf Rob, whom we picked up off a Cambridge bridge, where he was sitting in the honey glow of the street light surrounded by luggage. He had sneaked out of a hostel an hour earlier without paying his rent. Tongue-twisted, pallid, his hair sawn at the night before with a grapefruit knife, he is clutching a pigskin suit-holder in businessman's-overcoat beige with 'Louis Pierre, Paris' woven below the handle. In the other car, Linda the Outreach Worker, Fat Frank Who Never Speaks About His Past, and space for two King's College students who said they wanted to join in, were 'passionate about social justice' and absolutely to be relied on, then couldn't be bothered to get out of bed.

'And hairy places,' continues Stuart. 'Under your arms; if you've got hairy legs, on your legs. That's the difference between lice and scabies. Lice is when you're on the street and someone pulls a blanket out and you sit on it.' He holds up his hand, thumb and forefinger pinched together. 'Not as thick as a match – a third of a match long is fucking ginormous. A fucking monster lice that is. It's scabies, what are smaller, what goes under the skin. You scratch and that's what ends up. Literally, live under the skin. Where, lice – all you need is one lice. A male or female lays eggs. At the same time, the cold doesn't kill them. Last year, sleeping out under the bridge, Tom the Butcher had lice and they was hopping over his three mates next morning. It weren't because it was fucking warm!'

Stuart has been talking non-stop since 4.30 a.m. – I feel he has been talking ever since the Blinding Idea first came to him – yap, yap, yap, HIV, hepatitis C, why homeless people smell, why homeless people can't get their heroin doses right, why homeless people never *do* anything except shout obscenities and shit on charity workers, why homeless people always feel obliged to make ten times the amount of noise as anyone else, why homeless people blame everyone but themselves for being homeless, yap, yap, yap.

'Then you got drying out and foot problems. Homeless people get wet, you know.'

Who cares?

'Your foot just fucking ends up mouldy basically.'

I wish it would drop off.

'You know what it's like . . .'

No, I work for my living. I've got a house.

'. . . if you go out and your socks get wet, you come home and your skin's white, in'it? Imagine that when it's been raining for two or three days. It's all water and little mushrooms and no foot.'

The fourth passenger in the car, a man generally sympathetic to the poor person's complaint – a union member, a lifelong activist for the cause of Right and Fairness – has cupped his hands against the side of his face.

''Ere, Drew, something wrong? What for are you holding your head?'

'I'm trying to block you out, Stuart.'

Stuart keeps his thoughts sealed as we come down into London from the northern hills, but one might as well try to button up the ocean. His lips twitch. His face stiffens. He stares out of one window, then the other, looks at the lining on the car roof, fidgets with both sides of his hands. At Walthamstow Town Hall he draws a preparatory breath but stops. By Seven Sisters and Holloway it's beyond control.

'Not being funny, is that a prison?' he blurts.

'Holloway, mate,' confirms Drew.

'Here's another idea you should think of doing, Alexander,' he gushes forth, laughing with relief. 'Get a room full of, like, policemen and MPs and judges, then get someone else with, fucking, a couple thousand quid of smack and get them to put loads of little £10 bags in everyone's pockets.'

Brilliant, Stuart. Excellent. How do you think of them?

'Nah, serious, I am. Cos then they'd understand what John and Ruth was up against. Any good dealer could do it, cos a £10 packet is only about the size of a sweetcorn kernel, then at the end you'd tell them what had happened while they was all standing round having fucking sherry and them little pieces of toast with orange bits on, just to let them know how fucking easy it was. And you'd have to give them something to talk about, like with Special Brew Sue and Spider kicking off or food served by waitresses in short skirts. Nah! I know! Lap dancers! Cos you've got to create for them judges and nobby cunts the same environment – only it's not the same-same obviously – you know, for them, the equivalent level of dis-*rup*tion what John and Ruth . . .'

We pass Camden Sainsbury's. 'But smack's not a nice middle-class drug, is it?' Stuart says, giving me an accusatory look as if, but for the disapproval of people like me, heroin would be sold in polypropylene meal trays alongside Chicken Tikka For Two. 'All the publicity with Ecstasy. There's been like sixty deaths in ten years of E on the street, and whenever someone dies it makes the front pages of the newspaper, especially if they're under twenty-five. But more than sixty people under twenty-five die every year in England of heroin. You know, we're talking *a year*, and it's not a big issue! And crack – that's not a new drug like it's all made out. It's the same as freebasing which has been going on around the middle/upper classes since the sixties. It's in Cambridge. It come in through the colleges. You know, if they went and piss-tested all the college students I reckon they'd be really surprised at how many had crack cocaine in their system,' etc., etc., etc., etc.

You'd think the homeless would despise the rest of us, but it seems the thing they want to do most is talk. If only they could sit us down and let it all spill out – every twist of their history, down to the last murmur – then they'd be cured.

At Camden we get lost. Stuart, now on his second visit to the Big City, waves out a hundred directions that turn out to be totally wrong. I make a few suggestions that are correct. Then I make a mistake: we end up for a few minutes on the Strand.

Stuart laughs at me like a schoolboy.

As if about to come under fire we unload the battered sleeping bags and rolls of toilet paper outside the Home Office in a human chain. A desolate sort of place, 50 Queen Anne's Gate sits on a narrow street that splits off from Victoria Street above Westminster Abbey like a wind-blanched shoot from a robust and colourful stem. The building, shot full of windows, is a vertical extension of the pavement. Next door is the Wellington Barracks. New Scotland Yard, protected by armed officers, stands round the corner. We spread our luggage between two saplings struggling through the concrete slabs – the sort of things that look nice in architects' plans – and cover them in posters. Dawn seeps gradually among the narrow, torpid streets.

Stuart's mood has changed. He is no longer yapping. He busies himself with arranging boxes and fussing about how to keep order among the badges and petitions, protect sleeping equipment, arrange for our general security.

'There's something about that one,' he says, indicating Fat Frank Who Never Speaks About His Past. At this moment, Fat Frank, another street person, is in the ludicrous position of having his head stuck in the armhole of a T-shirt. His stomach is so obscenely large that his elbows bounce away from his sides like tangents in a maths textbook.

'Something, you know, I don't mean his personal hygiene, he might not be able to help that.' Stuart picks up a box of leaflets. 'Why wouldn't Linda sit next to him in the back of the car this morning? Linda's not normally scared of nobody.' Stuart is endlessly singing this woman's praises: someone who stuck by him in his thousands of hours of need. Because no one living rough feels threatened by Linda, her apparent physical weakness is her strength; or it has been so far, anyway.

Deaf Rob appears eagerly by my side.

'Gotta fin' my girlfrien', wha?' he says perkily, and starts away down the street.

'When will you be back?'

'Wha?'

'Well, where does she live?'

'Wha? We're goin' to move in together, wha?'

Does moving in mean sleeping on the same spot of pavement together? I wonder. He says he last saw her six weeks ago by Vauxhall tube station. Her name is Deaf Jackie.

I give him permission to go and off he marches, arms swinging, along the brightening macadam towards Westminster.

'That's what you'll find, Alexander,' observes Stuart uncharitably. 'It ain't loneliness what's the trouble when you're on the streets. It's some of the fucking people you've got to live with.'

Fat Frank, finally within the T-shirt, his freckled stomach pushed out above his belt like a great ginger egg, hoists up a box of leaflets and strides across the road to the tube station opening.

Stuart said he wanted this protest to do two things. First – the obvious – bring publicity. Second, the bit that interested him the most: to teach me and any other person who'd had life 'so fucking easy' what sleeping rough was really about. 'You fucking want to campaign about it? You get on the fucking streets and learn about it.'

And it is strange: a few moments after the cars that brought us down drive off, I become aware that already I have discovered something new. Because we do not have a place of our own, nor will have for the next three days, we must invent one. I catch myself, and the eyes of one or two of the others, searching for a section of the pavement with which we might want to become familiar. We are looking among the concrete slabs for the outline of a home.

Eight thirty in the morning – the show begins. The *Independent*, Channel 4, East Anglia News, Radio 5 Live, LBC – they've all shown up for our press conference. Me and Linda Outreach and Fat Frank get in our sleeping bags for the photographers and pretend (though, of course, Frank is only pretending to pretend) to be outcast homeless people.

HELP THE HOMELESS:
LOCK UP A
CHARITY WORKER

reads my placard. Linda's has

WHO'S NEXT?

'What's that mean, then?' smirks the Press Association cameraman as he takes the shot. 'Who's next in 'er sleeping bag?' The Home Office staff start drizzling towards work: some take leaflets, a few join in with us for a couple of minutes before stepping back into the flow again; others march past as if they were defying a picket and appear to be absorbed in a newspaper until their nose bumps into the front door. One or two stop to argue. Dull, stupid arguments: I've heard them a thousand times before.

'They were convicted in a court of law,' pronounces an upright man, white hair stuck to his scalp in plaster-of-Paris mounds. It is astonishing how often you hear this remark, always said with full verbal rotundity: 'Court of Law'.

'Which,' I reply, 'is exactly why we're protesting – it was a miscarriage of justice.'

'They must have been doing something wrong – no one else has ever been arrested for this,' from a young beardy face.

Don't people think before they start mooing? 'Of course people haven't been arrested for this before – this is a test case. Part of the government's ridiculous War on Drugs. That's why we've got to do something about it.'

A very tall, thin lady with a knitting needle in her hair: 'The staff *must* have seen something!'

Why must they have?

'Have you ever stood,' I ask her patiently, though perhaps not quite so fluently as I'm writing here, 'in the middle of 120 toxic, hooting, scatterbrained, psychopathological social freaks, bottlenecked into an old converted tap-dancing studio and tried to spot which two are doing something suspicious with their fingertips? The police surveillance camera showed one of their own officers walking within nine inches of a deal and not noticing it.'

A theatre troupe consisting entirely of ex-homeless push up, having heard about the sleep-out: they wear ping-pong balls strapped to the back of their heads, painted to resemble eyes. 'Ruth and John needed these,' they shriek as they dance about. Reverend Ian Harker, an East End vicar, arrives with a squeeze box. A muscular Christian like one of Charles Kingsley's Victorian friends, he plays some merry tunes. By elevenses our stretch of pavement is as jolly as a fairground. Twenty or thirty people are jostling on the pavement – Ruth's family, John's

A muscular Christian

family, my friends, Stuart's friends, street activists, drugs activists. Fat Frank has brought in a boy I nickname Dangerous Ginger. Springy walk, light red hair, a ski-jump nose, Dangerous Ginger keeps his shirt unbuttoned to the waist to show off his smooth chest even though it is distinctly cold.

'If you gave me a bomb, I'd put it under Number Ten,' he announces loudly, arms akimbo. 'I'd go right up there and smash all the windows. I wouldn't care. Your man Jack Straw would know about it if I was in charge.

'I hate people who aren't happy,' he bursts. 'Look at me: no job, no home, but I'm always happy. What have they got to be fucking unhappy about?'

Another protestor is Andria, director of the Mordaunt Trust, a charity for junkies affected by hepatitis or AIDS, and editor of *User's Voice*, a magazine for health- and policy-focused junkies. She has a laugh like a train coming off its tracks and has taken more than a professional interest in Stuart. Wonderful woman, but *really*! Fancy Stuart? She must be even more peculiar than Dangerous Ginger.

Deaf Rob reappears. Out of twelve million Londoners he has achieved the impossible – he has located Deaf Jackie. We all gawp. He fetched her out of a pile of dustbin bags by Waterloo. Is this another of the things Stuart wants me to learn? That the street homeless are not isolated wastrels. They are wastrels with a social fabric, and even in the vastness of one of the world's

largest cities they soon produce a sense of village community
amongst their peers and friends.

Deaf Jackie is a plump girl with bad teeth. Deaf Rob clears a space in the middle of our chosen square of concrete slabs, and props his discovery up on three sleeping bags, supported by a throne of pillows and clothing, like a fattened lunatic queen.

She has written a poem about Ruth and John, addressed to Jack Straw, and politely asks my permission to read it to one of the journalists.

'Let them free/For all eternity!' she chants, sounding as though she wants them hanged. In the background, I see Stuart, carefully facing away from the cameras, bow-legged, calling to Home Office workers like a seller of penny dreadfuls.

'Charity workers imprisoned because drugs found on homeless peee-pul! Knew nothing abaaat it! In prison for doin' no wruoo-ong! Thirty years working for the 'omeless – locked up cos they couldn't stop them taking druuu-*guhs*! Miiiss-carriage of juuus-tice! Thank you, madam, thank you, yes, I've been homeless meself, in prison also, miss, rob-bery and hostage taking, here's a leaflet, if you'd sign the pet-ition? Thank you! Have a nice day! Charity workers imprisoned in miiiss-carriage of juuus-tice!'

'Miiiss-carriage of juuus-tice!'

Sour with disapproval, a plump man with bookshelf glasses accuses Stuart of wanting to legalise heroin.

'No, sir, just cannabis. Smack means more junkies and less long-term economic production.'

Does the man know 'how many detox beds there is in Cam-bridge for all them junkies? Two, sir. And half the time when they've been in them beds for five or six days they're put straight back into the situation they were in before they went there. They fall off the wagon as quick as they got on the wagon. Where, the tax off puff would actually pay for all the treatment programmes and policing for heroin addiction. Legalise cannabis but come down like a ton of bricks on the class As.'

When I come back after fifteen minutes, Stuart and the man with the glasses are having an amiable conversation about South American politics.

The police arrive mid-morning. An officer, his belt trailing communication equipment and restraint devices, strolls among the sleeping bags to explain to me that the Home Office security staff have said they don't want us standing next to the building or crowding the doorway. 'See these brass plugs in the pavement?' he points. The very same that Stuart has been brooding about. 'You mustn't cross them. Not even by an inch if the Home Office doesn't want it. You've got to be on the other side of those.'

Except the vicar.

The Home Office guards don't mind the vicar. He can stay up against the wall as long as he keeps playing his squeeze box. The Home Office likes a squeeze-box-playing vicar.

'That's not good enough, is it?' explodes one of the Ping-Pong eyes, pausing for a moment in his leaping about. 'That's social fucking fascism that is.'

The officer smiles and says 'we' also have to put up riot fences. 'A fence behind you to ensure you're not trespassing. And you must have fences on either side, to protect you from the public.'

'Why do we need to be protected from the public?'

'They might step on you in the middle of the night.'

Finally, 'we' also want a fence in front, to shield us from the street.

'In case you roll off the pavement in your sleeping bags and get run over,' points out the friendly copper.

'You mean you want to cage us in completely?'

'I didn't say cage, sir, no. That was your word.'

Paul Boateng – junior minister, responsible for prisons – is spotted. I run after him. A well-poised, balding man in an expensive dark overcoat, he is striding alongside the wall of the Home Office trying to escape without losing his sense of elegance. He smiles. He has nothing to say. He really must be getting on.

Mr Straw, we are informed by one of the door staff, is not in the office today.

For an hour and a half Fat Frank Who Never Speaks About His Past stands like a boulder by the tube station, distributing leaflets. The press photographers get him in a good pose, massive back to the cameras, clutching the hands of two endearing blond boys. Then at lunchtime he leaves to do the shoppers in Hammersmith.

'Social fucking fascism.'

Only Stuart has become muted while the residue of his creation gambols round him. Despite the spring warmth, he wears the largest sweatshirt he can find. The journalists, attracted to Ruth's four-foot-eleven mother and her enormous velvet, pea-green hat (she is a mosaic artist – she made the decoration on George Harrison's swimming pool), manoeuvre to snatch her photograph alongside him, with his shaven head, broken nose and hotchpotch of dull blue home-made tattoos.

Saturday is cold. The hours drag by wearily. I stretch plastic sheeting across the east side of the barrier to act as a windbreak and to stop the litter bustling in. It works quite well for the wind that comes at us horizontally, but the gusts that billow over the top make two of the barriers bang against each other like an old sign-post in a Western. Around noon I go to Camden to collect signatures from young men and women in designer ripped trousers and thick-

Enormous velvet pea-green hat

rimmed NHS-style glasses. Fat Frank lumbers along the edges of Victoria, returns to Hammersmith, rolls off to Notting Hill. Deaf Rob and Deaf Jackie amble west. Stuart disappears later with Andria. (She returns him intact the following morning.) Dangerous Ginger strides down to Westminster clutching a washbag. Deaf Rob reappears having mislaid Deaf Jackie again among the twelve million. He has tumbled upon a middle-aged drunk, instead.

'Wha! Wha! He's gotta TV company! Gonna make a film! Put us in it! Wha! The Cambridge Two Campaign!'

A little man, he wears a broad-rimmed hat, white jacket and white gauze neckerchief, both grey at the edges but still dandyish. The spittle from his bottom lip drops on to our lunch. 'I borrow money off my friends,' he glows. 'I'll go up to a friend and ask for some money to buy a meal and he'll give me £200. It's quite embarrassing.'

His voice is a shock: clean enunciation, scrubbed-up vowels.

'Wha! I found him! Make a film about Ruth and John! Wha! I'm gonna be in it!'

I decide the little man belongs to the Anomalous Class of homeless: the collection of oddballs who really have *no* reason to be slumming it on the streets, yet aren't doing it because they like the image. They seem to prefer life this way. Living in the ordinary manner of housed people is to them like walking around with a stone in their shoe.

'Wha! Wha!' bleats the inane Deaf Rob until I feel like punching him. 'Film! Film!'

'It's true. I've got these television guys following me all over. Everywhere, except at the weekends. London Weekend Television and they don't work at weekends. Having a laugh, aren't they? Have you got anything to eat?'

He tells a joke: 'A man begging at Victoria Station calls out to a young woman, "Please, miss, got any spare change? I haven't eaten in four days." "Really?" says the woman, suddenly interested. "What's your secret?"'

'Wha!' laughs Deaf Rob, 'Wha! Wha! Wha! Film! Film!'

For a nice boy like me, sitting with the homeless is a bit like Miss Marple and St Mary Mead: in order to understand any fraction of what they are talking about I must relate everything back to my own world. For example, earlier this afternoon, after I'd stomped off from Camden in disgust, Linda and I were petitioning in Chiswick and I fell behind to read a good-looking restaurant menu pasted in a burnished brass box.

> Boccata roll with onion chutney
> Goat's cheese, spinach and tomato pissaladière
> Panzanella salad
> Baked pancake roll with a Cephalonian salad
> Baked honey-glazed Magret of duck

I couldn't let this list of dishes alone. *Boccata? Pissaladière? Panzanella? Cephalonian? Magret* – isn't he a French detective? *Piss*aladière? £11.95 for goat's cheese and urine dressing? But it bothered me. Thirty-six hours on the street and already the world had rushed so far ahead that I couldn't understand a menu. Then I noticed the sign-off line: 'Most teas and coffee's available.' Thickos! Halfwits! These prancing pseuds couldn't even spell a plural in their own language. My self-confidence restored, I marched off to catch up with Linda.

My conclusion? When you are homeless it takes between a day and a half and two days to discover ways to protect yourself from feeling cast out – in my case, by abusing menus in poncey restaurants that I would, but for my newly adopted campaign 'principles', probably patronise.

Another thing: this feeling of homelessness is insidious and creeping, because, of course, by no stretch of the imagination am I actually homeless. I will do this for three nights (I will not disappoint Stuart on that score), then I will go home and be admired. But, even so, I already feel a sort of pull, a sense of outsideness beginning to form. What's more, I rather like it.

I have learnt also that sleeping in a cardboard box is not uncomfortable. In fact, last night was the first time in months that I've slept more than six hours. 'I don't know what you bums are complaining about,' I tell Stuart.

9

Ram-raids and other hard work: Aged 24

Stuart, aged twenty-four, living in a bedsit on the east side of Cambridge: this was five years before he fetched up on Level D, six years before I first met him, seven years before we found ourselves camping in a cage outside the Home Office. Not the most stable period of his life.

When Stuart moved into this room he closed the curtains immediately. He wanted mopey darkness. The front door of the house was smashed up; the kitchen furniture, cracked and bloated. The wind pushed in off Newmarket Road, depositing leaves and biscuit wrappers in the hallway. In the backyard, plastic flapped among the debris. Stuart began chain-drinking: vodka, lager; lager, vodka; vodka, vodka. 'Two bottles a day, reglier.' The couple downstairs packed their bags and ran off within a week. 'Could have been cos of me, I suppose. Too drunk to notice.' Stuart moved into their old living room. In the morning he would find himself lying across the floor or over the arms of the sofa, the television still on, his cuts and bruises healing, and finish off whatever was left in the nearest unspilt can for breakfast. When he did go out, it was to the Co-op by the roundabout to buy frozen sausages, vodka and peas.

'I believed that if I didn't get involved with people, there'd be no one to wind me up and set the fireworks off.'

Once Karen came by the house unexpectedly and he rushed at her with a hammer thinking . . .

... God knows what he was thinking. He started to have visions of the Devil. John Smith saved him from this growing madness.

'A travelling fella,' Stuart explains, with pride. 'Part of the Gypsy Smiths of the Hertfordshire/Cambridgeshire borders. He was like the brother I never had. Respect, trust and honour, that's what keeps us together.'

Stuart takes a fastidious interest in words (except mine). Official ones, especially when they appear in brown envelopes, give him the quakes. He ponders their meanings to death. Gypsy ones, because of Smithy, he holds in the greatest esteem, though he hardly ever uses them himself.

'You see, the thing with travelling fellas is that they're a very close community. They're like Indians, they stick with their own – the only time they normally step out is with what they call "rattlies", a non-Gypsy bird who's willing to open her legs, who's up for a good shag. And, if they're serious about a gal or they going to marry a bird, a lot of them call them their "maud". And because I've never lived in a trailer or lived the Romany way or nothing, even though I've got Romany blood in me, I'm a "gorgia chappy" and I live in a "kennel".'

'What's a kennel?'

'A house.'

'What's wrong with living in a kennel? I live in a kennel.'

'They don't trust people who live in kennels.'

'What does Smithy live in?'

'Well, he's in a kennel as well, only he ain't, because he's most the time in jail.'

One day, Smithy drove Stuart to visit a Gypsy relative who gave Stuart a funny look. 'And Smithy jumped up,' recalls Stuart, voice rising an octave with pride, 'and said, "No, mate, he's 'kushty' [OK], he's safe with the 'gava' [police]. Ain't got to worry about this man in the 'gavakel' [police station]."'

Smithy took Stuart on drives to pinch things from village shops.

At a village supermarket they stopped off one day to buy cigarettes. It was just after closing and they were the last two customers. They asked for twenty B&H. The young cashier, who was on her own, had to leave her position by the grocery till where she was counting the day's take and step into the cigarette cubicle.

The cigarette display was locked.

Stuart and Smithy kept up a playful banter.

'Bit quiet round here, is it, love?'

She had to bend down.

'Where's your husband then – left you to do all the work as usual, eh?'

She laughed, hitched up her tight skirt, inserted the key in the lock of the secret storage cupboard.

When she re-emerged, Stuart paid and they left.

At 3 a.m. that night they smashed the door off the supermarket with a car stolen in the next village, broke open the revealed storage cupboard and filled two sports bags with cigarettes.

Driving back across the fens, they were as excited as spring lambs. Whooping and punching the air, they pulled the car over at a lay-by near the Tate & Lyle sugar factory and set light to the front seat. By the time the fuel tank caught they were halfway across the second field, Smithy carrying the two bags of fags and Stuart doing his best not to stumble in the ruts.

Over the next week they sold the cigarettes – £1.50 a pack ('£1 for the shittier brands') or £5 for four. Twenty went to Stuart's mum and stepdad. Ten to his sister. Her boyfriend wanted five. Smithy's Gypsy connections were like a black hole for the remainder. They'd stolen two hundred packs, risked a year in jail and made £183.

Another time, Stuart threw a TV at a policeman.

PC Shedding: 'As a result of information received we had reason to attend H——Junior School, H——. Upon our arrival at around 2.47 a.m., we approached the school on foot and due to the nature of the call began to check for any insecurities ... I heard another door begin to open about five yards away to my left, I moved towards this door and it opened further. I saw a dark figure appear at the door and shouted, "Stop, Police!" As I did so the figure threw a large object at me, which I later discovered was a television set. Then I ran round to the front of the school and as I rounded the corner, I saw two white males running from the front of the school towards the entrance to the playground. I managed to grab hold of and restrain one of the persons. I brought him to the ground and he began to struggle, as a result of this I restrained him using Home Office-approved restraint techniques.'

'I ain't got much of a run in me,' admits Stuart. 'I used to do the eyes and the ears, and Smithy'd do the graft, because I needed a head start if it come on top. And I was good at that. I've always been the eyes and the ears, but it was hard work.'

'So, was it Smithy you did the school with?'

'Not saying. No use asking twice. No. No comment.'

'I was on duty with Police Dog, Shadow,' the second officer at the scene remembered. 'When PD Shadow indicated a track, he continued tracking out of the school gate and turned left travelling adjacent to the pond.' Shadow chased the scent right up to the high street but it had vanished down the quiet, lamp-lit macadam.

'All I can say is you caught me bang in the act and I've got nothing else to say on the matter,' Stuart grumped at his interrogation.

It was Smithy who heard about the post office.

He shouldered into Stuart's fetid living room one day at about noon, when Stuart was still on bail for the school burglary, snapped off the TV, wrenched back the curtains. Sunlight flooded in.

'Wake up, you lazy bastard. I've got it. I've got it! *Twenty* . . . Wake up! Open your frigging eyes. *Twenty fu* . . . Fuck me, are you dead or what? All we gotta do is . . . Stu! *Twenty fucking thousand knicker!*'

Coates village post office.

PD Shadow
'You muppet, Alexander, it was an Alsatian not a pug.'

Stuart opened his eyes and felt round for the Stella. Half a can later, he spotted the weakness. 'Smithy, fucking brilliant, wicked. Just one small thing. What about the owner?'

'An old woman, on her own.'

'It don't matter if she's 104 with no legs. She isn't going to want to give it to us. She won't be able to give it to us. It will be in her safe, on a time lock.'

'Exactly,' crowed Smithy. 'We do it *before* it gets in her safe, on delivery day. I've got the times, everything. Every fortnight, Monday, 10.30 a.m.'

It was early in the day, but Smithy was usually a bit brighter than this. 'Smithy, on delivery day there'll be guards. Remember them? The big fellas what likes hitting people with truncheons?'

'No, Stu, that's the point. A friend worked there. The old dear doesn't lock the money. She puts it under the counter until closing time. It's down there, four, five hours, asking to be nicked. Twenty fucking grand. Then we'll go back to my missus' and have a proper party.'

In the swirls of dust and summer leaves, Smithy and Stuart cracked open another round of cans and celebrated. A big winner. Twenty grand! Arabic riches! Stuart would be able to buy a caravan, and retire somewhere quiet and sympathetic, like Swansea.

Three questioned following robbery*

DETECTIVES were today questioning two men from St Ives and a third from Whittlesey in connection with a raid on a sub-post office near Whittlesey.

Two raiders smashed their way into the post office at the Green, Coates, in broad daylight yesterday morning.

They broke open the door and made off with an unknown quantity of cash. One raider, believed to be carrying a screwdriver, forced open the till and grabbed the money.

The pair headed towards Whittlesey at 11.13am in an X-registration red Ford Cortina estate. It is believed they dumped it between Coates and Eastrea, changing to a red Escort car.

He and Smithy figured it out afterwards, as they lounged in remand. 'We were set up. How'd the Old Bill know it was us? We got away. We weren't followed. The descriptions from the witnesses were terrible. Every one was different about the two assailants. How'd they get to your missus' house so quick?' said Stuart.

'The police were waiting outside, hidden, when we got back,' he repeats to me, shocked by their duplicity. 'They didn't jump

* *The Evening Telegraph*, Peterborough, Tuesday, June 29, 1993.

on us straight away. His missus – he was bang in love with her,   85
and she had expensive tastes – she was looking right excited,
then, crash. Loads of Old Bill on me back. Like insects. Old
Bill crawling up the curtains, Old Bill under the sofa. Wherever
you looked, fucking everywhere. Old Bill in the sink.'

Stuart refuses to be drawn on the name of who set them up.
He is old-fashioned about such things.

'Let's just say it was funny the way as soon as we was sent
down Smithy's missus moved in with the fella who'd told us
about the job. I'd only been out six months from my previous
when I got banged up again for a five-stretch for this, and the
joke was the old lady didn't get no money that day. There
wasn't £20,000 there. The police had gone through the fucking
routine of pretending she'd got a delivery, hadn't they? Left
a few hundred quid in the till. Didn't want us to be put off,
did they?'

'Five years. That's pretty strong for stealing nothing, isn't
it?' I ask.

'Not really. I'd been doing loads of silly things. Stupid things.
They was getting pissed off with it.'

'Were you armed?' I suggest.

'No,' replies Stuart. 'Well . . . only with a crowbar.'

Stuart has forgotten to tell me something. (Perhaps, in fact,
he does not remember. He does not keep a scrapbook of the
newspaper reports of his notable moments as an ordinary
person would. Any cuttings he might own have long since
been destroyed in one of his periodic rages that purge his
flat of possessions.) What Stuart has forgotten to tell me is
that Smithy was no ordinary blagger. He was a multi-talented
man.

ARMED RAID: Pair jailed for post office robbery*

BUBBLEGUM KING STUCK BEHIND BARS

BUBBLEGUM-blowing champ John Smith is starting a five-year prison sentence today after an armed attack on a post office.

The city's Crown Court heard how the British bubble-gum-blowing record holder and his accomplice staged the attack on the post office at Coates, near Whittlesey, earlier this year.

The pair made off with more than £1,800 in cash and postal orders, after terrifying the elderly staff who ran the shop.

The court was told Smith fell into a life of crime after a series of TV appearances ground to a halt.

The 25-year-old is named in the Guinness Book of Records as the young British record holder after blowing a 16½-inch bubble in 1983 at the age of 15.

But by his late teens, he found his fame was drying up.

Brendan Morris, representing Smith yesterday, told the court how success at an early age had affected him.

He explained: 'He had a taste of the high life but no skills to sustain it.'

Poor fellow. Who can blame him for turning to a life of crime and terrifying little old post-office ladies?

---

* Duncan Milner, *The Evening Telegraph*, Peterborough, Friday, September 24, 1993.

10

Sunday is hard outside the Home Office. Excitements include three cups of coffee, a bacon-and-egg sandwich, closing eyes and imagining Spain, rolling up a sleeping bag, rolling up Linda's sleeping bag, counting signatures, recounting signatures, checking to see if any famous names are among the signatures and finding an actress on *EastEnders*, eating a lamb samosa from the work-every-day-especially-on-Christmas-then-rack-the-prices-through-the-roof shop round the corner – too bored even to read a magazine.

I begin to see why bag ladies have bags. When life is this dull, you have to invent purpose. Collecting torn-up newspaper gives you a hobby, provides an anchoring intimacy with your surroundings, keeps the streets clean. Or so you think. Then one day you wake up and realise that it was all a con: what you had thought was an escape from madness was in fact the arrival.

During the morning people stray off. Often it is just Stuart and me together keeping fort, and Stuart is talking too much again. If words were legs he'd be a billionipede.

Yap, yap, yap.

Andria says all ex-junkies are like this. After so much time brainless on heroin, they soil the road with spittle trying to make up for lost time.

Yap, yap, yap.

Andria is an ex-junkie. Once, she stormed the stage at the

United Nations and berated all the world's delegates on their inhumane policies towards her fellow ex-junkies.

Yap, yap, yap.

Andria talks a lot too.

Stuart has decided that Fat Frank Who Never Talks About His Past is a paedophile. He has no grounds for this. It is entirely based on 'me sixth sense'. Stuart can't even pronounce the word properly: 'pede-o-phile', he says, undoing the diphthong. He's 'really worried' because Mr Frank spent the night in Stuart's flat the night before we came down to London and might have looked at Stuart's address book and found telephone numbers. John Brock has children – did Fat Frank get their number? He's just had his arms around John's sons, hasn't he? Ruth has a daughter. Is Fat Frank interested in girls, too?

Stuart, I say in my roundabout way, calm yourself. He's smelly, that's all. There's obviously also mental health 'issues' as workers in the care professions call it when someone's as loopy as a carousel. But so what? You've got heaps of those too. In the meantime he's our best petition collector. He's gathered double the rest of us. A dedicated worker – don't alienate him. We could do with ten more like him.

But Stuart's not to be put off.

Why did the fucking nonce end up staying at Stuart's place? That's what Stuart wants to know. Does Stuart attract kiddy-fiddlers? Is there something about Stuart that makes boy-buggerers reach for him? Is Stuart to blame? Is Stuart a Perv Pimp?

Forget about Fat Frank. Stuart doesn't need hate figures. Just Stuart dissecting Stuart makes Stuart want to vomit.

In the afternoon comes the shock. The police contact me through a social worker. They have observed and waited, not wanting to intervene before now unless it is absolutely necessary, but a photo of the sleep-out, published in the *Cambridge Evening News*, has forced them into action. It is difficult for the social worker to be direct. Let him put it this way: there is someone, a homeless man, who is playing a prominent role in the campaign – do I know him? Yes, a very intelligent, capable, eloquent, but very erratic individual who lives in the vicinity of Cambridge. A character who is highly dangerous. 'Are we on the same wavelength?' I must kick him off the campaign immediately.

'Why?' I demand, outraged.

'Like I say, it's difficult because of confidentiality . . .'

'To hell with confidentiality. You've got to tell me. This is a democracy, not a fascist state,' I find myself saying in a ping-pongish way. 'The police can't just demand that I evict any campaigners they don't like.'

'If I tell, will you promise not to let it go any further?'

Fat Frank, it turns out, is not just dodgy, he is number four on the list of Britain's worst paedophiles.

The extra shock is that Fat Frank is well known to the homelessness services, and his social worker knew of Fat Frank's involvement in the campaign long before the sleep-out. But he couldn't say anything because he has a professional vow to keep his clients' secrets.

How tortured is that? Ruth and John are sent to prison for upholding the principle of confidentiality. Yet here, in this case of Fat Frank, concerning the same category of people – i.e. the homeless – social workers are forced by the same principle to put John's children at risk.

I do not tell Stuart.

At around lunchtime I want to cry. Perhaps it is tiredness – although, as I've said, I have slept extremely well on the street. Nevertheless, I have a sense that I am losing control. I can imagine that if it goes on like this there will be nothing left of me by Monday. I will not be myself. I will be like the dead, a function of other people's thoughts. Two days on the concrete trying to run a camp and I'm cracking up. I am sick of my friends. I am especially sick of Stuart. I have lost sight of my enemies. Everything is messy. Nothing is simple. I wish I could simplify the enemies of the success of this campaign like Stuart does. I wish I could gather them under a single heading. I wish I had the quasi-religious spirit of homeless people and conspiracy theorists to believe in the System or the Masons or the FBI.

Looking up, I catch Stuart watching me. It is still early afternoon. There is a long time and another night yet to go.

'You alright, Alexander?'

I nod. Is there any point in saying that if I have ever been close to punching him, it has been during the last yapping half-yapping-hour?

'Don't get stressed, mate,' he says softly and lifts his Stella. 'You done alright, Alexander.'

It is in the evening that Stuart finally 'loses it'. Walking along Victoria Street with Linda Outreach after dark I see him lurching towards us, pressing campaign stickers on shop windows, telephone boxes, the pavement, and rattling the HSBC bank doors and shouting through the letter box because he thinks there is someone hiding in the building. It might be amusing to watch, but there is a feral quality. A little tipsy myself, I see him as a Robert Louis Stevenson character, trying to escape the good manners and parental neatness of people such as Linda and myself. He is sniffing out an atavistic world, beyond words.

As he reaches me, his expression changes. Standing himself against a dustbin, he jabs a finger in my direction.

'You fucking, wanky, middle-class cunt-fuck, Alexander, always saying, "What's the answer?" That's the difference, in'it? No answers! You want to know how I become what I am? Write a book what don't have no answers. But that won't make your fucking name, will it? Nah, see? Fuck off. Go find your fucking answers.'

He gives the dustbin a thwack and then peers unsteadily through one of the rubbish slots. 'Not here. Stuart Fucking

Shorter, ask them, how can he justify his mother lying across his brother to stop him chopping him up with two catering knives? Ask the fucking answers about that!'

Back at the camp the others leave, muttering things about supper, when they see us approach. Stuart perks up when a police car arrives.

'Tell you what,' Stuart goads across the pavement at the huge officer who's rolled down his window to wish us good-night, 'since you got so much fucking time on your hands, answer this one for me. Ten people on the street beat the fucking crap out of somebody and they'd all get ten years for it, where, in prison, your mates put on shields and riot gear and fucking pour into somebody's cell and do the same thing, and they're doing a public service. Explain that. And then they wonder why the person they just beat up so there's blood all across the walls and screaming what can be heard from one end of the wing to the other doesn't turn into a nice boy. Do you know what I mean? Do you? Do you? Nah, of course not. *You* ain't got the faintest fucking clue, have you?'

The officer stays in his car, smiling back.

Never one to shy away from making a bad situation worse, Stuart picks on another topic. 'You *know* there are drugs in the hostels in London, don't you? You *know* they're full with drugs, don't you? Why don't you fucking arrest the hostel managers then, like they arrested Ruth and John? Give me the fucking answer to that, then, will you?'

He asks this fifteen times. I tell him to shut up. He starts on his middle-class geeky cunt routine again. What Stuart means when he says it's not the cold or the hardness of the streets that drives you crazy, it's the other people. It's the people like *fucking* Stuart, ranting and raving.

Shut up, will you!

'You fucking middle-class . . .' etc.

The policeman for a second time bids us both a pleasant night and drives off.

Stuart rubs his hands, retreats to the north edge of our cage and sits in his ugly twisted way, hunched over the kerb. He is an animal. A disagreeable oaf. I wish he would die. Right here. On the pavement.

That, at least, would be a publicity coup.

Across the road, above St James's Park tube – a deserted,

I wish he would die.

Soviet-style station – the Epstein carving seems tired of us. Epstein did two of these reliefs, in 1929. *Day*, round the corner, on the east face, is a man raising a naked boy into the air. When it was unveiled, it caused outrage because someone noticed that the boy had a rather large penis. Epstein denied it. The managing director of London Underground offered his resignation. A furious company director demanded to pay for the entire sculpture to be removed. A mystery person fired bullets at it in the middle of the night. In the end, the headmaster of a boys' school was summoned to decide the matter and Epstein was forced to chop an inch and a half off the offending projection.

Night is the one that overlooks us: a stolid, resigned woman, arms in lap, between her thighs. 'When will you lot go away?' she seems to sigh.

At around two, a large, once well-dressed man, seeping drink, bumps round the tube station corner, past the blue wheelie bins, and stops to glower at us.

'I was with the Provos!' he declares at last, sounding, because of his brogue, like a cross between a cold-blooded assassin and a lilting boat at sea. 'I know what the fucking government's like. Fucking down with the British! Good on you fellas whatever you're fucking doing. Do you know what day it was on Friday?'

Friday was St Patrick's Day.

'Fucking right! Down with the fucking empire!'

'I hear you, mate,' Stuart yells back, to my acute embarrassment. I consider myself a monarchist. 'We're with the homeless,' bellows Stuart, 'and it's the same fucking queen and government with us!'

Speak for yourself. Horrid republicans. I do not speak, however. I keep quiet. I am not a suicidal monarchist.

Stuart sits down again with an air of increased camaraderie and the IRA man bumps off towards Petty France.

Much later, after I have finally fallen asleep, Deaf Rob and Jackie come back and have an argument. This is spooky. I don't even know what has woken me to witness it, because the argument is in mime. The street light spreads an elfin glow over the entire camp. Traffic on Victoria Street sounds like rushes of gentle water. Deaf Rob, lying down, rocks from side to side. Deaf Jackie picks silently among their belongings, stepping over the rucksacks and the 'Louis Pierre, Paris' suit-holder as if each was in danger of being woken.

'Don goohh, donnn goohh,' moans Deaf Rob.

In the morning I will learn that he has stolen her hearing aid to stop Deaf Jackie leaving him. She is searching for it.

She makes a sound, but it is so quiet that I hardly know if she's spoken.

'Shaa*arrr up!*' bellows Deaf Rob. 'Can you *see*! They slee-ph, slee-ph, slee-*ph*!'

We've arranged things, at Stuart's recommendation, so that there are always two sensible people on site: either Stuart and me, or me and Linda, or Andria and Stuart, or Linda and Andria. While I was petitioning in Camden, Stuart and Linda kept watch. When Fat Frank was driving Linda round the bend, Andria and I held the fort. All Friday and all weekend, day and night, it has been like that, because it means we are never weak or caught off guard. It is because of this policy that we've avoided too much police interference, met Kevin Flemen, legal expert for the drugs organisation *Release*, been able to conduct newspaper interviews and arrange shots for photographers at any moment. When a radio programme happened upon us, just by chance, as they were cruising the backstreets looking for interesting snippets, a man called Brent, our kindly website designer, was there to say something sensible to *News Direct*.

News Direct turns out to be our undoing.

Monday morning. Never has a Monday looked so like a Friday – never a sun so glossy with relief and Epstein freshness!

We discover that Deaf Jackie's transistor radio has run flat. Who needs distraction and stupid music on a morning of loveliness?

We can't listen to the *News Direct* report.

Someone needs to fetch batteries.

Deaf Rob refuses to leave his sleeping bag. He's in Deaf Jackie's arms. Stuart's disappeared. Linda's left to get back to Cambridge. Fat Frank has rolled away. The only other member of our group is a newcomer called Scotty, an alcoholic who is already chuckling over his second can of Tennant's Extra.

Brent and I, bursting with goodwill, wander off to buy the goods. We will get trays of coffee and buns for everyone into the bargain. Yes, a surprise six-pack for Scotty also. On the house!

It is while we're gone that the Home Secretary Jack Straw shows up.

According to the garbled report I hear, he's been very pleasant. His car – 'a Jag, first class – it's the bollocks' – drew up alongside the pavement and two big men got out with him. Scotty recognised them immediately as bodyguards.

'I've seen you before,' says Scotty, spraying up his beer can. 'I was on the bench having a were drinkie when you and them walked by, and me mate said, "Who's that?" and I said, "That's Mr Straw with his security men."'

'You're on the ball, eh?' the Home Secretary replies.

Scotty's face goes purple with pride at the intimacy of this exchange.

To give him credit, Deaf Rob at least got to the point. I could imagine the guards tensing as he adopted his gunfighter stance, and fired off his Free Ruth and John speech. But Mr Straw just dodged the subject with his favourite 'The Home Office is not concerned in this case. It is a matter entirely for the judiciary.' Deaf Rob still doesn't know the answer to that one, and Deaf Jackie couldn't hear what the Home Secretary was saying anyway.

By the time Brent and I returned, the street was empty again.

Three weeks of preparation and £600 spent on publicity and planning, and who does the Home Secretary meet as representatives of the campaign? A middle-aged drunk, and two deaf homeless people stealing each other's hearing aids.

Stuart and I laugh about it on the train all the way back to Cambridge.

His primordial mood, briefly glimpsed, has gone.

We see a pair of hares boxing by a stream, and Stuart, exultant, calls out, 'OK, yaa! Right on, chaps!' and adopts a sniffy, Edwardian pose, holding his fists fingers down. He is going back to his flat to sleep and tomorrow on to Norwich. 'The Little 'Un – it's his birthday.'

'The little what?'

'Little *'Un*.'

'What's an "un"?'

'Me son, stupid.'

'You've got a *son*?' In four months he has never told me.

'Thirteen years of age.'

We scoop through the last stretch of country, past the Gog-Magog Hills and the Addenbrooke's Hospital cremation towers, while I take in this revelation. I don't know what to say. I fall back on platitudes.

'Have you got a present for him?'

Stuart beams. 'A golf club. He loves his golf. Always out on the golf course is the Little 'Un.'

11

'And this is the order of me prisons: Send, Baintnow House, Send, back to Send again, Eriestoke, Norwich, five lots of remand in Norwich, then I was sentenced for five years, so I started off in Norwich, transferred to Aylesbury, transferred to Glen Parva, back to Aylesbury, Littlehey, Grendon Underwood, Grendon Underwood to Littlehey, was released. Next sentence: Bedford, Littlehey, Whitemoor, Bullingdon, Long Lartin, Grendon, Long Lartin, Norwich, Long Lartin, Winchester, Long Lartin, Whitemoor, Blundeston, Wayland . . . I don't think I've missed any out. Oh yes I have, I been to Leicester three times as well.'

Rageous:
Aged 25–29

To be honest, Stuart's years in prison after the post office robbery infuriate me. I don't know what to do with them. Each time I rewrite them something is missing. He disappears from view metaphorically and literally when he steps down from the dock in Peterborough Crown Court after sentencing. The reason he vanishes, however, is not because he stops being noticeable, but because he ceases to be (to me) human. Instead of Stuart Unexpected – the soft-spoken, worried, edgy lover of archaeology programmes, the half-boast, half-benevolence – in prison, as he presents it, there is only Stuart Fury, the set of bloody incidents. Events replace character. For the next half-decade he responded to every significant difficulty with the intensity of a bomb going off, 'going right off on one', being 'not too clever', and it is a form of simplification that quickly becomes, well, boring. It takes away subtleties. In prison Stuart turned himself (trained himself, he would argue; perfected his technique) into the unpredictable wrecking machine that later made him distinctive on the streets. Personality is gone.

Stuart in prison was a category-A (where he soon ended up) pest. Category-A prisons are top-security institutions, for offenders whose escape would be highly dangerous to the public, the police or the security of the nation. When Stuart wasn't brooding in solitary, he was on the wing flashing through his nastier personas as if showing off his wardrobe: riots, dirty protests, smashing up the prison toilets, threatening to set fire to other prisoners – those are just the outbursts he can remember. Incidents that the rest of us would consider defining moments of horribleness are so frequent to Stuart that they soon become as unremarkable as last week's laundry. They sit sullenly between a bore and a swagger.

At HMP Littlehey, he could have worked in the kitchen (but that tends to be a job for sex offenders, who are considered cleaner and more reliable than ordinary convicts). Or he could have gone to the underpants factory (although the authorities admitted that producing 200,000 underpants a year was unlikely to give prisoners useful skills for the outside community). Instead, he ended up in the shoe shop and attacked the factory officer with a chair.

'I'm not exaggerating when I say between ten and fifteen, maybe twenty screws took me down the block. None of them got the helmets on, which I was quite surprised about. They've bent me up, put me in the strip cell, stripped me clothes off me, left me stark bollock naked, so I've ripped the lino up off the floor, shat on the floor, pissed on the floor. You know, just disobedience . . .'

'Just disobedience.' Childish, comforting, petulant, 'Fuck You' disobedience.

Ruth once told me when I went to visit her at HMP High-point that it is surprising how much of what you imagine to be your innate sense of self actually comes from things that aren't one's self at all: people's reactions to the blouse you wear, the respectfulness of your family, the attentiveness of friends, their approval of the pictures in your living room, the neatness of your lawn, the way people whisper your name. It is these exhi-bitions of yourself, as reflected in the people whom you meet, which give you comfort and your identity. Take them away, be put in a tiny room and called by a number, and you begin to vanish. It is almost the subject of a million magazine headlines – except that the magazines read, 'What your clothes say about you'; in prison, you realise they should read, 'What is left of you once your clothes have had their say?'

In *From the Inside*, the book she subsequently wrote about her experience in prison, Ruth is struck by the speed of this sense of self being stripped away:

> Following the screw back from the canteen shop to the cell, I realized I had developed a prison persona: hands in pockets, a slow uncaring walk, shoulders hunched, scowling and grumpy; a woman of few words but always a curse at the ready. It had happened in just two or three days. There I was, Wyner, prison number EH 6524: scared but not going to show it; ready for anything but behaving as if I didn't give a shit. My defences were up, and I knew I needed them, but also I feared that the real 'me' had been destroyed. Would I ever get her back again?*

'*Just* disobedience': to Stuart it's hardly worth mentioning. Of course you have to be disobedient. In prison, being a pain in the neck is one of the few ways to make the officers react to you as an individual. Disobedience is one of the few tricks you have left to hang on to the idea that you continue to exist distinctively and are still reliably connected to the person who bore your name on the outside. What comes from within turns out, in prison, to be not nearly as great as people hope.

'Next morning,' continues Stuart, 'I'm up on report, damage to the workshop, damage to this and that, in front of the governor. He's lost me loads of days again, more fines. Told me it was only because the officer didn't want an outside court that I wasn't being taken to an outside court. I said to the gov'nor, "You mean you ain't taking me to outside court, because you

---

* Ruth Wyner, *From the Inside: Dispatches from a Women's Prison*, Aurum Press, 2003

fucking put it on me. I told you what would happen if you fucking stuck me in the shoe shop and you turned round and told me I wouldn't do it. In other words you encouraged me to do it, because you should know better, being a gov'nor." You know, give him loads of verbal, sat there cussing him.'

Where does this man get his energy from? Is it as exhausting for him as (already now) it is becoming for the reader?

'The governor says, "You think you're a smart-arse, you." He says, "We'll see who's laughing. You're going to Whitemoor."'

Stuart leans forward, goggle-eyed. Don't I understand the horror of what he's just said? *Whitemoor.*

Stuart, I'm surprised they didn't take you into the backyard and shoot you.

Whitemoor. Stuart shakes his head in memory of the injustice of it.

'On me first night I melted a toilet brush up into a big point and melted two razors in it and I slept with the cunt under me pillow. You've got everything at Whitemoor. You've got terrorists, you've got psychopaths, professional gangsters what are called "faces". Then you've got their henchmen, your heavies, which are people that are respected by gangsters, the muscle for these people to work behind. There are wannabe gangsters, psychopaths, plastic gangsters, what are people who think they're gangsters, but like they're just smackheads, and when they're in jail, they ain't got a pot to piss in. They think they're Charlie Big Potatoes and they do loads of crime but what they got to show for it? At least your henchmen, heavies and gangsters – you never see them short of a few bob in jail. They're not running around asking people for dog ends like plastic gangsters. Proper gangsters would say to us, "Him, him and him over there, you wouldn't believe he used to have a half-a-million-pound house, and we used to do a lot of business with him." Because he got on the rock cocaine and sunk a thousand pound a night off on rock. It's really the older drug people: they're doing sixteen years for a stupid armed robbery, being really blunted, where before they were good crooks. But because of the party lifestyle, the Big I Am, they ended up losing everything. Then you got your people who are security threats, or have good sources and could gain escape, your murderers, your manslaughters, your crazies. People who are just unstable, unpredictable. Then, on separate wings in Whitemoor, the dirty nonces and the sex offenders and a fucking load of scum cunts . . .'

'Which lot do you come in?'

'I suppose I come in the crazies, really.'

Two days after Stuart arrived there was a riot.

The Times, 22 December 1993

Liquor trouble at jail

Prisoners brewing liquor for Christmas caused damage estimated at over £30,000 in five hours of vandalism at the high security Whitemoor prison at March, Cambridgeshire. More than 160 prisoners were involved in starting small fires; toilet fittings were smashed and doors ripped off their hinges. Three prisoners and three prison officers were hurt. Andrew Barclay, the governor, said: 'The catalyst, I think, was a search I carried out yesterday afternoon in C and D wings. They may have been drinking the hooch while the search was going on rather than pouring it away.'

'It just took off,' remembers Stuart with a tremble. 'Anything they thought would fit through the bars and reach the screws. Then fires started getting in. Bedding. Just going right off, smashing up their belongings.' The violence 'kept coming in waves'. The furniture and table-tennis tables flared up, the flames catching hold of the piles of rubbish that had been flung into the netting between the balconies, then the pool table was added, and fresh bedding, and the fire crackled two storeys high. 'If you don't fucking join in we'll all get done!' the leaders threatened. 'We want to get the fucking wing closed down.'

'I was petrified,' Stuart declares to my surprise. 'I didn't want to get involved. You know, you've got all these dangerous people, so embittered with rage and hatred – they were fucking scary. I legged it up the cells to the third floor what was the only place where the windows would open outwards.'

There he stood on someone's bed with his nose pushed between the bars, the smoke pouring out around his head 'and the fire engines down below and their stupid fucking flashing pea-sized lights like bits of glitter'.

Stuart made a few friends. Colin Richards lived on the floor above. He'd killed a policeman (accidentally, of course) during a robbery in Walton on the Naze and was paralysed from the chest down by the storm of bullets that the police fired in return. The wardens hated him. They never gave him the nappies he needed or the right amount of sterilised equipment, but he was a hero with the inmates, who, at mealtimes, gathered round to lift up his wheelchair and carry him down the steps to the dining hall, like a emperor.

Jeremy Bamber, who murdered his adoptive father, mother, sister and her two children, had to walk round with *National Geographics* strapped to his waist because so many people had tried to stab him.

In the block Stuart also met the only terrorist to have come out of the Iranian Embassy siege alive, and the two of them chatted in the exercise yard during their daily hour of 'association' time. 'He said to us, he had the most luckiest escape of any man he'd known, because it was the actual hostages who dragged him out. The SAS were trying to drag him back in.

All the others were shot by the SAS. It was the hostages who dragged him out with them.'

A Turkish drug importer, a mafia 'Baba' or godfather, nicknamed Stuart 'the Peterborough Gangster' because he was always in trouble, and 'I laughed back with him'.

'No,' said Stuart, 'I'm just a petty thief who ended up getting nicked and getting five years for jumping over an open-counter post office. I'm just a petty thief who's come unstuck.'

After the Whitemoor riot (or was it before? I lose track) comes the barricading in HMP Bullingdon, the hunger strike in HMP Winchester, the HMP Grendon fire-extinguisher incident, and soon your tolerance has disappeared. The perennial problem of the chaotic has crept in: this is a life with too much intensity. The wildness is fascinating in hints, but the days are over-concentrated and piled too high with outrage for extended listening. Such people might be rich for novelists; they are a downright liability for a biographer.

Even during visits Stuart took care not to give his prison persona any sense of real life. 'When we left because time was up,' recalls his half-sister Karen, 'Stuart used to walk to the door and he would never turn round. As soon as he'd said goodbye at the table he'd turn his back on you.' Nor did he send letters, except to his solicitor ('Never been a big one for the 17p stamp'); he never made phone calls. He did not keep a diary, either in a book or on tape. He never wrote notes. For some people, prison is the time of memory and record: Ruth Wyner, Jeffrey Archer, Fyodor Dostoevsky, but for people like Stuart it is the place where time doesn't quite count. The days are relentlessly dull, difficult to separate, just to be sat through, like a football player on the substitute bench.

'What's the best type of prison to be in?' I ask.

Stuart raises his eyebrows and purses his lips. 'On balance? Dispersals – high-security prisons – is better than locals. Because in locals, if you tell a screw to fuck off or there's a skirmish, you get bent up.'

'Why doesn't that happen in the high-security prisons?'

'Because in proper jails, people aren't going nowhere. You don't want to start arguing over a match or a roll-up. You don't tell the screws to fuck off unless you've had a really bad day. Whereas in the locals, you've got people who might only have a month. They go round giving it the Big I Am, and as soon as they get bent up and dragged down the block, they can't handle it. Just scream and scream and scream. When I was at Winchester, because it was a local jail, every day you'd hear screaming. But the good thing about that jail was the way the doors was designed so you couldn't see out to see what was happening. Even if I'd looked out through the crack in the doors, I couldn't see nothing in the rest of the block, cos the other rooms was in the wrong place. At least twice, and sometimes three, four times a day, screaming.'

'The good thing about that jail was the way the doors was designed.'

'Because it don't work, does it?' Stuart says suddenly in mina- tory mood, getting up. He pushes my tape recorder aside. He has had enough of trying to educate me today. 'Prison can't work. You can't make people change by bullying them and beating them with batons and locking them up in isolation for days and days, weeks, what would drive some people mad, living like an animal in a fucking cage. Do you know how many people get killed by screws in prison every year? Nobody would tell you something like that – but it's true, every year, murders. "Oh, sorry, gov, he choked on his vomit while ten of us was holding him down." "Oh, do *excuse* us, he broke his back – how was we to know bending him in half the wrong fucking way was bad for his health?"'

'John Brock says prison's not too bad,' I say.

'Yeah, but there's two levels, in't there? People like John is not what they class as a criminal. Any of the screws could have been in John's position. All John was doing was his job at Wintercomfort, so he was probably more like one of the boys. And even him – his first job on the wing – what was it? To wash the blood down in the seg [segregation] unit after the screws had fucking finished with someone in there. It's true what John says, you can do bird and not lose days if you don't buck the system, but unless you're willing to give information normally, they won't let you have a quiet time.

'Information about what?'

'Who's smuggling drugs, who's doing what. If someone's been done over, who done it.'

'And if you said "I don't know"?'

'You'd just get stitched up, get nicked, get a governor's report. You can have an argument with a screw, and tell him to fuck off, and the riot bell will come. Half the jail screws will come, you'll get jumped on, bent up like a chicken, dragged into a cell, get your clothes literally ripped off you, and then get charged with assaulting a screw as well. If a load of men jump on you and start inflicting pain on you, you're going to start struggling, and that's classed as assaulting a screw. You get those screws who will help you out if it's genuine, but them screws are normally the first ones in if it kicks off. There is no such thing as a good screw, and normally those that are the nice ones are also the first ones to come in with their shields and their fucking silly sticks when they want to bend you up.'

It makes sense. Put two macho groups together and give the first desperation and numbers, and the second truncheons and protective clothing, and the result is like a laboratory civil war. 'But there are times when someone deserves it,' I insist, thinking, you Stuart, my friend, you little nightmare.

'Well, no. If it's not alright on the street if someone does something wrong to just go up to them and beat them, why should it be alright in prison for one screw to decide that something's wrong, and then get a load of his mates to go and beat somebody up? As well as wearing all the protective clothes and shields. Who are they to say that that's the punishment that person should have? All it needs is for an obnoxious screw to have a bad day and you too have a bad day. It's easy for him to get all stroppy, for you to say, "Oh, just fuck off then," or "Shove it," and some of them literally just turn round and hit the bell, all the screws come running. You can take a fifteen-, twenty-minute kicking in the block. And the doctor will come down, "Yep, he's alright" Ask my mate Smudger to show you his arm. The screws broke his arm. Doctor had a look at it, said there was nothing wrong, and he still has trouble with it now. They broke his arm and then just left it to repair itself. Other countries just whip fucking prisoners, where in this country we call it Control and Restraint.'

'Wait,' I interrupt on another occasion, during another of Stuart's descriptions of slammers past and future (he wouldn't, he says, be surprised to die in one). 'Take me through the process of arriving.'

'Right, you go through reception, have a shower, go to your cell –'

'What's reception?'

'Right, reception is where you get all the, awww, it's not . . . I mean, it's just . . . nah, horrible . . . not horrible, horrible, but horrible, know what I mean? Not being funny . . . awww, you don't want to go there.'

It's no good. Stuart can't describe it. There are prison books and diaries that detail the process, which is quite a mild rite of passage, a dull-witted but clearly necessary stripping of civility – name taken, civilian clothes removed, prison garb handed out, number given, a shower and delousing – but nothing I've read captures Stuart's shudder.

'Then what? What's next after reception?'

'Go to my cell . . .'

'How do you get to your cell?'

'How do you think? Clank, clank, on the wing, up the steps.'

'What's the wing like?'

'Phhhaawww! Smell of piss. Just smells of piss everywhere.'

This was because of the practice of slop out, still common in the mid-1990s but forbidden now. Not allowed out to use the toilet during the fourteen and a half hours they were locked in their cells each day, inmates had to store their excrement in buckets until the buckets could be 'slopped out' in the communal latrine. The rancid odour seeped into every part of the wing.

> 0800 unlock, slop out, breakfast.
>
> 1115 dinner.
>
> 1330 unlock, slop out.
>
> 1600 tea.
>
> 1730–2030 slop out, serve supper.

'So there you are, the first night in your cell,' I pursue, strangely invigorated by this vision of urine sloshing through the building. 'What's it like? No freedom. Cooped up. Can you sleep? Who were you sharing with?

'Alexander, that's what I keep trying to tell you. I didn't spend the first night in my cell. Didn't like me cellmate. He was doing twenty-eight days. I'd just got five years and three months! "I'm not banging up with that cunt," I says. "He's packing his bags to go home while I'm still thinking where to put the toothbrush. It'll do me head in. I'm not hearing him moaning about oh, he's missing his wife and family or he's going home tomorrow." I wouldn't have it. Refused to go in. About turn. Straight to solitary, the block. I spent me first night of five years three months straight in the block – I lost seven days' remission straight off on me first night, and it was me birthday.'

What about bullies?

'First time someone tries to tax you in jail, attack them.'

'To tax' in prison is just as it is outside of prison: when a person nastier than you are takes away a portion of everything you own: a handful of tobacco, your phonecard, your Bob Marley cassettes.

'Attack them? What if he's an eighteen-stone yeti-man with pointy teeth?'

'If there ain't a weapon there to hurt them, and they're a right big cunt, just attack them,' Stuart says. 'Because if you're a bit weak-minded and give in, you'll have others – all the time. You'll *never* get away from it. And as soon as they let you out the hospital wing after that, you'll often find the bully will come and try and take everything again but just attack them again. And you'll find that if you fucking have a go at a bully twice, even if he beats you up, they don't come back a third time. Another way is to create a situation where they see you just lose the plot totally, even if it's against the screws, chasing the screws up the ladder with a lump of wood. Alright, you get a kicking off the screws, but it's a way of keeping the bullies back. It's a safer way of doing it. Because if you get involved with cons, it might come to the stage where you got to throw boiling hot water and sugar over them, and fucking stab them as well if they're a right big cunt, because I've seen people have sugar and hot water and fucking *still* batter people.'

Hence, as Stuart points out, the clear advantage of convincing other inmates from the start that 'you're fucking mad'. Then 'they'll leave you alone, in general. Also, since the Strangeways riot, there's so much pressure on cons to give evidence in an outside court, that if you do someone up, you'll probably get a five-stretch or an eight-stretch on top of your original sentence. Where, as long as you don't go up and punch a screw, seriously hurt one, just chase them, the chance of you getting an outside court are really rare. You'll get a really good fucking kicking. But what's a kicking when you've had so many?'

And what about education? Why don't more people in prison think to themselves, 'Well, OK, it's not where I want to be, but there's nothing else to do, so I'll take all the training courses so I can get a good job when I get out'?

Says Stuart: 'People say there's all these courses, but what are they? In the jails with the best courses, you have to put up with between 60 and 80 per cent nonces. You have to listen to fucking kiddy-fiddlers talking about kiddy-fiddling, fucking granny-rapists ganging up and taking straight cons out, just to do a class on how to cement two bricks together. A few have motor mechanics and woodwork and welding. The courses are only very basic, and sometimes you can get halfway through doing a course and then because of a problem on the wing, you'll get shipped out.' Most jails do an industrial cleaning course, but 'how many ex-cons are going to want to be industrial cleaners? And, seriously, what company director's going to want a load of ex-cons with fuck-off-sized Hoovers running round his office at 5 a.m.?

'Education facilities is always good in prisons with a large proportion of sex offenders,' complains Stuart bitterly. This is because sex offenders are generally older, better educated, less trouble and more intelligent. 'Ironic, in'it? They're in there with all the ones they've abused, because all their victims have been so fucked up by what's been done to them that they've become criminals too, and the abusers are still the ones with privileges!'

This fatalistic meeting between paedophiles and victims is

like Greek theatre. I press for more: moments of realisation, subtle incidents of revenge, poignant displays of despair, anything human. 'Frank Beck what did snuff movies died, the cunt, in Whitemoor, just before I got there, playing badminton in the gym,' recollects Stuart with bland satisfaction.

'What about murderers? Did you ever share a cell with a murderer?' I try instead.

'Murderers? The mad thing is, as soon as you mention the word "murder" everyone gets hysterical, really fearful. *MURDERERS!* Oh, dangerous, dirty, evil people. But the majority of people who I've met in jail who've been done for murder, you could release fifty per cent of them the day after they've committed their murder. Alright, yes, they have killed somebody, but they're so damaged, a lot of them, by what they've done and shell-shocked, they'd never ever dare commit another offence again. Fifty per cent of people in for murder are your ordinary people who just for *one* moment lost it.

'D'you know,' says Stuart after reflecting a moment, 'I thought screws was called screws cos, with their silly caps and that, that's what they look like.'

Occasionally, Stuart's family would find out about his outbursts. Several weeks after the event a letter from HM Prisons would arrive, explaining that the authorities had found it necessary to 'ghost' this scion of the family tree away to another establishment, two hundred miles south, or forty miles east, to Winchester or Lincoln. No details about why. At HMP She-Can-No-Longer-Remember-Which, Stuart's mother once showed up for a visit to find that her strange son was 'not available'. He'd been taken off, cell stripped out, washed down, 'ghosted' yet again, and another con in his place. The warders didn't tell her what had gone on even when she was standing outside the gates worrying herself sick. He was just 'not available'. Was he refusing to acknowledge her? Was he in hospital

Drawing by Stuart Shorter

with an infectious disease? Were the guards unhooking his corpse from a bed sheet wrapped through his window bars? Sorry, Mrs Shorter, no comment.

Stuart's sister laughs. 'The reason I've seen most of this country is going from prison to prison to see Stuart. It seemed like every Sunday. I remember at school we'd have to write in our weekend books what we'd done at the weekend. The others would have gone to the circus or the seaside and I'd have been to prison to visit my brother.

'We weren't never allowed to see him after he'd done things,' she adds, 'because I think they'd beat him so bad.'

Another woman, the girlfriend of a friend of Stuart's, helped out with the occasional bit of smuggling. 'I had to takes some puff in and Stuart had to get his friend down because Stuart couldn't put it up his bum himself. Couldn't face it. So Graham come down to the waiting room and I put it under a Coke can and slid it to him. He picked the can in one hand and with the other put the packet down the back of his trousers, up his arse.

'Another time, my boyfriend had these two really dodgy characters in the car who got out when we stopped at this town on the way and come back with black bags full of stuff – they were professional shoplifters. They just sat in the prison car park, waiting, while we went in for the visit.

'Money and puff, we used to take in. Ten- or a five-pound note, fold it up until it's as small as you get, then wrap it really tight in cling film and burn the cling film round it, because Stuart's got to swallow it, hasn't he? That's how he gets it past the screws who rub him down after the visit. You'd take it into the prison however you could. If you've got an onyx ring, that's obviously raised, put it under your ring to get it in, or in your bra. Next, go up to get your Stu a drink from the machine at the other end of the room, then hand over the packet when you come back and give it him. Simple.'

Most smuggling does not go on in the visitors' room. It is

done over the perimeter fence, at least in the lower category prisons. Girlfriends, parents, friendly businessmen, strong children
– they stand in the fields outside and lob whatever's been
requested (usually stuffed inside tennis balls) into the com-
pound. Then the prisoners on gardening duty (known as
'Wombles') clean up the mess and get it back to the cells.

One Saturday afternoon, a few months before Stuart was due
to be released, his name was shouted over the tannoy because
his visitor had showed up. Stuart was surprised. It's only with
a visiting order that a visitor can come in and Stuart hadn't
sent out any visiting orders. No one was allowed to visit him.
He had to borrow a pair of decent jeans off a mate because he
wasn't prepared. He hadn't an ironed shirt ready nor had he
shaved in a week.

He never got to the visiting room. Just before he reached it,
an officer guided him through an alternative door into a private
area he didn't know existed. To his astonishment his mother
and stepfather were sitting there, together with the principal
officer of the whole wing.

'The hard bit to me is that Dad was crying. Dad broke down
in tears. First thing I said is, "Is Marcus and Karen alright?"
Me little half-brother and sister. Me dad's really upset.'

His mother said, 'Nah, they're grand.'

'Who's died? What's up? Who's ill?'

And his mother said, 'It's your brother, Gavvy. He's killed
himself.'

RECIPE FOR HOOCH

For one person, 'to get pissed, not drunk'.

> *'You ever tried it, Alexander – proper prison hooch? We'll do
> that some day. Make a bucket and get rat-arsed.'*

Bucket or industrial container 'what's not been punchered by
the screws'.

2 × spoonful of Marmite, bran flakes or yeast tablets
'smuggled if you're banged up. From Tesco's if you're not.'

1 × big bag of sugar.

Orange juice, apple juice, 'a bit of what you fancy'.

Potato/handful of rice.

5 litres warm (not boiling) water.

Mix 1 litre of the water in the bucket with Marmite and sugar,
add orange/apple juice for flavouring and potato for starch.
Top up with remaining water. Leave, loosely covered, for two
weeks. 'You know, it's not very nice to drink, it gives you gut
ache and everything, but it does the damage. It's good stuff.'

METHOD FOR MOONSHINE

> *'Distilling? Yeah, you can do that too. Remember me telling
> you about Colin? The one who was in a wheelchair and had
> catheters? I just used to go see him . . .'*

1 × bucket of hooch, as prepared previously.

1 × pressure cooker with adjustable temperature setting. 'The
kitchens of HMP Long Larton – you can nick them from
there.'

1 × catheter tube.

Ice.

'It takes a bit of fiddling, but then what you got to do in prison
but fiddle?' Set the pressure cooker to 78°C, pack the catheter
tube in ice, and arrange so that the vapour passes from the
cooker through the tube. 'Then drink the dribbles what come
out. Nah, the screws were horrible to Colin. They wouldn't
give him clean catheters so he always had infections and that.'

12

The Unmentionable Crime:
Aged 20

The Unmentionable Crime, the crime of Stuart's life, the crime-about-which-he-would-ask-that-the-world-be-forgetful (although, when he does get on to the subject, it is hard to get him to shut up again) occurred four years before the post office robbery: it concerns the Little 'Un.

Sitting here in my study, working on this book for the last four years, growing a little squalid in my habits, feeling I'm finally getting the hang of the man as I reach the last half (by which I mean, of course, the first half) of his life, the table and floor covered in photocopies of articles about prison food, glue-sniffing, joyriding, ram-raiding, suicide, and manuals on drawing, and the thesaurus, the thesaurus, the thesaurus, I am often appalled by Stuart.

The Unmentionable Crime appals me. His behaviour in prison appals me.

At this point I get sick of the whole project, wonder why I bother, go off, get drunk, stomp about this study with its flower-covered throws, round carpet, pink fan on the wall, think, 'There, idiot, another year wasted. Stupid man.'

Then I wake up in the morning and think, 'Hey, might as well start again.'

I can't hope to justify or explain Stuart, I realise, nursing my headache: just staple him to the page.

Stuart has specific conditions for talking about the Unmentionable Crime. Only in the morning, and only on a Thursday. He wants the afternoon to recover. Thursday is the day after Dole Office Pay Day, so he will still be able to afford £30 for his dealer. As he recovers he will need a hit.

'It was a fucking charade, me and Sophie.'

Sophie was his girlfriend, mother of the Little 'Un.

'Because she was so kind, I just kept taking the piss out of her. We'd get in loads of debt, then I'd go and live in a bedsit for a while, glue-sniffing and drinking. Then I'd move back with her and stop the sniffing but carry on drinking. I was in and out, in and out, in and out, in and out.'

Over Christmas, the pair struggled for money. But, 'to prove her love' for Stuart, Sophie spent £900 on a credit card to buy him a motorbike. It was a Yamaha RS100, with a burgundy gas tank. She insured it, taxed it, bought a crash helmet, 'the whole lot for us, and within six weeks I'd blown it up and shagged it out, crashed the bollocks out of it. You know, it was fucked. Six weeks, and I'd hammered it into the ground. I was on it like twelve hours a day, racing taxis around the town. Thrashed it to pieces.'

One night, 'out of me head on glue, I went round this girl's house and she wouldn't let me in, and she was with her boyfriend. I didn't like the boyfriend, so I smashed all the windows in her house, dived through one of the smashed windows, picked a piece of glass up, and threatened to cut meself open with it. She used to glue-sniff with me. Then she'd met this fella and blanked everybody, and I had nowhere to sleep this night. I was sleeping in an old abandoned house, and it was really cold this night, so I gone round hers to sleep and she wouldn't let me in, so I've just gone off me head. And I tried cutting meself. But I didn't press hard enough, did I? Just ended up with a graze around me neck.'

The police shook their heads in disbelief, 'wrapped their dustbin lids around me head a few times' and sent him to Norwich County Hospital for a psychiatric report.

At the end of the interview, Sophie asked to speak to the psychiatrist in private, too. She told her that Stuart scared her rigid.

'I think he's going to try and kill me,' she said. 'He's frightening me. When he's not living in the bedsits, he walks around the house with knives, and he walks up behind me. I can see the madness in his eyes. I'm really scared, but I don't think he realises what's going on.'

'What did the psychiatrist say?'

'She told her to go away and stop being so paranoid,' says Stuart, baffled by other people's irresponsibility.

'Anyway, one night down at the pub a man says to me, "Oh, didn't you know? Sophie's fucking Graham."'

When the pub closed, Stuart walked the streets. At around 1 a.m. he returned home and for a few minutes watched television. 'And there was boxing on. I don't know why, it just wound me up even more.'

Finally, he went upstairs to the bedroom.

Sophie's adulterous, ignorant body lay spread out across the mattress, asleep.

'So I give her a little nudge, try and kiss her, she says, "Oh leave me alone, you're drunk." I tried getting really fresh with her and she turned round in the bed and said, "If ya fookin want it you gotta rape me." Then 'parently, I went downstairs, come up with a kitchen knife, and says something like, "If you don't give me all the fucking money you've got, I'm gonna kill you and everyone in the fucking house."'

In law, a Schedule 1 offence means many things: it covers kiddy-fiddlers, nonces and other 'dirty scum fucking cunts', but also any serious crime against children, sexual or otherwise, including ones that appear to the rest of us mild. For example, a sixteen-year-old boy who goes to bed with a fifteen-year-old girl is a Schedule 1 offender.

The police arrived at Stuart's house in convoys, lights pulsing in the midnight, sirens howling. 'You know, I don't know if I do hear voices in me head or not, but a few months before this happened there was a *Bill* episode on the telly, where a Polish fella holed himself up in his house with a Second World War German Luger gun. There was a big stand-off with the police, and I'd obviously thought a lot about that house siege situation, because I knew what was coming next all the time, you know with negotiators and putting the fear in. I'm not proud of it, but it just all took over.'

For an hour Stuart waved his knife about, shouted at the police to fuck off, then abruptly decided to give himself in. 'But just as Sophie's gone out before me, the cop grabbed her, so I've kicked the front door shut, run in the kitchen, grabbed another knife, run upstairs, in the bedroom, barricaded meself in the bedroom, lit six fires in the bedroom and stood there inhaling big blooms of smoke.

'Well, they've come up with all the riot gear, and they've took the top half of the door down, and with the suction of air, it created a flashover, and this big ball of fire, from all the fires, went right down the room, and I went with it. Right into the riot shields.

' "Out, out, out, everybody out, out, out!" One of the coppers is whacking the fuck out of me arm.

' "We've got him, we've got him, we can't disarm him!"

'Well, they've disarmed me, they've dragged me out, they threw me head first down the stairs, as quick as I've hit the bottom of the stairs, some cunt, it's felt like he's jumped from the top of the stairs with his riot shield and landed on me, then they've dragged me outside, jumped on me again with the riot shields, punching and kicking me, dragged me in the back of the van, given me a right hiding on the way to the Old Bill station, calling me a bastard, kicking me in the bollocks and in the stomach, stamping up and down on me fucking head.'

Stuart's crime is not abated by the excuses of suspected

adultery, quick defeat, disturbed youth, attempted suicide, self-hatred. When the police arrived at Stuart's house, he had done something unspeakable. 'I'd got the Little 'Un in me arms, and I've still got this knife with me at the time, and I've stood by the window and I've said, "Right, if anyone comes in the fucking house, I'm gonna kill him."'

As is usual for those involved in Stuart's explosions, the officers received commendations for bravery. Just a few hours before, they'd tucked their children up in bed, sat down with their wives, prayed for a quiet, gentle night. Then this hell-hound had burst on the scene, flinging knives and fire.

Stuart had threatened to kill his own son.

That made him a Schedule 1 offender, and among prisoners words lose the range of meaning that free people give them.

From HMP Grendon to Whitemoor, it indicated one thing: Stuart, nonce-hater, was a nonce.

13

Meekness:
Aged 20–24

During this sentence for threatening to kill his son – his first large sentence – Stuart slumped in his cage.

After the beating up in the back of the police van, he was put in a strip cell with nothing except a nylon gown, a thin mattress on the floor with two blankets 'what were supposed to be unrippable' and a bucket for excrement.

Stuart shat on the floor.

No one particularly minded.

This was the remand wing of the prison, where juvenile offenders were kept until trial. Stuart could hear inmates shouting out of the windows at night at each other, guitars being played, Radio 1 till three in the morning. Sometimes the clatter of an officer's feet down one of the landings, a crash, cries, swearing, catcalls, then feet being dragged backwards, after which the sounds would gradually pale off again.

Stuart lay down, naked, not on the bed.

'Remand is when nobody knows what's going on. If you're three up in a cell, one of you might be expecting a probation order in two days' time. Another one might be expecting ten years, fifteen years, so he's really hyper and lairy, cos he's got to do that bird, so he's got to harden up. And you might get someone who could get twelve months. All it takes is for one of you not to get on – someone who winds you up or someone who farts. Punch-ups. Not just someone giving a dig. Suicide.'

His meals in the strip cell came with regularity.

8 o'clock: Porridge, tea.

11.30: Fish, cabbage, mashed potatoes.

17.20: Fish pie, mushy peas, chips.

One time he tried hiding. He pressed himself flat against the wall so that he couldn't be seen through the warden's spyhole in the door, and stayed silent when the watch came by on the half-hour check and shouted out his name. A minute later the spyhole in the roof snapped back. 'Having fun down there are we, Shorter?'

8 o'clock: Porridge, tea.

11.30: Stew, proper peas, chips.

17.20: Shepherd's pie and swede.

Another time he crawled under the mattress and lay as flat as possible.

8 o'clock: Porridge, tea.

11.30: Sausage, egg, bubble and squeak.

17.20: Sausage hotpot with a potato topping, mash, cut grey beans.

On the third day Stuart saw a six-foot beetle jump out of his shit bucket. On the seventh, two wardens lifted him up from the floor and gently guided him down the corridors to the hospital wing, where the cells were the same but the wardens were called nurses. Stuart's loopiness was now getting out of hand. He was moved again, hallucinating and incapable, to the hospital wing at Glen Parva Prison, near Leicester, and kept under sedation for nine months.

It was at Aylesbury that Stuart began mutilating himself in earnest.

Self-harm is epidemic among prisoners and the homeless and is not just about taking knives to your arms, biting your calves like a battery hen and stubbing cigarettes on your skin. Those are the easy-to-spot tricks. There's a whole continuum of others. Further down the line are the hard-to-spot ones, such as swallowing glass, injecting acid, inserting needles into your groin. After that come the part physical, part tempting fate ones: picking stupid fights, taking huge concoctions of drugs when you don't know what they are, walking too slowly in front of an oncoming vehicle. Then the tricks that provoke disgusted/humiliating/belittling/contemptuous/abusive responses, which may or may not lead to physical pain.

And so on, until you arrive at the other side, among the purely abstract self-harming: the grinding over your failures, the refusal to remember anything good, the determination to ensure – if anyone falls into the mistake of making it clear they actually *like* you – that the next time round they change their opinion pronto. Emotional self-cannibalism, in other words, like those tessellated pictures of a person grappling with a mirror image of himself.

That's the range, from chickens chewing off their legs to Escher drawings.

The point that strikes me most about Stuart's discussions of self-harming is his emphasis on separation. As a child, he says, he learnt how to separate himself from an ordinary mood and enter into a rage. He has also separated himself from his childhood (and many of the other periods of his life) by removing all recollections of pleasure from them. At times when he loses his cool, he says he often separates himself into two people who argue with each other even as he is ranting and raving – one of the people is telling him not to be silly, the other is urging him on. And, as he slices himself open like a chef producing pork crackling, Stuart is able to step back from the agony. 'Doesn't it hurt?' I ask him. 'Yes, but at the same time the pain is pleasurable. Not sexually pleasurable, but it's not like ordinary pain. It's like you are separated from it.'

There is also a sense of unity. The physical act displaces the

mental pain, says Stuart. It unites everything under one heading. 'I know someone who used to get a hard-on out of pain.
It's not like that. The physical pain is a release. It takes away
what's going on up in me head.' Injecting yourself with pure
citric acid (used to dissolve street heroin, so he always has
lots of it lying around) is for Stuart a way of drowning out or
simplifying the mental mess – giving it a physical, tangible focus.

Stuart does not remember the first time he cut himself up at
HMP Aylesbury, or even why. His more recent scars form a
sort of diary: the blunt pale tissue at the top of his bicep is
where, a few years back, he stuck a finger in so he could splash
blood at a policeman who was trying to arrest him. The jagged
slash on his right forearm (he is left-handed) is four inches long
and still fleshy red. The shape of the mark tells him it was
either glass or a razor that buckled during the job. That it is so
low down his arm indicates an unusually powerful disturbance.
Normally he likes his scars higher up, where they are easier
to hide. An X-ray at the hospital recently revealed he had a
twenty-year-old fracture in his skull caused in the BC (Before
Cutting) times, when he used the alternative method of 'lifting
up a table in me maths class and banging it up and down on
me nut'.

'If you took all the clothes off all the people in Cambridge,'
declares Stuart, 'you'd be amazed how many of them had scars
underneath.'

When you began at Aylesbury, I ask again, was it anything
like the woman I have read about who started one day when
she was chopping carrots in the kitchen – and just decided to
keep chopping? Did it start as a suicide attempt? Was it 'a cry
for help'?

'Alexander, I keep saying, No. If you're fucked up in the
head there's no explanation. You might think about it one way
one minute then two hours later you'll think about it totally
different. It's too confusing to even try and put your head
around it. Now, can we leave it alone?'

'Sorry. We'll drop the subject. We'll talk about it some other time.'

'Don't mean to be rude. But – you know.'

I say that I do know.

'What implements did you use?' I ask a moment later.

'Grendon was me cushiest jail. Horrible fucking gaff.'

Stuart liked HMP Grendon at first. A therapeutic institution for mentally distressed prisoners, it is regarded as the most pleasant prison in the country and there is a waiting list for men who want to be transferred there. (Stuart had asked to be considered during one of his rare moments of lucidity while at Aylesbury.) He joined in the group therapy and did his life story. When the session was over, the therapist hurried after him in the prison corridor and said, 'Don't you see? That explains it all. That's why you've been offending.'

To encourage tolerance and openness, paedophiles, 'granny-bashers' and 'straight' convicts are mixed at Grendon. Every session Stuart had to listen to someone spout off about how they had raped old women with kitchen implements or murdered pre-pubescent girls on the Underground, and then whine about the miseries of their childhood.

'What you read in the paper is about a fifth of it. Some of the descriptions are fucking horrific. Some of the things these women experience are unthinkable.'

Stuart demanded to be returned to an ordinary prison.

The final days of his sentence, when he was in HMP Wayland, Stuart was banging off the walls to get out. It wasn't two months: it was seventy-five days, or 1,800 hours, or 108,000 minutes, or *one-third of a million* times the three seconds it takes to read:

8 o'clock: Jam sandwich, tea.

11.30: Corned beef in soup, peas, potatoes.

17.20: Corned beef shepherd's pie, chips.

And

8 o'clock: Porridge, tea.

11.30: Fish, cabbage, mashed potatoes.

17.20: Fish pie, cut grey beans, chips.

Stuart had seen other prisoners released. Some went mad with joy, cackled, whooped it up, took a billion addresses, made a trillion promises, then forgot to say goodbye. Others fell into terror. A lot overdosed: as soon as out of sight of the prison walls, they celebrated with a hit that would have pushed them close to the edge even in their drug-tolerant pre-prison days. Now it killed them.

A month before he was released, Stuart's father, Rex, died.

In terms of facts alone, I know more about Rex Turner than Stuart does. Stuart estimates that, in total, he was in this man's company for less than three months. An easy come, easy go sort of man, after he married Judith and had Gavvy and Stuart, he went – off with a younger woman, and was rarely seen again. 'He'd had these strokes and it fucking done me head in, because I'd never had a chance to talk to him. I'd only seen the man four or five times in me life and the last time we had this big fistfight. Then me mum was going down seeing him, and at the time I was getting really concerned that my stepfather would leave her, because she was offering to go and look after me real dad because he was so ill. I'd got so much respect for my stepfather by this time because of the way he'd looked after me mum and held the family together through all the problems I'd given them. I really had a lot of time for him.'

But Stuart never stops talking about Rex. As a young child, his father's violence horrified him. As a schoolboy, Stuart wavered between hatred and admiration: one day shouting that everyone could fuck off, he was going to live with his dad, and bumbling out of the school gate in tears; another day conning his grandmother into letting him look through a suitcase full of his parents' wedding photographs, and ripping them to pieces.

'But he must have had something to him otherwise me mum never would have loved him and had us kids by him,' says Stuart. 'I think I never loved me dad as much as I do now.'

The last sight he had of Rex was when the prison let Stuart out for the day to visit him in a hospice in Portsmouth. At first Stuart didn't recognise his dad, he was so shrunken and pale, 'a fucking vegetable'. Still only in his mid-forties, he was chewing on a grape stem because he was too weak to eat the grape.

After the funeral (attended, again, on compassionate day release) Stuart arranged in order of importance all the things he was going to do as soon as he recovered from his 250,000 pints of lager laced with vodka post-release hangover: go straight, become a mechanic, go straight, buy a flat, go straight, have a spliff on the footbridge behind his mum's pub, go straight, make the Little 'Un take an MBA and go to business school.

As his mother drove him away on the day he was let out, Stuart broke a cardinal prison rule: like Lot's wife, he looked back, at the building he'd just left.

14

'Clothes washers – there's a fucking mystery.'

Stuart peers at his broken wing mirror, glances over his shoulder, and creeps into the slow lane of the triple carriageway – at every sideways movement, flicking on the indicator. Stuart is driving us to Norfolk like a pair of old men.

'I mean, you put ten socks in the machine, and only seven comes out. Where *do* they go? And I'll tell you another thing, if you take the machine apart they ain't inside it neither.'

This Volkswagen Polo in which we are sitting is one of Stuart's rare legal cars, in that it was *purchased* (from his sister), its transfer *declared* to the DVLA, and the fact that it has alloy wheels does not mean somebody else's motor has been left with its axles balanced on bricks. They, too, have been *bought*. As for the rest: there is no insurance, the tax will be out of date in ten hours and seventeen minutes, Stuart shows a disappointing lack of interest in when the MOT is due, and he does not have a driving licence. Indeed, Stuart cannot have a driving licence. There are already so many penalty points lined up in police stations waiting to be put on the licence the moment the licence comes into existence that, even if such a licence ever were to exist, it would at one and the same time be impossible for it to exist. Only Stuart could manage to give his relationship with vehicle documentation a flavour of quantum mechanics.

But the fact that the acquisition of this vehicle was honourable is, as social workers like to say, 'a start'.

The inside of the car is nasty. The shelf under the glove compartment has given up. Fiercely coloured wires that look important have disconnected themselves from mysterious spots behind the heater unit. Put your feet on the dashboard to escape them and the cigarette lighter pops out. In the middle of the front seats, slightly advanced from where your bottom rests, there are stains, mostly round – the best one can hope for is that they are spills from lager cans. In the tray around the gearstick are more stains, this time three-dimensional. With hairs in.

Forty minutes into the journey and we have puttered as far as Exning, fifteen miles away. Stuart glances in the broken mirror again. He is just checking, he says, for pursuit cars. He crashes the gears. A punk in a red turbo hatchback harasses our tail, lights flashing, bobbing like a hornet, then zips past and vanishes in a belch of oil. 'Mad, dangerous bastard,' tut-tuts Stuart.

At Newmarket we slot cosily between a BP oil tanker and a juggernaut full of pigs, and Stuart relaxes. 'That's another thing about washing machines, right?' he shouts above the thundering din. 'I was watching this programme. There was this geezer what put three, like, washing-machine *drums* together – you know, just the skinny metal inner bits, not even the concrete or nothing – and said it was a sculpture! And somebody bought it!' The car weaves between the behemoths of doom as he shakes his head in disbelief. 'It's got me thinking. All I got to do is buy a job lot of clothes washers – probably get them for a fiver each – from the yard in Peterborough. Not being funny, it's what artists want to buy these days.'

He has, he bugles on, found out that the costs to rent a barn as a scrap washing-machine outlet are 'quite reasonable', and is pleased to observe that security will not be a significant issue (who – except artists, of course – would want to *steal* such stuff?). He knows also that the business must be within five miles of Cambridge (because, although artists 'often live in fields', they prefer cities), but he has concerns about getting enough car-parking space for the convoys of eager sculptors.

'That's what really annoys me, you know, Alexander. I'm always having these ideas, ways to make money and that. But I'm always getting told they're wrong. I never get no encouragement. Never no encouragement at all.'

Stuart's mind is turned constantly to jobs these days. His ideas trip from one scheme to another and each one sounds the sort of thing that gets exposed by BBC investigative journalists who will want to shout at him through letter boxes.

'Why don't you just get an ordinary job?'

I never get a good answer to this question.

When he worked at the recovery firm, he got himself sacked because of the amount he was spending on heroin, but he's off the smack now. When he came out of prison the first time, for taking his son hostage, he didn't buckle down but instead teamed up with Gypsy Smithy and rammed village shops and plotted against post offices.

Why didn't he take his chance to earn an honest crust then? 'You'd just spent five years in a cage. Didn't it put you off crime at all?'

'Hated jail,' agrees Stuart. 'Drove me mad being inside. Locked up like a fucking animal, getting beatings off the screws. But when I got out I needed money to drink.'

'Why didn't you get a job?'

'How could I? Always drunk.'

The only other time, as far as I can make out, that he's got near to proper employment was when he was sixteen and was offered a placement at Woolworth's Goods Yard in Cambridge. He lost that before he'd even started because he spent his first day sniffing glue on the other side of town.

'Nah, that's not rightly fair, I done valeting work for a mate of me brother's.'

'So? Why aren't you still doing it?'

'Head-butted the bloke.'

Excellent. Of course you did. Just the thing. Stuart's version of putting your head down and getting on with it, I suppose.

'It was when me sister was about fourteen, fifteen, and he tried to fiddle with her. So instead of going to work one day I phoned him up to ask him to come round, and as he come in I done a flying head-butt off the top of the stairs, banged his head near enough through the sitting-room window . . .'

Stuart clashes the gears as we join a line of traffic clogging up Thetford Forest, and head up among the twisted Norfolk pines, towards the Brecklands.

'. . . blood everywhere, the front door, the window, the floor, everywhere. And then you know, later, aah, I dunno.'

'You "aah, dunno" what?'

'Nothing, Alexander. Just . . . later, when she was eighteen, me sister said she was too scared to say it, because she didn't want me to kill . . . you know she was very confused . . . when me brother killed himself . . . and she sort of said to me, she says, you know, me sister, she's scared to say it, because of what I'd done to this fella, rather . . .'

'You don't have to say anything, Stuart. We can get to it another time.'

'Yeah, Alexander. Thanks, Alexander.' He settles in behind a tractor. 'Mind if we give jobs a rest now?'

'Nah!' exclaims Stuart.

Twenty miles on, we have spotted a roadside sign: 'CHAIN-SAW CARVED MUSHROOMS'. Troubles promptly forgotten, Stuart falls to gawping at the road ahead. What could it all be about? 'As one victim to another,' his body language seems to marvel, 'what's a mushroom done to deserve that kind of abuse?' Not even in the worst days of street-fighting did he ever experience ill-treatment on this scale.

We pull into a lay-by among the pines to stare at a display of wooden sausages with hats on. They appear to have jumped out of the back of the Volvo estate parked to one side, and arranged themselves as if for a school photo. Behind them all, a man in a butcher's apron is leaning against a tree, counting through a wedge of notes. What on earth provoked this wizard? How did he discover that what people really wanted along this stretch of road was to pay £45 for two-foot-high fake wooden mushrooms 'sculpted' by a chainsaw? Stuart and I are drop-jawed with admiration.

'Fucking nice little number you got going here, mate! Get many cunts falling for it?' Stuart's voice softens and rises a note when he is being polite. 'Do you know about clothes washers? No? Thank God for that, mate.'

On the other side of the road, in the woods, Stuart notices a Gypsy camp. 'Did you know Gypsies steal homeless people?'

This makes me laugh so much.

'Yeah, pinch them off the streets. Force them to work. Make them lay Tarmac.'

Gypsies achieving the impossible: marching befuddled alchies and junkies off to labour. Stuart doesn't know why Gypsies always want Tarmac, but if this camp is representative I can see why. What else is there to park caravans on in a Norfolk forest? And the piles of burnt-out cars such people always like to have nearby – a male Gypsy needs Tarmac to roll them around on too.

'Have you ever been stolen?' I ask Stuart.

'Nah, they want a worker, not a waste of space.'

All these distractions have made me forgetful. I haven't explained why Stuart and I are driving through Norfolk (if you can call this slug speed driving). The purpose is to get out of Cambridge, leave behind the campaign, banish Stuart's miasma of troubles, to go away for a few days to a house in the country.

Secretly, I have also asked a bunch of friends – a writer, a custodian of an academic trust, a Research Fellow in art history,

experts in the underprivileged life, all of us – to judge whether this man is really worth a book.

Stuart swears for a full five minutes, in appreciation.

He extricates himself from the car. ''Enry Eighth! 'Enry Eighth! Think about it. England was a fucking big forest before that. Couldn't see nothing. People bumping into trees all over the shop.'

'What's that got to do with it?'

He hauls our bags from the boot. 'These big houses is what used up the wood. And some of the beams I'll bet are fucking big. They're made from boats. Fuck me, that roof's a hundred feet, in'it! You'd need a pint after bunging that much thatch on! Archaeology's the best, in'it?'

Recognising my computer printer wrapped in my duvet, Stuart gingerly picks it up and rests it on the bonnet.

'Yeah, it's these houses what got rid of the forests. That and the . . . you know.'

'No. What? I don't know.'

'Yeah, *you* know . . .'

'No. Not a clue.'

'Think, what's made out of wood?'

'Stuart, what are you wittering about?'

'Nah, Alexander, thought you'd gone to university. Don't they teach you posh cunts nothing? The mushrooms. Fucking wooden mushrooms everywhere in them days. Ouch! No, honest, Alexander! 'Enry, ouch, that hurt! You punch fucking hard. 'Enry, he give one to one of his wives what he was always having, then they all had to fucking have one!'

We push through the gate, bundled up like donkeys with weekend supplies.

'Hello, James, you're very tall. What's the weather like up there? Alexander was telling me you run an Indian museum,' Stuart mumbles, his mouth muffled by pillows. James is also the linguist who described Stuart's voice for me in Chapter 4. 'Hello, Reuben, you're an art person. Very interesting.' Then he looks at Reuben closely for a second. 'You indulge in the substances, don't you?'

'Hello, Dido.' He has no trouble with the pronunciation of Dido's name. He does not accidentally or humorously call her Dee-do, Fido, Dildo or Dodo. Stuart is conscientious about names. He believes they are important to a person's self-respect and, to Stuart, there is nothing more important than that.

'Lovely house you got. Alexander told you I'm an alcoholic, didn't he?'

Stuart likes to say the worst about himself at the first opportunity. 'I'm a Schedule 1 offender also, and a thief. But I won't cause no trouble. Can I do a tour of the estate?'

In the orchard, Stuart trips and waddles through cow parsley. 'That's a pear tree? Make cider out of that. And them apples on the ground, put them on a table at the gate with a tin of baked beans. Make a good impression on the neighbours, save them going shopping, apples is heavy. Not a fucking full tin of baked beans, Alexander! Empty, for the money. People are honest in the country.'

As we progress around the garden, the flavour of the place begins to rub off on Stuart.

'Laurence Olivier played tennis here, did he?' waving an imaginary racket above his head. 'Really? On this very spot? Love twenty-five!'

'They like swimming, too, people in the country,' he continues, unstoppable. 'It's cos the smells what get under the skin need to be washed out. So tell your friend to put a swimming pool there. What's that? A bomb shelter? Make it changing rooms. See, you just gotta think, gotta have your head screwed on. I wasn't delivered with this morning's milk!'

In the stable each brick is worn to scoops between the pointing. There is a line of hay feeders made from an oak plank severed off the side of a tree. The worm has eaten everything but the shape. There is just the apparition of wood.

Stuart agonises up a ladder and gets his legs to the fourth rung so he can pontificate into the hay loft.

'Holiday lets. Honestly, not being funny, I'll build them meself, for free. You let me stay in this attic for nothing, and pay for the wood and nails. Can't do electrics. My mate Tommy will do that. I'd get housing benefit transferred, so you wouldn't lose out, because I've been wanting to get out of Cambridge and this'd suit me fine. There's loads of government ini-*auau*-tiatives . . .' he babbles on, his tongue entangled by enthusiasms. 'And I'd be away from the dealers and the criminal elements which is good because me head's going a bit doolally at the moment. Yeah, something's coming. Don't know when, don't know where.' He tests the beams with his knuckles. 'You'll need plumbing. You know that? But that's OK, plumbing's easy. Watched me mate Terry at it. Oh . . . I'm stuck.'

Stuart's legs start to flail. They don't work in reverse. I step in and guide them down, left, right, left, right, rung by rung, until Stuart's back to floor level again, covered in dirt and abandoned cobwebs.

I agree with the police. Stuart should not be allowed within ten yards of a motorised vehicle. He is a danger to civilised living. A brand new ride-on lawn mower: a red beast with a fat plate of cutting blades dangling between its wheels – seething to get loose and scalp the soil. Stuart has discovered this in the potting shed. He clambers on and yanks the levers.

'Oh, *fuck*!'

I do my best to repair the damage.

He fiddles with the seat spring. 'Oops.'

I attempt to jam it back to rights. When I put my mind to it, I can always fix things better than Stuart.

He turns the key in the ignition. The engine makes a noise that I have never heard before.

'Er, Alexander?'

He is a Job's curse.

Eventually, he rumbles out of the potting shed at slightly above his motorway pace, me walking ahead, like one of those people with a red flag who used to lead cars a hundred years ago, while Stuart revs behind, cursing and apologising whenever he hits a rock or tree and the blades shriek as if they're wrenching the appendix out of an earth god.

Merrily, Stuart dispatches swathes of the tall grass, and vetch and dandelions, chickweed, fat hen, speedwell, elder, four nicely ripening Gardener's Delight tomato plants, hoary plantain, fumitory, horsetail, then back to grass. The lawns and meadow haven't been mown in months. While I lug the cuttings half a mile to the compost heap, he changes direction and slashes across towards the specimen trees. In the nick of time the art historian deflects him towards the giant hogweed. It is about to flower and this, despite their splendid lunar extraordinariness, is a bad thing. Stuart jumps up before he can be told and assaults one.

This afternoon is one of the few times I have seen Stuart unreservedly happy.

'Lapsang shoe-pong? Ve-rry tasty.'

We are all having tea on the freshly skinned meadow. Stuart pokes his finger in his teacup. It is tepid: it is suitable. He sinks the lot and lies back in the grass.

'Fucking amazing. A-*fucking*-One,' he says lazily. A moment later: 'I don't believe she burnt them.'

'Who? Burnt what?'

'Princess Margaret. Her legs. It was given out the reason what she was in the wheelchair was because she scalded herself getting in the bath. But how you gonna get in a boiling bath with both feet – take a running jump? Do you know what I think? I reckon she might have tried to torch herself. Another cuppa? Yes please, ta, James.

'What you reading, Reuben? *Hello!*. So false, false tits is. I like a bit of natural bounce. If they're going to sag, they're going to sag. That's just the way it goes, in'it? See, women haven't got to impress the men. Women have the one thing that men always want: TLC. A cuddle. That's the thing a man misses. That physical contact is more important than the sex. Though,' Stuart adds reflectively, 'I'm not saying the sex isn't important, because if a man don't get rid of it – either by hand shandy or by a quickie, it has to be done – his balls end up on the floor. See, me, I suffer from premature ejaculation meself. As soon as it's up, it spits. I'm mature enough now to say, well, that's just the way it is. Is it frustrating? Yeah. And if it's frustrating for me, think how much more frustrating it must be for the woman.'

In certain slivers of his personality Stuart is profoundly well balanced.

'Once when I was begging late at night, three girls come up. They had Christmas hats on and shiny stuff. Pink tops. Short skirts. And I'm not lying, they started masturbating in front of me. Truly, lifted up their skirts.'

'Bet you'd like some of this, wouldn't you?' they chanted at him, pushing back their underwear. 'Yeah, looks good, don't it? Ooooh! Aaaah! Well, you can't have it! You can't have it!'

Then they danced off.

Stuart does not seem to be disturbed by this. 'Giggling, they was,' he notes. 'But some women are fucking vicious cows. Homeless women perticulier give as good as they get. There's one I come across, a crusty – you know, the smellies who don't shower and wander from one town to another. This one, if anyone tried it on with her, she'd claw their eyes out. Most women you find on the street aren't timid, they've got their body to use, and they're hard inside.'

In the evening, we move back inside the house, eat Convict Curry and lounge around the fire. Stuart the Yapper is still going strong. ('Nah, James, you don't want to put that log there.') It is like a scene from Agatha Christie's *Thirteen Problems*. Everyone in the living room, cosy, entertained.

('Nah, not there, neither.')

Or a Boccaccio setting, after the population has fled Florence and keeps each other occupied by telling stories.

('James, what you like? You gotta stick that branch between them three logs, and those other twigs on top.')

Except in this case no one but Stuart can get a word in edgeways.

('Ooh. It's gone out.')

'And the working classes?' he gabbles on. 'That's the trouble about them. If you come up with anything rather than going and working for somebody, you was never encouraged to go and do it. But to be honest with you, if I'm pissed up and in one of my drunken, don't-give-a-fuck moods – you know how you get – and someone comes by who talks like they've got something stuck up their arse? You know, I say out loud, "Here comes a Nobby Cunt." '

'What! That person was just minding his own business. He didn't come up to you and say, "You sound like a yob." '

'That's where you're all wrong. The middle-upper class never spoke to the kids on the council estate, even though a lot of them went to the same comprehensive school. It was because you didn't have £50 trousers on, and your fucking shoes might have holes in, they'd just walk by sniggering and laughing.'

In Stuart's vision of the British class system, everyone from lower-middle class upwards is, at best, furtively upper class. From swells in bowler hats to oiks with two Fords on a herringbone drive, all are Nobby Cunts. 'Upper class' does not mean the highest level of non-aristocracy to Stuart, it refers to an entire social landscape, never quite in focus, of lost and unavailable chances.

'Yeah. The other day, me and this friend of mine, we were saying, all the people we used to take the piss out of for being nobs and cunts and arse-lickers, the truth of it is, most of them now have got really nice houses, driving really nice cars, and here we are still sitting in a pub being angry and bitter about the class war. Who's ended up losing out?'

He mentions that lately he has been on TV, which brings up another odd fact about Stuart. He is on public record much more than ordinary citizens. It is true of so many chaotic people: they are far more likely to be given historical permanence than your average taxpaying citizen. Their exploits make headlines, their sleeping habits get annual weepy features in the local paper, they are interviewed for TV whenever the police do a crackdown on anti-social behaviour, their haircuts, tattoos and facial piercings are photographed for postcards and people doing art-school assignments. By the time Stuart gets to front an eight-minute, nationwide documentary on BBC2 about home-lessness and police bungling in Cambridge, he is so blasé with publicity that he almost forgets to mention it.

'Quite funny, really. Last year, it was. Or was it the year before?'

The programme is called *Private Investigations*.

'Stuart, why didn't you tell me this? Have you got a copy of the programme? I must see it!'

'Sorry, Alexander, forgot to get a video. It's only TV. You musta been on TV before . . . *haven't* you?'

And so our evening continues. Stuart's gasbaggish mood never lets up, leaving us bemused and dazzled and furious and entertained and lectured and with tired ears.

'You know what you lot want to do?' yawns Stuart at last, getting ready to go upstairs to bed. 'Fix this place up. Rip them roses off the front of the house, cos they trap the damp. Turn the sheds into a youth club with them flats I was talking about. Seriously, I've got it all planned out – where the mower was, that'd be the disco. You'd earn a packet. Then the ponds. Know what you should do there? Fill 'em in. Then you could make that fieldy bit into a go-kart course and charge a fiver a go. It could be really lovely here.'

'You fucking ponce, I'll rip your head off!'

He rushed for the door, kicked aside the table, squashed a window pane as he hit the wall, sliced his finger on a shard of glass.

'Ring the fucking Old Bill on me, then, Alexander!' he

hollared. 'The fucking Old Bill know all about me! I'm gonna fucking tear your throat out!'

It was 8 a.m. in the morning. Everybody else asleep.

The bottles of beer and bowls of congealed Convict Curry stacked up by the inglenook – he scattered them across the floor.

'Think you're fucking clever, eh? Think you can fucking talk down to me, eh? Eh? Eh?' He jammed me up against the broom-cupboard door, his fingers digging around my windpipe, squeezing sharply with every 'eh': 'Eh? Eh? Eh?' He sprayed spittle over my glasses. I tried to take them off. I jerked like a chicken.

'Fucking stupid name, Alex-*and*er, fucking poncey name, Alex-*and*er, eh? Eh? Eh?'

Afterwards, I decided what I should have done: I should have reached down and stroked his thigh. That would have shocked the name-snob ponce-hater. Face wide with horror, I then would have jabbed my inkpen in his eyeball and flicked the jelly out. That would have made me happy.

I'm proud of myself for what I said next.

'Go on, do it,' I gurgled. 'Do it, do it, do it.'

'Eh? Eh? Eh?'

Jerk, jerk, jerk.

'Hit me, hit me, hit me.'

My memory about the rest of my stay at Fir Grove is in shreds.

Stuart, asleep upstairs throughout the uproar, was woken by silent blue lights flashing across the ceiling of his room and jumped out of bed and locked himself in the wardrobe.

With the arrival of seven policemen, shame set in on me. I wandered about the orchard and paddock at a distance from the officers, hands in pockets, worrying at my foolishness. Why had I tried to imitate Stuart? Who did I think I was? How embarrassing!

'Right, officer,' my attacker was vociferating, 'this fucking ponce . . .'

'Now, sir, I don't think that's a helpful attitude.'

'Right. This ponce . . .'

'Let's try and calm down, shall we, sir?'

'I am fucking calm! He was trying to stop my missus getting the things what's in this house.'

And why shouldn't I? The woman was an ex-tenant of Fir Grove who'd refused to pay the rent. She'd also tried to punch her landlady. I wasn't going to let them drive up and steal back a load of stuff they'd forfeited. All I'd said was the two numbskulls would have to sort the matter out with the owners before they could start grabbing whatever took their fancy. At that point the male of the two subspecies assaulted me.

'Then you had fisticuffs?' said the officer, deadpan.

The subhuman jolted forth. He jabbed his finger in my direction. 'He fucking provoked me!'

'Provoked you, did he?' The policeman's interest perked up. 'How did he do that?'

The man swelled his shoulders, his neck got thicker. 'He took his fucking glasses off!'

'Shut it, sunshine, or we'll nick you.'

I love the police. I wish we lived in a police state.

'Lovely visit, that, thank you.'

We are driving back to Cambridge. A lady in a three-wheeler shoots past, then a scooter.

'Not being funny, allowing for where the house is,' he muses, 'you putting a padlock on the gate this morning might be a deterrent to them tenants in your own mind, but your padlock isn't going to stop nobody. It don't make no difference to a thief, a professional thief. We'd just climb over the fence . . .'

'We're not talking about professional thieves,' I snap. I confess, I am slightly wounded that Stuart has not paid more attention to my brawl.

'No, no! But it won't stop nobody. They'll just climb over and walk up.'

'Of course it won't stop anybody if they're determined. The point is to stop them driving in. It's a small thing, but . . .'

'But it's not. See, that's the difference between the way you and me think. Anybody who knows anything will tell you all you need is a screwdriver. As quick as it can be done is as quick as I can click my fingers. It's off.'

'That *is* the point, because we're not talking about thieves. We're talking about two-bit losers. Just trying to stop them making a nuisance of themselves.'

'They're screwing with you again, they're screwing with you again!'

'Why? How do you know? You didn't even meet them.'

'Exactly! Just because you met somebody, doesn't mean to say you know anything about them.'

'No, but you're one up on the person who hasn't met them.'

'They only let you see what they wanted you to see.'

'OK, what should be done, if not a padlock?'

'What? Seriously? Change nothing. They ain't going to do nothing. Stop worrying. But the one thing I would suggest is that maybe them at Fir Grove get a couple of infra-red beams, straight across, and a Chubb lock, like on each door, and the windows: at the back you could put bars. The wires from the detectors? Put them in metal tubes what can't get short-circuited . . .'

Isn't this the most boggling conversation ever heard? But it is *echt* Stuart. His maddening insistence, his pleasure in technical detail and system even when it leads him completely off the point and convinces you he doesn't actually understand the subject and he's just being windy, his concern over false appearances.

Sometimes Stuart seems like an irritable fisherman. He bobs about, on the disruption of his life, a small, unsteady figure, fishing for order. Then he gets into a rage, 'goes right on one', and it is as if he's taken out the gutting knife and mashed his catch to pulp – every sign of hated, repressive, reminding order is gone again. Because order has also been the abiding malevolent force in Stuart's past – police order, prison order, court order, order in the care homes run by council-sponsored paedophiles: the order of 'the System'.

This tussle between disorder and order occupies a large part of Stuart's time.

Plots, for example. He likes plots. The police, he is certain, have teamed up with his girlfriend and the ventilation repairman to record him in compromising conversations. The second room on the first floor of the building opposite contains a drugs squad stake-out. A city councillor who came by to visit last Thursday was really planting heroin. I am not writing a book about him, I am eliciting confessions that will be used to justify locking him up for good the next time he finds himself in court. These little fishes of order make sense of some loose ends. When the fit of paranoia passes, he throws them back and the elucidations disappear again.

Other catches are more helpful – at least, to a biographer.

'When did you discover violence?' I ask. Give him a moment to cast about and reel his thoughts back in, and what's he caught? A great sturgeon of order. The exact day he made the find. He knows the very day, the exact moment, that he went from a ten-year-old to a lawless, grade-one, society-loathing bastard.

15

'It's me muscular dystrophy,' trumpets Stuart. 'Haven't I told you about that yet? That's why I walk funny. Humeroscapu-something muscular dystrophy. It's a real gobstopper, but I don't want to look it up. What you don't know can't hurt you.'

He is lying in a metal-barred bed, in a small public ward in Addenbrooke's Hospital, clear disproof of his own defiance.

The three other beds in the ward are taken up by silent ladies in various states of pretend coma, their noses pointing at the ceiling. A nurse is standing next to Stuart's bed, tapping his drip feed. His pretty half-sister is perched on the other side. As usual – surrounded by women.

'I only come in because I wanted to get a cuddle and it spits too soon,' he says, turning to his mother. 'I thought, maybe it's cos of me muscular dystrophy. Cos your dick's a muscle, in'it?'

'Stuart! Shhh!'

'Well, no bird's going to look at me if I can't keep her happy, is she? Know what I mean?'

'You are *such* an *embarrassment*!'

The outpatients nurse who'd first had to listen to these happy explanations about his useless member hadn't been par-ticularly interested in the case to begin with. Then she'd taken his blood pressure, screamed, and rushed him to Emergency. The normal heart rate is around seventy beats per minute. Stuart's sagged in at thirty. By the time his mother had been contacted, the surgeon had already cut two flaps into Stuart's chest and embedded a set of wires into his thigh. Stuart had come to hospital to cure his premature ejaculation and discovered he'd almost lost his heart.

Not that this seems to have dampened his enthusiasm. 'Do you want to see me new ticker? It's in me leg,' he says with pride. His attitude to his body has never been one of reverence. The wires come out above his knee and are attached to an electrical box that emits curiously unreassuring blips, as if each one is considering whether or not to be the last. It is a temporary pacemaker, to keep him alive over the weekend. Now that he is in good hands, there is nothing to fear.

'Doctor says he can't understand it. He says I should have been blacking out all the time, which I was sometimes, but no more than I always do.'

Stuart is looking surprisingly respectable. Recently, another friend he's made on the campaign drove him to Birmingham so that he could get his FUCK tattoo covered up by a thick twining pattern that looks as if it's been grafted from the neck of a Maori warrior. His usual stubble is shaven off; his T-shirt is remarkably white and washed; his skin is without its normal ghostly pallor.

'They tried twice to put a proper pacemaker in me tit, but it wouldn't stick to the veins because of all the citric and smack I've injected. They just crumbled. Ironic, in'it? Gotta laugh, haven't you? Want to see the scar?'

Two of the Silent Ones in the surrounding beds open their eyes.

Stuart's mother quickly tries to change the subject but ends up making the situation worse. Remembering that Stuart has once before felt chest pains, she muses, 'But what I can't remember is, was that during the first or the second time you were in prison?'

'Second,' says Stuart immediately. 'Here, that's another story for you, Alexander. Funny as fuck. Right, Long Lartin? When I was doing me five-stretch for the post office? I started getting these pains in me chest then, but the screws kept "losing" my request to see the doctor for an ECG. So I had to think of a way to fuck them off so that they'd move me to another prison where I could see a doctor, but not do something what would get me in so much trouble that I'd get another sentence on top. That ruled out the usual, like hitting a screw. I thought about it for fucking ages, then I saw that every day at four o'clock these four screws went into their office to have their tea. Regular as clockwork. You could set your watch by it. That's what give me the idea. So I got these two buckets and went to where everyone was having their dinner and said as they come out, "If you want to have a shit, shit in that one; if you want to have a piss, piss in that one." There was enough fucking volunteers! Mixed the two buckets into one, and stuck it next to a radiator for two hours to make it sweat. Ppphwwwwaaawww! And when it was ready, at teatime, I took it to where the screws was just sitting down to have a cuppa. I didn't say nothing. I didn't give them time to do nothing, duck or nothing. Just went in and threw the bucket all over them. Just went bosh. One, two, three walls I done, bar the wall I was stood at. It made like a big, fuck-off "O" shape of shit, all round the room. Hit everything. Got all four of them.'

Three days later, he was allowed to have his ECG. Result: normal.

Stuart's mother gathers her coat and bags, and gives a last comic look at the comatoses, as if to say, 'Poor you – soon it will be night-time and you'll be here on your own with him,' promises to come again first thing in the morning, and walks off in the direction of Dermatology.

'Like I told you before,' Stuart resumes, 'if you don't actually hit a screw, just do something mad like throw shit at them or chase them around with a lump of wood, it's a good way of getting things done.'

Muscular dystrophy – is that the one that has posters of an attractive female cellist with a strip torn down her back? Or is that spina bifida? Perhaps muscular dystrophy is the one that kills kids, drowning them in their own spit, after a lifetime of twisted wheelchair misery? Or maybe that's multiple sclerosis.

I look it up on the Internet. Muscular dystrophy is wheelchairs and wasted biceps.

There are lots of types. MD is one of those broad medical terms which uses up labels like a new star formation. Limb-Girdle affects the limbs by eating at the muscles of the pelvic and shoulder girdles. Distal begins in the hands and feet and works inwards. Oculopharyngeal, the eyelids and throat. Some of them set in when the person's a child, some when you're as old as sixty. Duchenne's is the nastiest, and the most common. These victims of God's omnipotent love die in agony and terror in their teens.

When Stuart was three, a doctor in the same hospital he's in now had pulled him about like a doll, pinched his fingers, flicked his arms, made him stand up and down as if he were on a baby parade ground, tutted over his weak, side-to-side walk and nodded with approval when Stuart fell over . . . but got up again more or less like an ordinary human being and not with the Duchenne's weird trick of 'climbing up his own legs'. 'If you're going to have muscular dystrophy,' said the doctor, looking up at Stuart's mother with relief, 'he's got the best sort to have.'

Fascioscapulohumeral muscular dystrophy affects the muscles of the face (*fascio*), shoulder blade (*scapulo*) and upper arm (*humeral*). Transmitted through a damaged genetic structure, there is a fifty per cent chance that the offspring, male or female, of an affected parent will inherit the disease, which is why Stuart never wanted to have kids. Some people with FSH, if they treat themselves well and are lucky, can live as long as the rest of us and not notice a single symptom. Stuart's father, Rex Turner, who also had the illness, led a busy schedule throughout his life.

Cambridge Evening News,
Tuesday, 2 January, 1973

**Jailed man told: Illness no
excuse for crime**

A detective was forced to leap for
safety as a 29-year-old muscular
dystrophy victim drove through
a police roadblock, Cambridge
Crown Court heard yesterday.
Rex Turner, who admitted a
series of thefts and driving offences, was jailed for four years with
a warning from Judge David
Wild that his illness was no excuse
for preying on his fellow citizens.

The court were told that
Turner had appeared in court
31 times before and committed the crimes, thefts and driving
offences while on bail for another
offence.

Turner's counsel, Mr
Frank Keysell, said that parts of
Turner's body were wasting away
and his anti-social behaviour
might have been the result of his
realisation that he would only
have a short active life.

Stuart has made a bad mistake treating his muscular dystrophy with disrespect. Because of 'me eccentric lifestyle' it has
ceased to be a minor complaint. It has taken offence at being
soused in strong lager and illegal substances for the last twenty
years. It is starting to look more like the considerably worse
Emery-Dreifuss muscular dystrophy. It has started to attack his
heart.

Stuart is alone in the ward. The lady patients have vaporised.
He is drowsy. For much of the time that I sit here on this
second visit he sleeps. When he is awake, we tease each other,
or I get him some food, or he tells another prison anecdote,

which seem surreally out of place in this sanitised hospital
room.

'I knew a fella at Littlehey who stuck three children on a pike fence. His excuse was that he was out on acid. I used to talk to him, you see, and a lot of people started giving dirty looks. He'd said that he'd killed a child, but it wasn't deliberate. It sounded quite feasible.'

Of course it does, Stuart. Nothing could be more understandable.

'Then it turns out he's up for sticking three kids on a spike.'

'All at once?'

'Same evening. Three children in one night.'

'Because of acid?'

'Yeah, but that's no excuse. I've done acid. The only thing with it is, he was one of the best prison artists I've ever seen. He was really gifted with waterpaints. The rough side of hardboard, he used to paint on that. Even though he was a really bad nonce, other people used to pay him £50, which is a lot of money in jail, to do portraits of their loved ones, he was so fucking good at it. He was wicked at art.'

He fiddles with the tube in his arm to admire the injection technique of the nurse, then drifts off. My manly, emotionally embarrassed bonhomie is more than matched by his quizzical detachment. This is interesting, he seems to be saying about his predicament, I wonder if I'll die from it.

In the afternoon, he is transferred to the specialist heart unit at Papworth, a small town outside Cambridge, where he undergoes a third operation.

When I arrive to visit the next day, he is back in his room, propped up in a metal cot, a white bib around his chest, and a doctor, stethoscope strung round his neck like a seamstress's tape measure, is giving him the third degree.

'Do you understand what the situation is?'

Lisping with humility, Stuart says that he does: 'Yeff.'

'Good. What has happened so far is this: the first two tries were not successful. Because of your drug abuse, your veins were too weak to hold the connection. That was why you were brought here. This morning we tried a third time to fit a permanent pacemaker, and because of the difficulty I decided to use a top-of-the-range piece of equipment. Fortunately, we were successful, and you now have £5,000 worth of technology embedded in your chest. I want you to look after it.'

'Fankyou.'

'If it goes wrong and you have to come back here for me to take it out in six months,' he adds, 'I can't afford to give you another. I have decided that.'

'Fankyou.'

'That means no needles.' He points at the still glisteningly fresh tattoo covering Stuart's right arm where FUCK used to be. 'No more of those.'

'No.'

'No injections.'

'No.'

'What do you use?'

'Meffadone,' mumbles Stuart, 'what I drink, and Es, and amphetamines . . . and smack,' he admits. 'And citric.'

'Pure?'

'Yeff.' Part of his new speech impediment is due to the anaesthetic, I tell myself hopefully. This fit of respectability will soon pass.

'You can't do that any more. You understand? You'll have to stop, and stop today. Not next month, not next week – today. The risk of infection from injections is too high. Even with sterilised needles, you can get diseases pushed through from the skin. If you get an infection in this piece of technology I'll have to have you back here and I'll have to take it out, and, like I said, I won't give you another.'

When it comes to reclaiming Stuart's artificial lifesaver, he is determined not to miss a trick.

After the doctor has gone, Stuart tells me that the thought
of having to stop injecting pleases him. Now that he's been
told that his next dose of heroin could kill him, he has the in-
centive to come off completely. He'll 'never touch the stuff
again'.

I note that Stuart has curiously mistaken what the doctor has
said – it is not the heroin that is dangerous, it is Stuart's method
of putting it into his body. No one has ruled out smoking or
eating the stuff. He can still snort whatever he wants. But I
don't say anything. Drugs have almost killed Stuart more times
than he can count and if he stops doing them simply because
he's too dopey to figure out the doctor's real message, then that
is as good a way as any.

'What did the man mean about your uncle?' I ask.

'Uncle Nigger?' Stuart perks up.

Uncle Nigger turns out to be Uncle Roddy, who earned his
nickname as a child because he fell in a puddle one day and
came home covered head to toe in mud. Of all his father's
family, Stuart was closest to Uncle Nigger. Uncle Nigger used
to give him lectures on how to grow up responsibly, and then
go out and get himself nicked for car theft or burglary. Uncle
Nigger ended up in a wheelchair because of his muscular dystrophy, and died on his fifth pacemaker.

'The day I'm like Nigger is Death Day. I'm *not* going to be
no *Uncle Nigger*.'

Stuart's wounds, where the surgeon has cut flaps into the
flesh of his chest on both sides, are causing him agony, but
as a known drug addict, he isn't allowed proper painkillers.
Painkillers might be combined with illegal substances, or overdosed, or sold, ground up and injected.

'Oi,' Stuart whispers, 'did you get what I asked you for?'

I nod and fish a bottle out of my bag.

'Quick, before the nurse comes, empty the water jug. They'll never know the difference.'

Stuart, abruptly energetic, takes the emptied jug back and hurriedly splashes it half full of the new clear fluids. Plymouth Gin: £14.99. Nothing but the best for a delicate patient.

'Fancy a sip yourself?'

Over the next two months, I see little of Stuart. There is an enormous amount to do on the campaign. Ruth and John's application for an appeal is in July. The committee has news-letters to write, MPs to contact, vigils and protests to organise, press releases, press releases, press releases: Michael Winner has supported the campaign; UNISON is backing the cam-paign; Alan Bennett (spotted by me, skulking in my neighbour-hood bookshop) has signed our petition; Joan Baez is advertising the campaign on her American tour; Victoria Wood and Simon Hughes MP have taken a stand outside Number 10; one of our main antagonists, a city councillor in Norwich, needs to be deflated, which means a press release to reveal that this gentle-man once smashed up five police cars with an axe during a drugs raid in Norwich. Another, a sniping, thorn-in-the-side Cambridge councillor, has made loopy hints that the campaign is sending her death threats. A photograph of a gathering of people that includes her has been put through her letter box, she says, and her head is ringed. On the back, the words 'You're Dead'. She is telling people that because of the drugs Winter-comfort should be closed down. But I am becoming meaner at this game of local-politics brawling. I have learnt that the best way to defend your morally noble cause is to get nasty fast. Head-butt him while he's still rolling up his cuffs, so to speak. I contact *Private Eye*. A piece appears in 'Rotten Boroughs' noting that the councillor is on the advisory board of a hostel for the homeless in another part of Cambridge in which nine people have died of drug overdoses in the last year and a half. At a supper party some weeks later a council official whispers congratulations in my ear. She has, he says, lost an appointment to head the city's housing committee, because of 'bad publicity'.

Stuart, worried by his own disruptions, drops away. He should be joining in. But he's gone, vanished.

July comes.

The week of the 11th arrives.

The day of the hearing finally dawns.

The campaign committee – fifteen of us – drive down to London three hours too early, spend the dawn rubbing our hands around hot cups of coffee and sticking posters to the railings, then wade *en masse* into Court 5, where three amiable judges chat for two hours, Michael Mansfield QC mumbles rotundly through his arguments, the prosecution pats a few counter-arguments back, and Ruth and John are pronounced

Seven months after disappearing into a small hole in a provincial crown court to start five and four years in prison, our old friends re-emerge back to their families' embrace, under the neo-Gothic portico of the Royal Courts of Justice, arms aloft, laughing faces lit by flashbulbs.

Daily Telegraph, 12 July 2000

Charity Pair are freed to appeal over heroin case

After 207 days in prison, two charity workers were freed on bail yesterday pending a full appeal against their landmark conviction for permitting drug dealing at a homeless day hostel ... On the steps of the High Court in London, more than 50 supporters, who have campaigned for their release for seven months, cheered as Wyner and Brock appeared with their families clutching bunches of flowers.

Wyner, a mother of two, who was the director of the Wintercomfort charity in Cambridge, said: 'I am looking forward to spending some precious time with my children and some private time with my husband. Now I just want to go home and have a decent cup of coffee.'

Brock, who suffered a breakdown in jail and is being treated for depression, clutched his wife and sons, Lloyd, 16, and Dylan, 11, outside court. 'I am just very glad to be back with my family,' he said. 'The opportunity to be with them might be brief and so at the moment it's a cautious celebration' ... His wife, Louise, 39, who has decorated their home in Cambridgeshire with yellow ribbons, added: 'I just want to take him home.'

Ruth comes out, overtly at least, as she went in: defiant, self-controlled, calculating how best to survive the next step of the fight. Within a few weeks she is writing up her prison diaries for publication and has started working for a prison reform charity. Her determination is a source of awe. Knock her down with a breaker's ball, squash her flat with a ten-ton steamroller and still she stands up and carries on walking.

John, a more normal human being, is destroyed. Emptied of direction, desolate in his impotence, he goes back home and sinks out of view.

'How do you feel?' he is asked by a respectable woman at the first post-celebration campaign meeting.

'Like I want to kill a certain person,' he retorts. 'You know who I mean.'

We all nod, although there are at least four candidates who come to mind. But that's not the point. What matters is the wholesomeness of this response. Good for John, we are saying to ourselves – honesty, truthfulness. He's reached Step One on the Road to Recovery.

'Then I'll go out and piss on his corpse,' he adds.

The lady bristles. John's wife is abruptly alarmed. 'You don't mean it like that, really.'

'That is exactly how I mean it.'

The subject is quickly changed to the unexpected cost of a recent minibus bill.

Even in the hellfire of unrequited justice there is expected to be propriety.

I browse through Stuart's diary during these remote weeks. 'FACIO scapulo humeral muscular DyStRophy' is now spelt correctly. 'STUART LOOK ⟶ SET ALRAM. MAKE SURE ALRaM Button is up not Down. When WeaK up is needed.' I can understand this entry now. It means not that he is too weak to manage the 'alram' button, but that when the disease is 'on a bad 'un' and feels like it is stripping the muscle from his bones, a twenty-minute bus journey into town – to fetch his methadone prescription or attend a job-training course – can exhaust him so much that he has to sleep for twenty-four hours when he gets home. The moments of weakness are, understandably, more common than usual these days. He is another rung down towards what he calls 'Death Day' – the day when he can no longer make it from his front door to the bus stop in the centre of his village without the help of a wheelchair. On that day, he insists, he will screw up his body for one last flowering of strength and (with the help of a crate of Stella) cripple his enemies, so that it is they who end up in the wheelchairs – so that they may spend the rest of their lives 'knowing what suffering is about, like they made me suffer' – and then kill himself.

In one sense, suicide is always reminding itself to Stuart: the scars on his neck from failed shots at it, the watchfulness with which doctors hand him his necessary pills, the memories of his brother's suicide during Stuart's second prison sentence, the longing for an apocalyptic revenge against his unnamed 'enemies' that would leave him no option but to dispense with himself immediately after.

In another sense, suicide pops out at him by surprise, like a jack-in-the-box. He is almost as startled by it as his friends are. With Jack-in-the-Box Suicide, if I have understood Stuart properly, he is suddenly overwhelmed by a desire to die *now*, this *instant*, and by any method to hand. Or it might be the other way round, with equal unexpectedness: he realises that an opportunity has suddenly presented itself and rushes to take advantage. No time for hesitation. No time for a note. Got to get it done before some grave-saver spots what he's up to. He is too excited, has too little time, to plan this properly. Result: a failure. Every time, a failure. Every time so far, at least. In Suicide Land, Stuart has no more self-control than he has here.

That is why it is wrong to assume that a failed bid is, as the nauseating cliché will have it, only 'a cry for help'. It could be – is usually in Stuart's case – just the opposite. Its failure is the result of too great a desperation to get the job done.

The latest attempt occurred several weeks ago, using a weekend's worth of heroin. It wasn't a ten-minute decision. Not even thirty seconds. Just a snap of the fingers. 'Here's the spoonful of molten smack and citric. Let's have a good time,' he thinks to himself. 'No, let's kill myself with an overdose instead.' Thump. In it goes.

He doesn't remember the reason – there was no specific reason. Just an unbearable sense of hatred and waste. But because Stuart didn't know what he was about to do, he didn't use a syringe with a large enough capacity to kill him on the first injection, so he had to fill up again. By the time that was done, the heroin he'd already taken had long ago made him unsteady and he couldn't find the original vein. All the others in his arms and legs had also disappeared. He ripped off his shoes and socks and stabbed between the tendons on his feet to find another entry point, wasted half the vial, realised he had only a few seconds of consciousness left, twisted round and emptied everything that remained into his right buttock. He was out cold for twenty-four hours.

Other attempts appear as scars, weals, parentheses in conversation, absent days in his diary. But, at the same time, according to Stuart's weird sense of etiquette on such subjects, only one son in a family is allowed to kill himself, else it puts too much strain on the parents, and his brother, Gavvy, like Jacob in the Old Testament, has stolen Stuart's birthright. That's why, when I first met him begging outside Sidney Sussex College, he was planning to get himself punched and kicked into non-existence by taunting drunks from the pub.

'Aah, suicide – it's a difficult subject. Do you mind if we give it a rest now?'

All this interpretation gives me a slight thrill. Beneath the mould in the bathroom of his flat, the melamine sideboards, the fussing with welfare payments, the tedious addiction to drugs and alcohol, Stuart is a biblical character. His symbolic sense of justice, the expressions of hatred, his carelessness with life and longing for calm – cut out the 'fucks', add a few 'thous' and he belongs in the Sinai Desert.

16

161/205				Friday 9
8	Phone	KAyT	1	yer To
9	Day	She	nerly	DieD on
10	me			
11				
12				
1				
2				

Despite his poor handwriting, Stuart is generally tidy in his diary, which allows for further exegesis. June begins well. He has arranged a home visit from his social worker, plans to sign up for disability living allowance, books in with his doctor for a drug detox programme. Then, Friday the 9th, the entry above: 'Phone KAyT 1 yer To Day She nerly DieD on me.'

The weekend is empty. Monday's a mess. Stuart's attention has clearly gone. The coloured highlighting vanishes. He doodles:

160

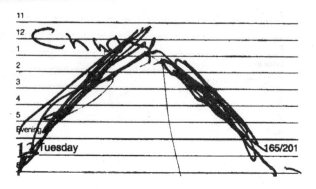

He dozes off:

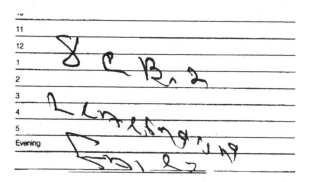

(Which translates as: '8 p.m., go to CB2 café for a campaign meeting. Get there early.' He did neither.)

Temporarily he revives:

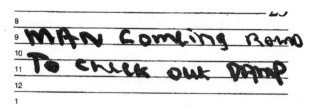

Then he collapses altogether:

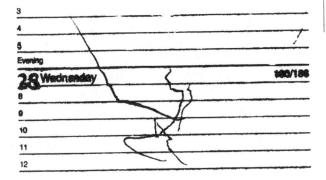

The recollection of this business with Kayt has cast a strange, fading rhythm over Stuart's days. He is like a man falling asleep on the bus. The next month, triumphant for so many of the campaigning people around him, is blank.

In August, he reawakens: the highlighters are back – yellow for health, green for social, orange for duty.

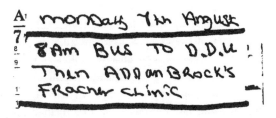

And:

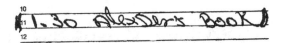

'K-A-Y-T, she spelt it,' explains Stuart, weighing up my room with a single glance to confirm that I have not got up to any decorating silliness while he's been away. 'I told you about that already, remember?' He pushes back the brown cover on my armchair and heavily flops down. 'She was the one I cut me throat over, what got me me flat. I first met her in Hospital Town after I put meself on the streets the second time, because she'd had to have her stomach pumped.'

Of course she did, Stuart. You wouldn't want to meet a nice, stable, ordinary girl, would you, now?

'This wouldn't have been around May, by any chance?'

'Yes. How'd you guess?'

May is the anniversary of Stuart's brother's suicide, and it has set up a sort of periodicity in his life. His sense of disturbance is at peak amplitude; it is just the time when he is inclined to be pounded on the head by furious memories, to 'kick off', 'be not too clever', and find himself in hospital meeting unsuitable women. I have noticed this, or been told about it, with a number of chaotic people. The ones who end up on the streets following a major, well-defined disaster – their wife left them, their mother died, their business collapsed, their brother took an overdose (it is always a death of some sort) – acquire a new pattern in their lives, a sort of fundamental harmonic. As the anniversary of the event comes close they get agitated, swing off course, ingest rock-star quantities of narcotics, slurp enough beer to fill a football stadium, and soon all sorts of things are going wrong – smashings, bashings, evictions, convictions, vibrating from one mood to the other, maximally displaced. Then, after a couple of weeks, the annual peak passes into middle distance and once more there are moments of calm. The lesser harmonics reappear: the weekly disruptions around pay day at the dole office, the more or less bimonthly fussing of housing benefit, occasional affairs, breakdowns of relationships. The odd arrest.

'So, like I was saying, I'd met this Kayt, and fallen bang in love with her. But, like, three times on that night I'd have to get her to promise me before I let her go that she wasn't going to kill herself. At the time I was trying to get it together so much myself, I was just doing the meth, not using the smack or nothing, and I had just got me flat.'

'Your current flat?'

'No – how could it be me current flat? I haven't cut me throat yet, have I?'

'Silly me. OK. Go on.'

'It's no use you asking questions before I've got to where the answers is kept. This were just after I come off the streets. I decided I couldn't handle it no more, I've gone to the council, explained to them I was disabled and apparently, because I had muscular dystrophy, it was detrimental to my health to be homeless for four months.'

The council, obliged to house him, found Stuart a bedsit just around the corner from the hospital.

'So, me and Kayt never had a sexual thing, only the odd kiss and cuddle, and we had a few little disagreements, where I wouldn't see her because it was doing me head in, I was so in love with her. Then we had a little argument at Strawberry Fair [an outdoor music festival in Cambridge that Stuart ranks high in the list of the glories of the year], and I said I'd never speak to her again and that, then I went and wrote her a letter and said I was sorry. This perticliar night someone's turned up and she's gone off with him. I was in me flat and, at the time, I believed that I'd brought the Devil into that flat because I'd painted the walls burgundy, and I had black-painted wood. Black for the blackness, and red for the blood, the Devil's colours. I believed it so much at the time, I was having conversations with meself about it. So I got pissed off with just being in the black and red there, gone back down the pub and sat drinking and talking to a friend of hers, saying how I was bang in love with her, and she's come in and says, "Come on," she says, "Come on," so we went back to mine. And I'd bought a bottle of vodka before I went to the pub, and I drunk a quarter of it, so there was three-quarters a bottle of vodka.'

Back at his flat, Stuart and Kayt drank the rest of the vodka, took methadone and sleeping pills, 'which I knew she was scripted for. I had just me boxer shorts on, you know, and we lay on the bed.'

The next morning Kayt didn't wake up.

'I'd set the alarm, but when I woke up all the lights were flashing on me clock, so we'd had a power cut. I didn't think much of it. I looked at Kayt, asleep there and I just thought, ah well, she's fucked from a heavy night, and I sort of dozed off cuddling her again. I don't know how long later, because like I said the clock was all in bits, I woke up and I've shook her and I couldn't wake her. I've slapped her round the face, and couldn't wake her. I've picked her up and she's felt like you'd expect a dead person to in your arms. I've slapped her round the face again, I've tried finding a pulse, I've put me cheek to her mouth and when I pulled her eyelids back, her eyes were rolling in the back of her head. So I just laid there cuddling up to her. I don't know how long, an hour, two hours, I don't know how long. Then she just started making a really funny noise, like hhhhuuuunnn, hhhuuuunnn.' The sound Stuart makes causes him to bare his teeth and strain his neck.

The last sight Stuart had of Kayt was when the emergency services turned up in the early afternoon. There was only one ambulance man, 'but she must have been half conscious, because whenever he tried to open her mouth, she kept trying to bite his fingers, because she was having trouble breathing'.

At the hospital, her parents refused to allow Stuart in the room to see their daughter. They said the sound of his voice made them want to be sick. 'I didn't know what state she was in, but everybody's telling me what happened, they weren't *asking* me, they was telling me, and what they were telling me weren't fucking right at all.

'I should have phoned the ambulance when she started making that funny noise, I know that now. But I didn't, I phoned me mother, told me mother what had happened, but my money run out in the phone.'

Stuart started receiving anonymous phone calls: a man

muffled and distorted – sharpening knives, biffing baseball bats – accused him of deliberately drugging her 'so that I could have me wicked way with her. And all cos her clothes were ruffled. Parents never believe their child could do something wrong, do they? Their children couldn't have taken drugs because they fucking begged for them or slept with a dealer to make him give her some. There's got to be some nasty other person to blame.'

Two weeks after the anonymous threats began, Stuart marched into the pub where he knew Kayt's father and brothers drank every night, smashed the end off an empty pint glass in front of all the customers, and shouted, 'You want to fucking get me? Is that what you want? I'll do the fucking job for you!' Then he rammed what was left of the pint glass into his neck.

That's how he got his current flat. The council had to move him away from his old flat near the hospital 'to a place what was stable and safe and over the fucking other side of town'.

Stuart frowns and takes on an expression of concentration. 'I tell a lie. I did see Kayt one other time. It was last week. It was on the street.'

'Did you speak to her?'

'Yeah, only she reckons she wasn't Kayt. She reckons she was from Devon. The funny thing is that her name was Kayt, and if she wasn't Kayt then she was her fucking twin sister – same teeth, same way on her shoulders when she was walking.'

'Well, did she recognise you or didn't she?'

'She come up to speak to me, only she reckoned she'd never seen me before.'

There are times when the metaphysics of the street is beyond understanding.

17

'You don't go quietly. I never did in them days.
Didn't agree with going quietly. Gobbing off and
spitting. As you do, as you do.'

Funny Days:
Aged 15–21

The first time Stuart became homeless he was 15 and high on glue, not heroin.

Aged fifteen, full of zing. The streets were not exactly cosy, but they were not friendless either – a sort of home from home – they suited his temperament. He wanted to live. His brain wasn't fogbound by thoughts of death.

'Where did you spend the first night?'

'There wasn't a first night.'

'But there must have been a night when you stopped being at home and started sleeping rough.'

'That's what I'm saying, Alexander, no. I'd been running away since I was eleven.'

Half-sister Karen's first memory of Stuart 'was I was in bed and they were all arguing downstairs. The next thing I remember is Stuart running into my bedroom, up on to the bed, and he had this old silver radio with a handle on it, and he was going out towards the window, to jump out the window, and my mum come behind him and grabbed him and they started scuffling in my bedroom.'

Weekends, schooldays, during the holidays, it didn't make any difference to Stuart. He'd balance on his window ledge and leap out into the garden. His legs might buckle into the flower bed and the pain of landing split his groin, but he recovered quickly. Contrary to what the doctors had said, Spaghetti Legs was getting stronger. 'Fuck them if I didn't. Ever since I can remember, I thought of it like a war, me against the muscular dystrophy. I'd push meself and push meself. I'd show them I'd win! I wasn't going in no fucking wheelchair! Fuck them!'

He scrabbled up from the dirt, blundered as fast as his new bruises would allow down the incline to the estate road, past the air conditioner at the back of the Queen's Arms, the VG Stores, with their blue stickers advertising cheap fruit, and the aged quietude of Midston churchyard.

I have a great sense of Stuart and silence on these nights. The village, wrapped in sleep; owls glide between the yew trees, badgers poddle across the graves. Then Stuart, cleaving the peacefulness. All people, gone. No educational experts, medical specialists, bullies, policemen. His mother's disapproval, hot on his heels, runs out of breath after half a mile. It is Stuart and the earth, just those two.

He usually didn't reach the cars passing through the village in time. Their yellow lights rose and dipped among the hills, then somehow always swirled past in a bellow of noise just before he reached the crossroads. He'd push himself furiously along the country lane towards the night workers on the A10 clanging by in their vans: a crop-haired, foul-tongued, crippled boy.

Half an hour later, he'd be grabbing his way into a passenger seat.

'Where you going, mate?'

'Anywhere. You take me – I'll go.'

Or:

'Hop in – going as far as Royston – that any good to you?'

'I'll go far as China, mate. Got any baccy?'

Back in Midston, Stuart's older brother, Gavvy, who shared Stuart's room, slept on. His mother Judith: deep in dreams. Little sister Karen and the youngest, Marcus, dozed in the toddlers' quarters. Paul, Stuart's stepfather, was out on nightshift: he was an axle and cross-beam welder and laboured all night in a noisy car factory. He would whisper back in the morning.

The phone call burst Judith's sleep. Before she knew where she was she was bolt upright, snapping on lights, address of the police station that had just found Stuart making whoopee on the streets snatched on to paper. Gavvy was put in charge of tiny ones, especially difficult daughter (another village nasty growing up there – thank God Gavvy knew how to control her, there was never a peep of trouble when *he* was in charge). Then Judith hurried out into the night to begin disturbing the neighbours with a car ignition that rasped and rasped and rasped and refused to start.

Not that it always was a police station that had got hold of Stuart. Sometimes the call came from a stranger whom Stuart had befriended or from Judith's mother on the other side of Cambridge. Often, Judith would discover he had gone missing before she'd got to bed herself. Paul would rush back from work whenever he could and he and Judith would spend two hours or more searching the lanes for Stuart, but 'it didn't matter how much you looked, you wouldn't find him'.

Judith sighs and shakes her head. 'I was always totally amazed at people, because Stuart was a real little scrawny old kid. Getting lifts from all over the show. People who didn't want to know what a child was doing out and about at that time were actually giving him lifts in the middle of the night.'

Today, Judith is heavily lined, with a ready bronchitic laugh and cigarette permanently attached to her right hand. 'Before he started running away he used to get frustrated with things but that was the muscular dystrophy. The boys all playing football: every time he swung his leg to kick he went over. And if the boys all ran off up the road Stuart couldn't keep up with them, he'd be angry with himself. But he was such a caring boy.'

She often marvelled to the police officers as she was standing in the lobby waiting for her son to be returned to her: 'It was when he was eleven that it happened. Always such a caring boy, then all of a sudden, this sweet little boy who'd always been so

caring become a little horror! Unbelievable. The change, to this
little horror. The change in him was unbelievable!'

Stuart's favourite dosshole when he managed to avoid the police
was a squat: a row of battered houses by the railway tracks.
'The punks – they told me where it was, though I was a skinhead
at the time, myself.' It was 1984. The year the Libyans shot
WPC Yvonne Fletcher. There were still Victorians in old
people's homes.

In Stuart's squat, the top ceiling was held in place with
scaffolding. There were no boards or banisters on the lower
floors; the doors and door frames were wrenched out 'because
when some of us needed to keep the fires going, we used to
nick the coal off the railway line, if we could be bothered, or
just burn whatever wood we could get in the squat. It stunk of
piss and shit cos all the toilets and bathroom were blocked.'
Then, one day, 'the Old Bill come and hammered hardboard
over the entrances'. Someone tried to start the squats up again,
'ripped all the windows up and whacked all the bricks out the
walls, but them squats were finished'.

Another time, 'I was in a squat, which was a college house,
and the students had left all their stuff in it because it was
summer. You could guarantee that every couple of days the
police would come and pay a visit at six o'clock in the morning
looking for people on warrants or looking for runaways. So in
the middle storey if you didn't know where you were going you
fell right through the stairs. We'd made big booby traps on the
stairs, big holes hidden in the steps. Even in the one by the
railway, we left one door that hadn't been burnt at the top of
the stairs, so at night when everyone was in, if people had been
out robbing and there was nicked gear, then you just put a big
lump of wood against the wall and on the door and the Old Bill
couldn't push the door open. It would take some doing to get
that door off.'

'How long did you stay in the booby-trapped place?'

'You know, to be honest, that sort of question don't mean nothing to a person like me. That's what you're going to find difficult to understand. You grew up with order so you're going to want order to explain things. Where, me, anything ordered was wrong. It weren't a part of my days. My life is so complicated it's hard for me to actually say what happened in them days let alone in what order.'

'But some sense of time – you must have had that?'

'Nah. Some minutes was long, other minutes was short. I know that. Sometimes I was in the park, sometimes I wasn't. Sometimes I was in a cell, sometimes I wasn't. Sometimes, which were supposed to be weeks and months – I don't think they happened at all. The one constant was, I hated the Old Bill. Anything for an argument with the Old Bill. Then, I hated going to jail, but I hated the Old Bill as well. Funny days, weren't they?'

Stuart squeezes his diary out of his jacket pocket, squashes it over his knee and writes with tongue-bitten concentration. All this talk of arrest and policemen has reminded him that he wants to speak to his MP.

During the day the fifteen-year-old Stuart rared through the streets, blind smashed, and dozed out the sunny afternoons on the green. Stuart was a glue-sniffer – as heavy as you can get at it without bypassing the rest of life and fixing yourself directly to a gravestone. He had perpetual headaches; his lungs started to give in. 'I was at it eighteen hours a day. Three tins of glue a day. I was on death's door.'

'Do you know anyone who's died from it?' I ask, rather shocked by my boldness.

'Fellow called Nutty Norman. He'd tattooed his face up. That was part of his problem, that everyone was staring at him. From my experience, everybody I know who's tattooed their face up, they either end up in a nuthouse or they end up very volatile. In jail you see, like, some fellas, they've got swastikas tattooed on their forehead or on their cheek, so they get loads of shit off the blacks all the time. I know a fella who's got both cheeks tattooed, right across his forehead, tattooed here, teardrops, and he's paranoid to fuck. You know, 99.9 per cent of tattooists won't tattoo on your face, but there's always the one who will.' Nutty Norman hanged himself, high on glue, aged twenty.

Most of Stuart's tattoos were done at this time (including FUCK) using a pin. 'Just put a bit of cotton wool round it soaked in Indian ink, and stab it in.' The five dots above his knuckles, arranged as on a dice, are the five Fs: Find 'em ('em being girls), Follow 'em, Finger 'em, Fuck 'em, Fling 'em. The tattoo I'd thought was a swastika when we first met, two years ago, is an ordinary cross with a pattern round it. A saint – a stick man with a halo above the head – is popular with home tattooists. Unfortunately, Stuart's version is decapitated. 'I don't know why. I think I got disturbed or caught or something,'

he says, peering round to look at the sorry sight on his left bicep. 'Probably got caught,' he concludes. 'Must have got the ink confiscated.'

Another of Stuart's friends died from sniffing Tipp-Ex. 'Clogged his lungs up and he died. You pour Tipp-Ex on your cuff, then put your mouth over it and inhale it. They found traces of Tipp-Ex in his lungs. Fourteen, fifteen years of age, he was. He's gone to the chippy to buy the family's tea, and he never got home. I lost five friends through glue-sniffing, aerosol- and Tipp-Ex-sniffing, and every time I used to glue-sniff I was hoping it was my turn. For the amount of years I was doing it I don't know how I didn't die.'

Each winter Stuart gets minor bronchitis in his left lung because of the damage from solvents; part of the reason he had a bad memory, he thinks, is because of glue; it is possible that his black mists, his outbursts of rage, his love of knives and the severity of his crimes are to some degree related to the brain damage caused by toluene, the volatile substance that gives the high.

'My favourite's Fix-a-fix, which come in a bright red and green tin, if I remember correct. It's like a paste. Timebond's a paste, but Timebond tastes uuuu-ughw. Evostick, in a red tin, you get a real heavy head after you've finished, where Fix-a-fix is the sweetest going.'

Stuart tried lighter fuel, 'but just didn't like it. Some puncture-repair kits aren't too bad,' he muses.

Almost any household item containing volatiles can be used: nail varnish, clothing dyes, dry-cleaning fluid, windscreen de-icer, hair fixative, car paint, aerosol painkillers. Some people spray lighter fuel into lager or Coca-Cola; others suck on fumes from rags soaked with petrol and paraffin (Australian Aborigines are particularly partial to this). According to research, the typical gluehead is an adolescent, lower-class male with low interest and motivation, whose father left or died when the child was young, who is excluded or rejected by his peers, and short of stature – i.e. Stuart to a T.

Stuart doesn't remember exactly when he started sniffing. 'You're lucky if you can remember many instances of glue. The ones you normally remember are because you ended up getting arrested.' But after the age of fifteen most of his free time, and all of his artistry, was spent trying to find good places to get high. In a deserted house 'all falling to bits', he hallucinated that he saw 'cameras, a film set. Outside it was all overgrown grass and I believed that was an air bag. I ran and dropped straight out the window, landed on me back in a bramble bush on this heap of bricks and laid there all night. I fucking broke me back, couldn't move, until the next morning I managed to get away.'

Another time, he crept into a cemetery, 'hoping to see ghosts come out of their graves'.

'If you go and glue-sniff in woods, the trees come down and shake your hand. You see trees with mouths on 'em. It's mad. If you could paint what you see when you're glue-sniffing like me in the woods, tripping, it would make wicked art. Through hallucinogenics, I've been to Toyland, I've been in a movie as a stuntman, had conversations with bushes. Have you ever done acid?'

'No.' Stuart, please!

'Imagine taking ten acid strips, it would probably fuck your head up for about ten years, but you still wouldn't get one-tenth of the hallucinogenic as you get off glue.'

Anywhere with lights was good, because of the images they provoked during a hit.

One girl was rushed to hospital after meandering across a road into the path of an oncoming lorry. 'The police are lying,' she protested. 'I was never near any motorway or roadway. I was minding me own business just having a sniff and going about this field picking some lovely yellow and pink flowers and suddenly this bloody lorry was coming straight at me across the grass.'* Another boy was arrested for weaving his way through

* Denis O'Connor, *Glue Sniffing and Volatile Substance Abuse: case studies of children and young adults*. Aldershot: Gower, 1984.

six lanes of traffic – he thought the car headlights were the illuminations on Blackpool Pier. Habitual users often report that glue makes up for a sense of loss: it makes their nan, or their dead/eloped/imprisoned mother, come back to life.

There is an endearing innocence about glue-sniffers, which Stuart still tries to recapture now and then (he has admitted to doing it twice since I've known him). Foul-mouthed, slouching punks with noserings and 'h ᴚ T E' written across their knuckles, take glue in order to have fantasies about going to the seaside and being nice to their mums.

Even the patterns of glue-sniffing arrests and referrals by police have a naivety about them. An early report in the *Lancet* observed that the number of incidents always drops during mealtimes, when the children put down their solvents and skip home to have tea.

'The main thing is to keep moving about,' advises Stuart. 'When you do it all the time, if you go back to the same place too much, you can have repeating trips and they get boring, so you change your place. Anywhere. Trees, derelict houses, even in the centre of town.'

'What happens in the centre of town?'

'Normally get arrested.'

One of Stuart's best mates, Eden, gave it all up to become a Muslim.

PUNK DOES A BUNK TO JOIN MULLAH'S ARMY

Punk rocker Eden Fernandez has swapped his love of the Sex Pistols for a Kalashnikov rifle and a life of perpetual danger as a fanatical Muslim guerrilla fighter.

The 23-year-old tearaway, who used to spend his days sniffing glue and roaming the streets [looking] for gang fights, has astonishingly been accepted into the brotherhood of the Mujahadeen rebels who are struggling to overthrow the Communist regime in far-off Afghanistan.

The tough mountain men could hardly believe their eyes . . .

WORRIED

Eden's mother Janice, who still lives in St Ives, is also proud of him. 'I'm so pleased that he has found something at last that he really does believe in,' she says. 'Of course I'm very worried about him fighting in a war, but at least I know he is happy living his new life. If he had stayed in England I don't know what would have happened to him in the end. He was always very kind-hearted, but he did get into a few fights and he did drink far too much.

'He was like a square peg in a round hole . . . I'll send him a blanket and just pray he can survive through the winter.'

This article appeared in the *Sunday People* magazine in December 1989, when Stuart was just starting his prison sentence for taking his son hostage.* Stuart looks closely at the accompanying photograph of Eden on a mountain top. 'There, I thought I remembered it right. You can just see a bit of one of his tattoos on his neck.'

'What does it say?'

'"TERMINATOR".'

The second photograph shows Eden peering down a gun. 'There's another tattoo on his forehead, only they've made it faint in the photograph,' says Stuart.

* Fiona Wyton, *The People Magazine*, 3 December, 1989.

'What's that say?'
'"FUN".'

Looking for new ways to provoke Stuart's memory, I pick out his pre-con sheets – the catalogue of his past offences that is shown to the judge before every sentencing.

THIS PRINTOUT IS PRODUCED FOR THE USE OF THE COURT, DEFENCE AND PROBATION SERVICE ONLY AND MUST NOT BE DISCLOSED TO ANY OTHER PARTY.

says the note at the top of the cover page.

'It's a bit thin,' notes Stuart with disappointment. 'It only goes up to '98. There'll be a good few more pages since then.'

The punishments begin mildly and creep upwards over the months.

Aged fifteen, he was arrested eleven times. A twelve-month conditional discharge and £20 for his first offence, a case of criminal damage. Stuart is a little vague about the details: 'Knocking school property around, I expect, something like that. When you say "the first time I was arrested" what you got to understand is that in one year alone I'd run off eighty-six or eighty-nine times, so I been in the police station so many times. Don't ask me about the time I first got arrested. How can I remember?'

A month later: forty-eight hours at an attendance centre for four more counts of criminal damage. 'At that age I was naive: I admitted it.' He and another boy put a paving slab through a shop window and stole a half-bottle of gin, a packet of cigarettes and a pouch of tobacco. 'Fucking stupid, really. I helped drink the gin.' They stumbled about the town and damaged a telephone box. 'What else did we drink? I don't know. Might have bought some Coke. Whatever you drink with gin. I've never drunk gin since, to be honest with you.'

Soon after, he stole a tin of glue from a DIY shop. 'I'd

already been in to try and buy a tin of glue earlier, and they'd refused me, so I've gone back to the same place, nicked the tin of glue, tried to run, they've grabbed me.' One of the young shop assistants started pushing Stuart around because he kept trying to escape out of the door, so Stuart whacked him back and the boy's elbow went through a glass door 'and then a scuffle spilled out into the shop, tins of paint, bits and pieces . . . that was the criminal damage'.

This story confused me. 'So,' I said, 'let me get this straight – you went back to the same shop that had already refused you, and therefore knew you had to be watched if you returned, stole exactly the same thing that had got you under suspicion in the first place, then tried to escape by running away?'

'Yes.'

I know the shop he's talking about. There's a big car park in front of it that has to be crossed before reaching the street. For someone like Stuart, who had to leave his first school because it had too many steps, it was sheer lunacy to think that in such a place he could get away from a horde of able-bodied staff led by an enraged young manager.

'Why did you do it? What happened to your brain?'

'I don't know. I told you – I'd lost it.'

A great many of Stuart's stories show this odd side of him: a grim wilfulness, a refusal to be thwarted. Sometimes it comes across as a display of spirit; sometimes as idiotic defiance in the face of failure. He simply keeps going until either brute force or exhaustion steps in and puts a stop to him.

In the evenings, Stuart had gang fights. He was a Nazi skinhead at one time, 'or I thought I was. Only for about six months. Then I was a ska skinhead, I was a mod, I was a punk. I was an oi boy. I was nothing.'

'What do you mean, nothing?'

'I was never really into the music. It was the way of life and

'Why did you do it? What had happened to your brain?'

the dress sense, you know, "Fuck you, up the world." I never really understood what being a punk was all about, and I never understood what being a National Front skinhead was all about. It was the same with a lot of us. There was a National Front skinhead called Laurence I knew. And he was black! He got stabbed by seven Pakis!'

'What about you – were you racist?'

'Yeah, I was a right racist cunt,' agrees Stuart, and then pauses for a moment: 'No, that ain't rightly true, because when I was in care homes there was different nationalities. I didn't get on with them all, but it was because you didn't get on with them, not because they was black, that you called them black cunts. Not to their face all the time, because, you know, it weren't the environment to do it.'

It was prison that taught him tolerance. 'Once you go away, you've got every nationality there is, and you start learning that there's good and bad among everyone. I think the word racism is used too freely. Too many people use it when it's got nothing to do with racism – it's the fact that they're a horrible cunt and the person don't like them.'

Stuart misses those early days on the streets. They had an individuality about them that he thinks is lacking for children today. 'In the mid-eighties, there was a real big anti-establishment thing going and everybody had their own identities,' he pronounces, like a man about to say that when he was a boy he had to *walk three miles* to get to school, *respected* his elders and for good measure got a smack across the backside, which never did *him* any harm. 'You had rockers, casuals, punks, mods, three different types of skinhead: ska skinhead, like I said already, right-wing skinhead, scooter-skinhead; you had Hell's Angels. You used to have what we called posh punks. All their punk gear would be clean. They never looked dirty.

'If you got a picture of a sixth-form college now,' he concludes sentimentally, 'you'd be lucky if you found two people who didn't look exactly the same as everyone else. But in them days it wasn't boring and materialistic, like today.'

'Then you'd get together and beat the hell out of each other?'

'Yeah.'

They'd meet in the shopping centre. Skinheads and punks at one end, the mods down one side, and the casuals with their Pringle jumpers at the other end. They'd have knives and bricks, broken bottles, knuckledusters and lumps of wood with nails in.

'Hang about,' I interrupt. 'With those weapons, why aren't you all dead?'

Stuart's answer is as if fresh from the battle.

'Because if you have a proper group, if there's like ten of you fighting, people are getting thrown about left, right and centre, getting knocked about, and there ain't much room. You'll find that the one who's got the weapon is standing at the front and he's the one everyone goes for and he's only got time for one swing. It's the ones behind him, at the back, that hurt you. The fellas at the front with weapons are the stupid ones and they normally get thrown.'

'Like getting past the row of archers in a medieval battlefield?'

'Yeah, like Henry the Fifth,' replies Stuart, startling me with one of his flashes of History Channel knowledge.

'Then, next thing you know, the Old Bill's turned up. If a group fight happens, you know, there's a build-up to it. It don't just fucking kick off there and then. There's a lot of verbal. Members of the public see and phone the police. So by the time it gets going it's over with as quick as it started. And if someone looks like they're really getting hurt, quite often people shout "Police!" anyway, and everyone just fucking runs off in different directions. You might meet one of them you was fighting in a side street and have a scrapper down there, or whack him with a bottle or pick a bin lid up and whack him up the side of the head – then get back to running again. It's a funny thing that – a lot of the excitement of them fights is in the running away. Of course I've had a bottle over me head, but in one on ones, not gang fights. I've never got hurt as bad in a group fight as I have in one on ones or a couple against ones. And I've been stabbed. I've had a brick over me head twice. The first time I had four stitches. I was glue-sniffing with this old boy and he whacked me over the head with a brick and it snapped in half.'

On the second of these jolly brick-bashing occasions, 'I was fighting this fella and he was beating me quite bad, all me mouth and nose and eye had gone, and cos I wouldn't stay down he picked this brick up and threw it at me fucking head. Opened me head up. He just walked off and I head-butted him in the back of the head. Because I never stop. Once I get going, I go and go and go. That's part of my badness, is I lose sight of me goodness completely and then I can't stop.'

I remark that it must have made life wearing to be always watching around, waiting to be assaulted by mods and casuals.

'But that's the mad thing. We all knew each other. There was a big punk/skinhead mate of mine, he got done by four of the old casual boys. It'd been sorted that we were all going to have a big bundle this Sunday night and we turned up, and the front row of the casuals was all people we knew. So the old boy who got his head kicked in by the four old boys just picked whichever one he wanted and had a one on one. People had fucking bits of wood with nails in, bricks, all gone for a fucking tear-up, but we all knew each other.'

'You didn't want to do it?'

'What was the point? What was the point in beating each other up when we might all be in the remand hostel next week?'

After a fight, Stuart would dodge back between the street lamps to the derelict houses by the railway, bang up the stairs, encrusted with blood and spittle, still stinking of glue, and fall asleep across the bare floorboards. The trains hummed past on their way to Ely and Birmingham. The stairwells marinated in urine.

'Oh, it was horrible that place, it weren't nice, it was a health hazard.'

'Did you ever sleep outside, on benches?'

'Yes, and I'll be honest with you, I'd never sleep on a bench in a park again, because when they've come out the nightclubs it can be really violent. I've been punched.'

Neighbours coming back from Cambridge on the bus to Midston would report sightings of Stuart to his mother. 'You've got to sort your boy,' they'd say, although on the whole he was still liked in his home village by the older, less vigorous adults because he put their rubbish out and would do a bit of gardening for them when he was around. One or two said that Judith should wash her hands of him, to which she replied, 'How can you wash your hands of your own child? He's my flesh and blood. He's my son. Just wish I could do more.'

She has often said to Stuart, she tells me, 'I wish I could pick you up sometimes, turn you upside down, shake all the bad things out of your head and put you back up the right way again.'

Always attractive to women, this was when Stuart made a catch of Sophie, soon to be mother of the little'un. She was the night manager at a local homeless hostel.

At the time, he was living in one of the hostel rooms. She invited him to come across the road to the pub on the pretext of celebrating her birthday with a drink, then a few hours later guided him back under the street lamps to the staffroom.

'I was sixteen! I thought I was the fucking bee's knees! I was fucking sixteen and she was twenty-four!'

Sleeping with 'clients', as homelessness agencies please to call them, is a sackable offence. So, ever courteous r.e. the fair sex, the next morning Stuart packed his change of clothes and moved back on to the pavements.

The two met whenever they could. Sometimes, on Sophie's nights off, it would be in her small flat. If the two other managers who shared the night duties weren't looking, they hustled into one of the hostel rooms.

Stuart's mother was not pleased.

Stuart's mother said Sophie was a dirty pervert.

But within a month Judith had grown to like her. Even if Sophie's taste in boys was a little unusual, she was efficient, generous and determined. To this day, in spite of all that has happened, Sophie never forgets the birthdays of Stuart's mother and sister.

This is not to say that everything was fine and dandy at the start. There were warnings of what the future might be like. Once, one weekend in the summer of 1984, Stuart went down to see his father, Rex, in Portsmouth. Sitting in his father's bedsit, he was talking to his father's latest girlfriend, when Rex came back from the pub, slammed the front door, stumbled into the room and hit the woman in the face. Enraged, Stuart attacked his father. 'Smashed all his room up. Then he tried strangling me, so I smashed up his telly, his video, went berserk, then went outside and smashed all his cars.' The next afternoon, Stuart met Sophie in Cambridge. To cheer him up, they decided to get drunk and bought a gallon of cider and a bottle of wine and went down to Grantchester Meadows, overlooking the River Cam, where they sat among the nettles and willow trees. But, as so often happens with Stuart, when one thing goes wrong, other errors of judgement start to cluster around.

His temper boiled over. They argued. As they were shouting some students fluttered by on a punt, with champagne glasses and boaters, and started mocking their accents. Stuart jumped into the river in his fourteen-hole Doc Martens shoes – tried to chase through the silt and water after them. At which point everybody, including Sophie, burst out laughing.

Stuart wheeled round, grabbed hold of her, and hurled her into the river.

Sophie sank under the surface and the blast of water billowed out, speckling him and the white dress shirts of the students with polluted river. Then she spluttered up, yawping with shock: 'You're exactly like your fucking father!'

'*You're exactly like your fucking father!*' the students mimicked, rolling with laughter.

'You've just done what you always have a go at your father for doing,' she screamed.

'*You've just done what your father done!*'

'What you going to do, hit me now?'

'*What you going to do, hit her now?*'

Too ashamed to argue, and drenched in weeds himself, Stuart lurched off. Up the road, he came across a car accident. A man had knocked someone off his moped, so Stuart started telling the driver off, and when the police arrived he told them off, too.

Result: Ninety days for breach of the peace at Send Detention Centre, a hard place. One of Maggie Thatcher's quasi-military boot camps for young offenders, run by men pretending to be sergeant majors.

To me this sounds a stiff punishment for what was little more than a loss of temper, but Stuart considers it perfectly reasonable. 'Look how much trouble I'd been in. Like, in a twelve-month period, I'd been in court about six, seven times, maybe more, and never for one offence, it was always, like, two or three offences, you know. That's how the cookie crumbles, in'it?'

When Sophie's contract in Cambridge finished, she took a job in Norwich, where her parents lived. Stuart hitched up there to be with her after his release – through Thetford Forest, past the Snetterton speed track and Wayland Prison, where he would soon be an inmate himself.

She and Stuart moved from bedsit to bedsit; then to a two-roomed flat. Sophie became pregnant.

'That was on me seventeenth birthday. We'd gone out and had a good shag that night, and Sophie said to me the next day, "Stuart, I think you might have got me pregnant." I just laughed, and said, "What do you mean?" She said, "Trust me: women's intuition."

'You know, at seventeen, I thought I was Mr Stud. You know, little seventeen-year-old, got this twenty-five-year-old bird pregnant, and I thought, "Yeaah, what a stud!" Couldn't wait to tell me mum.'

Tell his mum he did. He couldn't stop blabbing about it.

But despite his cockerel strutting, Stuart did not look forward to the birth. To distract his attention and because he was inclined to such things anyway, he started trying to twoc cars (*t*aking *w*ithout *o*wner's *c*onsent).

'I was shit at it,' he admits with resignation.

'What did you do with the ones you did steal?'

'Took them down dirt tracks and just smashed them up.'

'Was it fun?'

'What?'

'Was it fun?'

'I don't know. It was just a way of life, whether it was fun or not. It's just how me life was.'

In February 1988, aged nineteen, he was caught. To guard against future charges that might land him with more time inside when the police looked through their unsolved crime records, Stuart asked for a number of other offences to be *t*aken *i*nto *c*onsideration, otherwise called 'tics'.

In April, he was convicted of one twoc and four tics.

One hundred and ninety hours of community service does not seem quite in Stuart's line, but the magistrate must have thought there remained grounds for hope. He began the sentence in the probation-office café, until customers complained that he put them off their tea; then he moved on to grass cutting.

Aged twenty-one, he put the finishing touches to his master-class on bad parenting by – as we have already seen – shoving his son up through a window at surrounding police cars and threatening to kill him.

18

Ten years later, aged thirty-one, Stuart woke up with a torch shining in his face.

The intense beam lit the floor and the walls, 'blinding but not blinding, if you know what I mean'. It wasn't *in* his face – not startling him – he didn't need to blink. It *slapped* his face. Cleaned out all the shadows. *Scalded* the backs of his eyes. It was an almost refreshing light.

He was in his room, he saw that now. But he was not in bed. He could not be in bed because his bed had disappeared.

And the light came from outside, he saw that too. It pierced through the reflective sheeting on his window that the neighbour had put up for him to stop people looking in – the same neighbour who'd promised to make (but never had) the boing, boing, whoosh, folding James Bond bed. Had Neighbour messed up the reflective sheet? Stuart's first thought. The trick in these situations was to think rationally. Had he put the reflective sheet on backwards, for example, so that now it had grabbed all the light in the world, sucked it into Stuart's room and trapped it, turning Stuart's flat into a light bomb?

Where had all his furniture gone? Why would someone want to steal his bed, even as he slept on it, so that now he, Stuart, who had muscular dystrophy as everyone knew, and therefore needed his bed, was without boing, boing, whoosh *or* ordinary bed?

If he was not in bed or on boing, boing, whoosh, he must be on the floor.

He was not on the floor.

He was standing against the wall with a twelve-inch knife taped in his hand.

Boing, boing, whoosh; boing, boing, whoosh. He understood now. That was the sound of the police helicopter hovering outside. *It* was responsible for the bleaching light.

He had not just woken up. He was emerging from a Black Mist. Somewhere, smirking in the back of his mind, was a recollection of Neighbour's arm with – curiously – a meat cleaver attached to the end of it. Or had it been an aluminium baseball bat?

A face appeared: at the window. A policeman's face, hazy, shaking with the maddening noise. Face mouthed something at Stuart. There was more than one policeman behind Face. Beyond the window, Stuart realised, his self-control starting to slip away again, among the dustbins, on the roofs, battering down his front door, digging under ground with huge drills and tunnel props and hard hats, there were at least forty more.

'I, Stuart Shorter, care of R—— Street, Midston, Cambridge-shire, make this statement believing the contents to be true to the best of my knowledge and belief and would say as follows:

> Sankey was my neighbour. We spoke on friendly terms as neighbours, we would go around each other's house for a beer every once in a while, every couple of weeks or so. Sankey is very gobby.
>
> [Due to an argument at Christmas, two weeks before the incident] every time I saw him he would just stare at me, blank me out or play paranoid head games with me. His mate Tom said, 'You want to watch him.' He also said, 'He is pissed up. He has already been throwing punches.' I said I was getting pissed off with it all and said to Tom that it would have to be sorted because it was doing my head in.
>
> [On the night in question] Sankey stuck his head out of

188

his window and shouted, 'Are you calling me a fucking
butty boy?' Within a minute or so he came outside, then
said, 'I am not going to hit you.' This put my guard up
immediately.

I said to Tom, 'I am getting fucked off with this, let's
get it sorted.' Sankey said that we could go into his flat. I
said, No, I did not want to go into his flat and I knew that
he had an aluminium baseball bat in there by the door.
Instead I suggested that we go into my flat. The three of
us walked into my flat. I could feel myself getting irate. He
picked up something in the main area of the flat which
incorporates both the bedroom and the living area. I was
sure that he picked up a knife, as there was a knife on the
table, then threw it towards the settee.

He then walked over again to the knife and picked it up
and walked towards me. I was stood near the bed. There
was a knife under the pillow, it is always there.

Sankey Doyle's movements are very quick. He came
towards me very swiftly. I was sure that he had the knife
but I could not see it. He was hitting me, pushing or
punching me. I was dragged on to the bed and in any event
it kicked off. I grabbed the knife from under the pillow,
turned round on the bed so that I was on top of him. I was
then swearing at him and abusive, stating that he had better
leave me alone.

The knife I had was an eight-inch blade, perhaps twelve
inches in total. All I wanted to do was scare him enough
with it to get him out of my flat. We rolled over again and
this time he was on top. I put my arm up against his chin
and put his head up against a wall. At this stage I do not
know what was said. My knife was in my left hand, it was
raised.

I went to Stuart's flat with his mother, while he, banned from
returning to his village, was staying at her house in Midston.

The front door, beaten to slivers when the police had tried
to extract him in the ordinary way, had already been replaced.
The flat number had been rescrewed on by the council and a
new letter box to match. A new window was in the frame,

although it had been hurriedly done and the pane had cracked.

Everything else was chaos. Shattered glass was spread across the floor. Bottles, knives, driving theory test books, computer manuals, a roll of carpet that he'd bought to redecorate his hallway – all stuck pell-mell in a hedgehog pile of broken furniture and table legs in the middle of the room. The council workmen had had to hack their way not just through the front door, but down the whole corridor, which Stuart had rammed full of everything he could find – his mattress, his chest of drawers, side table, bedside lamp, even old letters and Bic biro pens – in an attempt to barricade the police out.

There was no blood. Stuart's mother told me, usually there is blood. She wondered if the cleaners had also been in, just for the blood, and left all the rest.

So this is how it is with chaotic people, I thought to myself. Even though Stuart's off the streets, in a flat, and regarded by the local homelessness agencies as a great success story – indeed, practically the only one on the books – he has not changed fundamentally. Where everyone else has one disaster, his sort has seven hundred, all at the same time.

If Stuart is a success story, then it is pointless to imagine that we can ever really help these people without breaking the national budget. The depressed businessman, the bankrupts, the cuckolds, the father who's just lost his daughter in a car crash – perhaps these late-arrival emotional wrecks can be turned round fairly quickly if they want to be. But the chaotic? It isn't a bedsit and employment that they need; it is a new brain.

At best we can keep them steady with drugs. At worst, we must throw them in jail, and hope that we are not in the room when they decide to hang themselves.

The image that stuck with me was the kitchen window. Stuart had wedged into the window frame a plastic plate-drying rack and a small set of pine shelves, the sort girls use for china puppy dogs. It wouldn't have kept out a baby.

From under one edge of the pile in the centre of the room, I retrieved a Dictaphone I'd given Stuart several months earlier. By the wall, among the broken glass, was the cassette, half used, with 'Alexder Onely' written on it.

Hello, Alexander, it's Stuart. You know I was supposed to speak one night when I was feeling really down, confused and . . . everything else. You know, admitting I've had lots to drink and all that, but I can't help but reflect on a programme called *Care* what was on Sunday night, today's date being Wednesday, 11 October. I think about that programme, and when I see the fella with the bottle of vodka and the pills at the end, after reflecting that he went and gave evidence against the magistrate . . . well, in my case I went to the police about my brother and my brother's friend, and how I'd had no justice, only abuse, and then going into care having [been] asked to do things that I wouldn't have thought was possible that anyone could ask of an eleven-year-old . . . and then Midfields home and assaulted maybe because of my doing, maybe because of the way I was, being locked in what they called the Red Room and telling me doesn't matter what I done, there was nothing I could do that they'd let me out unless I calmed down. I just head-butted and head-butted and head-butted and head-butted and head-butted the window what was supposed to be unbreakable.

Coming back to that programme, *Care*, I couldn't watch the abuse of that, the child, had to keep turning over. I couldn't watch all that. Too hurtful, too soon. But the way the drink and the violence and the lies and the hatred became his life. The more he spoke, the more you felt he was disbelieved, and that nobody listens to anything you have to say. So you just carry on and carry on. You don't want to be here any more, you feel dirty and disgusting. You feel, what's justice? So you sit there and you talk about it to the police, you go and kick the paedophile's door down who abused you with your brother. He's still out there walking. Yet there are times regular when I sit in this flat and I look around, and I look what's here in my life – do I really want to be here? If the truth is known, I've used alcohol every night recently, just to go to sleep. If I've got my drink inside me I sit here having mad conversations with meself, talking about mutilating myself, killing myself, killing those who I think have done me wrong, from me babysitter to tracking down those who were responsible who abused me in care to executing the police officers who never gave me any justice. I wanted just to lay down and die. I felt so dirty, and fucking horrible and hated and attacked anyone I got close to. I can't even have a relationship if I want it because I think sex is dirty and disgusting. I just wish once there could be an escape from this madness.

19

'It's a question I often ask meself: what would I do with me? And I don't know the answer. I don't know what I'd do, except run away.'

A Plucky Little Lad:
Aged 10–15

I have taken to working in bed. Trying to write Stuart's life 'like a murder mystery what Tom Clancy writes' has defeated my study room. Stuart doesn't like guns, can't do karate chops, finds sex disgusting and, despite repeated exciting promises to put his enemies in wheelchairs, whenever things turn 'not too clever' the only person who gets rushed off in an ambulance is himself. Trying to expose the 'murder' of Stuart's innocence/ potential/responsibleness, if any of these was murdered, rather than simply never present, is befuddling. I want to kick him for suggesting such an idea. I'd like to thwack him over the head. *I* shall commit the murder.

The room I began in is now coagulated with photocopies and library hardbacks with titles such as *Institutional Abuse; Suicide in Care; Miserableness, More Misersableness and Gloom* and folders, forgotten folders, confusing folders, folders labelled 'Research I Spent A Month Doing And Then Never Used', and (especially thick, this one) 'Completely Unhelpful, Untrust-worthy, Fatuous, Overwritten, Verbal Diarrhoea Printouts From The Internet', or folders with no label at all, because I've accidentally flicked the label from its clip-on plastic display and it has spun away like a sycamore seed. When this happens I have to scrabble around the carpet, crack my head on the chair, squeeze an arm behind the piano till my elbow sticks, all to discover where the tiny ticket of paper has fluttered off to, and which I could have rewritten in half the time, but which at last, triumphantly, with a furious face, I find poking out of the turn-up of my trousers. Then I see that I have lost the folder.

This has clogged on for months. Now, when I glance into my study, it seems to me more like a cave, with strata.

So I have extracted everything I can find relating to Stuart's school years and escaped next door.

With the curtains closed, my bedroom sinks into muffled twilight. The lamp gives the air a comforting orange-yellow tint, and the world outside, slicing through in the gaps between the curtains, sounds tinny and unreal. Occasionally, I hear my neighbours' voices: the Professor of Theology and his wife, just back from holiday with a scroll-handled urn for their Tuscan garden; the Australian lawyer, who has spent so long fighting Cambridge City Council to get compensation for child-abuse victims that it has destroyed his marriage; my landlord's shadowy grunts from downstairs.

It is a freer Stuart in here, unmanacled from books, less hounded, as he angrily calls it, by my attempts 'to simplify' him. When the dark descends outside, I turn on my overhead light, which has coloured bulbs, and the Christmas lights that I have strung along above the mantel, and the room around me turns a clubbish, library red.

'Stuart was a happy little boy. A real happy-go-lucky little thing.'

His mother says this was the way he started. Each time we meet, she gives one of her respiratory laughs, leans back in her chair or sofa, puts on a faraway expression, lights another Benson & Hedges, and repeats: 'Yes, a happy, lively little lad. Always up, building things. Absolutely loved it. Anything that he could build he used to like. He'd sit for hours on his own, playing cars and building roads in the dust and the dirt. Yes, quite amazing really.'

Each school morning he waddled, something like a goose, from his parents' house to his classes, half a mile into the village along the country lane and up a short, steep hill, satchel swinging, hand in hand with his brother, to Midston Primary, a skinny, chipper fellow, pleased with the world and with himself. His favourite subjects were battering the water in the swimming pool as if it had done him a disservice and calling it 'crawl stroke'; making fat, greasy marks on pieces of paper with coloured crayon, calling them 'MuM'; and sums.

Stuart was talkative, curious, loud, irresponsible, restless, fond of practical jokes, enthusiastic, determined, even wilful, unusually attentive to other people's changes in mood and overfond of embroidering stories. He made friends easily. But despite Stuart's suitability for the school, the headmaster soon noticed something was amiss with the little barmaid's boy. It wasn't just his funny gait: he couldn't kick a football – when he tried he usually missed, coiled up like a rope, pulled a funny face and fell on his nose. He had trouble with steps, too, and no school on a hill could be expected not to have at least a few hundred steps. Slopes were fine. Stuart had got to the school quite happily. It was steps. The sudden updown, rather than the teeth-gritting push forward. Even the three steps into the front classroom seemed like pitting a boy, a very skinny boy, against a mountain. Stuart had to haul himself up by the banister like a fairground tug-of-war strongman.

Then, one day, Stuart overreached himself in gym. In a fit of exuberance, he shinnied halfway up a rope, lost his grip, fell to the ground and bit through his tongue. Another boy was sent running up to his mother's house.

Stuart was dying.

His spine was smashed up.

His arms and legs were splattered over the wall bars.

When Stuart's mother finally reached the sanitorium, Stuart was sitting in a plastic chair in the corridor, perfectly calm and essentially unharmed. He was not even crying. Indeed, the PE teacher, who agreed that ropes and five-year-old boys have an unhappy tendency to part company sooner than they should, told her that after the initial shock he had not cried at all. His face was covered in drying blood, that was all. He did not need to go to hospital.

But it was the final straw for the education authorities. They had seen an ill boy from the start and they weren't about to give up their disquiet just because he could take a tumble as well as the next kid. He had tumbled, that was what mattered. The boy was not fit to be with normal children. They had Stuart transferred to a school for the severely disabled.

Cerebral palsy children, whose lips flopped and wobbled in proportion to the degree they'd been asphyxiated at birth, jiggled around little Stuart. Epileptics dropped like stones, usually picking themselves up again immediately they hit the floor and walking off, but occasionally remaining frozen, faces discoloured, jerking rhythmically until, beset by massive contractions, foamy saliva ejected from their mouths. Then, flaccid and comatose, they'd seep back to life. Spina bifida kids, more twisted than coat hangers, insinuated themselves through the new school's corridors – one was only two feet high, with a huge hump on its back pushed to one side as if all the burdens of the world had been stuffed into a knapsack. Approach from the front and you saw a little girl locked inside this perversion. Another boy, with muscular dystrophy – Stuart's brother in illness as it were, the symbol of his future – always sat against the wall during classes watching Stuart pallidly, oozed into a wheelchair.

To get to the school now, Stuart had to take what the local children uproariously called 'the Spaggy Bus'. To Stuart's ears, the sound of this small, twelve-seater coach with low-slung doors at the back and side knocked out every other noise as it wrenched among the pretty lanes towards his house, throttling up the hill, and stopped with a wobble outside his picket gate. The pneumatic doors wheezed open, Stuart would clamber on board and join the others – the driver was a woman called Ruby, who had a big head of red curly hair – then the doors clicked shut and off they'd scoot. It was lucky Stuart did not get carsick as some of the others did: the journey took an hour. If the local able-bodied children spotted them they'd run alongside, laughing and waving their arms, their faces bobbing up to stare aghast at the freaks behind the windows.

Stuart loathed that journey more than the school. It had not just the handicapped on it, but also the full-blown mentally retarded. ('They weren't physically, but mentally spasticated,' as Stuart puts it.) Of course the village kids didn't know that. To them, they were all the same and all hilarious: Stuart, who had fallen off a rope, was the same as the Down's children, with their old man-moon faces and lidless eyes, who fixed him in ridiculous shouting conversations. To get away from them, Stuart would change seats and end up next to an autistic case who never spoke at all, just tried to hide in the luggage rack. There was no telling who or what would get on at the next stop. When it came to churning out mental and physical distortions, the villages around Cambridge appeared to have an insatiable imagination. It might be a birdlike girl who looked as though she'd just tumbled from a nest, or a boy bristling with body braces, stinking of urine, which meant that Ruby had to lower the hydraulic lift at the back of the bus and ease him in as if he were a parcel at the sorting office. Then, just as the mood settled back again, and Stuart managed to distract himself by pressing his face against the window and daydreaming about an odd-looking car he'd just seen parked by the roadside, one of the Tourette's two seats behind would burst into giggles and repulsive abuse, like a sneeze.

A lot of the children on the bus didn't know what was wrong with them.

'My dad said it was because my mum ate too many potatoes.'

'*My* dad said, in the womb, I couldn't breathe properly because I had me face sticking in my twin brother's bottom. What's wrong with you, Stu?'

Sometimes they confessed to each other that they hated handicapped children.

'Oi, Breakable Sally, are you going to go to normal school?'

'No.'

'What about you, Tom-without-a-heart?'

'No.'

And, 'Stu, what about you, Stu? Stu the Fighter! Are *you* going to go to normal school one day?'

The Roger Ascham School, named, rather oddly, after a fifteenth-century longbow expert, belonged to a set of 'special' establishments. In the jaunty words of the *Cambridge Evening News*, some of the pupils at the Ascham 'are spastics, some suffer from spina bifida, some have water on the brain'. Just across the playing field was the Lady Adrian, for children with 'moderate learning difficulties'. Half a mile north-east, the Rees Thomas dealt with the mental cases.

Between these places and schools for ordinary children such as the one he had just come from, there was no contact. 'It was,' says Stuart, 'two different worlds.'

'Yes, and even then he wasn't unhappy at first,' marvels his mother. 'A plucky little lad. His legs were all over the show, bless him.'

He became used to his new status as a cripple. He even began to enjoy it. He was by far the fittest in the school, the Olympic athlete.

The only material left from Stuart's schooling at the Ascham are six school reports. The first thing to notice about these is that they exist at all. Nothing in Stuart's possession usually makes it beyond a year. Furniture, books, clothes, his long-suffering television: all soon smashed up, burnt, taken away for evidence or lost. Paper objects, crammed into the pockets of his green bomber jacket alongside bus tickets, screwdrivers, tobacco, yesterday's lunch, this morning's beer can: after two days, they begin to resemble seaweed. Yet these six school reports, quarter of a century old, are neat and flat.

'Yeah, Alexander, you'll find this lot interesting,' he insisted when he handed them to me one day, standing at the front door, lopsided with fatigue because he'd spent half the day at the drug dependency unit and the afternoon sorting out a housing benefit claim. 'Nah, can't come in. Reggae Night at the Man in the Moon, in'it?'

He seemed reluctant to give the envelope up.

'Wonder what you'll think of them,' he pondered, clinging to one corner while I, slightly embarrassed, pulled at the other. 'Funny little old boy.'

His school reports, his social care reports, his collection of letters from his solicitors when he was in prison and copies of his prison complaint forms, also stored in an envelope in my possession: these official documents he preserves.

Finally, my cling exceeded his.

'What do you call that fucking horrible thing you're wearing, anyway?' he demanded by way of revenge as, triumphant, I slotted the envelope under my arm.

'It's my dressing gown! Don't be so insulting. It's made from pure silk.'

'You got flu? What you in bed for then? No wonder you ain't never got no money, Alexander.'

Back in my bedroom, I lay the reports out on the duvet cover and try to put out of mind the rude ogre who has just been at my door. The A4 sheets of paper are heavy and slightly furry, like moleskin.

The Roger Ascham School
Report for year ending July 197.5.   Name S.T.U.A.R.T....TURNER
Class..4......   Number in class..9...

reads the heading of the first.

There is something odd about this, which I don't catch at first.

Below, the sheet is divided into subjects, leaving an inch of blank space for the teacher's remarks. This is the next surprise: they are excellent. It's no wonder Stuart didn't trust them. Nobody could connect the man now loping across the city with two suicide scars around his neck with the six-year-old goody two-shoes who smarms across this piece of paper in dark blue Biro.

Comprehension: (Oral) Very good. He has a good vocabulary & expresses himself well. He is observant + logical & he has a good memory (Written) He has made a very promising start.

And, in summary, at the bottom of the page, in pale blue:

a very helpful in the classroom.
Head Teacher's remarks:
Stuart's behaviour and general attitude are now very good.

The next report is in a different hand. Aged seven: 'Stuart enjoys arithmetic and has made good progress.' 'Stuart's comprehension is good, whether of the written word or of stories.' He 'has a lively mind', he 'adds much to the class discussions'. Aged eight: 'Excellent progress', 'remarkable progress', 'very good work', 'very creative', 'great understanding'. In PE, Stuart 'has done particularly well at swimming and archery' – rather an alarming sport in a school for the disabled, one might think.

Aged nine, he changes his name.

I see what is wrong with the first report now – the name, 'Stuart Turner'. After this it never reappears in his life, except on his collection of official documents and, ironically, at moments when he wants to disguise himself.

'One night,' explains his mother, 'Stuart was about thirteen and had got it into his head that it was his stepfather's fault that I'd left dad. I sat down with him and I said, "Look, we were living, you and Gavvy and me, on our own when I met your stepdad. Rex weren't there," I said. "Your stepdad's not the reason that Rex's not here now. I've never told you about your father. I've never run your father down to you. What's gone on in marriage was between me and him, I always thought. But I'm gonna tell you a few home truths now, just what it was like." So I told him that night and he looked at me, I can remember him just sitting with his head down and he kept looking up and I said that was what life was like. He was amazed.'

'Did you tell him about the violence?'

'Yes.'

'That he beat you up?'

'Yes. You've got him on such a pedestal, I said, because you thought your dad would make everything right.'

It was a few years after this conversation that Stuart came out of his six-month sentence in Send Boot Camp (where beatings occurred daily) and went to visit Rex in Portsmouth and Rex beat a woman up in front of him. 'That's why he went mad. He'd put his dad on a pedestal and then finding that Rex proved right what I told him – Stuart did have a job coming to terms with that.'

'Did these things happen when Rex was drunk?'

'And when he was sober, but far worse when he was drunk.'

'What provoked him?'

'Nothing. You couldn't put a finger on anything. He was just so unpredictable.'

'Why didn't you leave earlier?'

'Because in them days, thirty years ago, there wasn't the help for women on their own with kids. And your loyalties are that you try and keep the family together. And you just think that they'll change. And you're young, you're naive and excited and bloody stupid. You are! I've never seen anything like that behaviour. I didn't come from a family like that. I don't even think my mum and dad argued, certainly never in front of us kids. Rex didn't care about anything. I just found it totally amazing. Karen says to me, "Ah, Mum, I've always liked naughty nice boys, haven't I?" Yes, I understand just what she means! "It wasn't all bad, Stuart," I says. "There was obviously good times, it wasn't all bad. Dad and I had some good times."'

In my view, Rex Turner should have been dispatched at birth. He was a savage. Stuart's grandparents heard the screams from two houses away when Rex kicked their pregnant daughter in the stomach. One of brother Gavvy's first memories was of leaning over the banister, aged three, trying to crack his father on the head with a broom as he beat their mother up. Rex was a man who injected poison wherever he went, and for generations after he'd passed.

'But what right have I got to condemn him?' says Stuart. 'Everything he did, I did worse.'

Stuart's mother met his stepfather, Paul Shorter, in 1973. A burly person with tattooed forearms, Paul was first a plasterer, then took a job welding lorry axles. Paul was a kind, placid, hard-working man, untalkative to the point of muteness, and loyal. One time, says Stuart, 'Paul, me dad – I call him me dad – and Mum had a serious car accident. This was driving me to see the headmaster because I was being real disruptive in school. Me dad went to brake at the junction, and the brakes went on the car, and we went out on to the main road, hit a lorry, practically head-on, ripped the whole side of the car off, car somersaulted from front to back, then ended up in a ditch upside down. Paul had done all his back in but he got me mum out. They had trouble finding me, but he got me out, then he collapsed himself. So obviously he did care about me.'

Another time, a friend of Paul's came to the house. The friend was having troubles with his wife and worrying about leaving his children. 'It don't matter for you if you was in my position,' the man reflected, 'because Stuart and Gavvy aren't your sons.'

Paul flipped: 'Don't you *ever* say that again!' He pounded his finger on the kitchen table, 'they *are* my sons!'

Paul took the battered Turner family to a new house, on the other side of Cambridge, in a village called –

'If you don't mind, we'll change the name,' interrupts Stuart hurriedly.

'– Midston?' I improvise.

Stuart nods. 'I've caused me mum and dad enough grief as it is. Can we leave them out of it now?'

A few days after Judith married Paul, Stuart and Gavvy secretly agreed to honour the new husband. The first Judith

heard about it was when the headmaster at the Roger Ascham
rang up and asked if it was all right to address her son as

Name .St.u.a.r.t...S.h.o.r.t.e.r.

I throw on some clothes to leave my bedroom for half an hour,
and walk across to the university library.

In one of Stuart's reports, the composition teacher has written that Stuart has

Ladybird 7a.   discovered   the   joy   of reading.

Ladybird 7a turns out to be part of the Key Words Reading
Scheme, and is called *Happy holiday*.* It's on restricted access.
I have to examine it in a special room of the library reserved for
books with weak bindings and publications of a sexual nature.

Happy holiday is the story of two children, Peter and Jane,
who go to the seaside to visit their aunty and uncle. The cover
shows Peter and another boy standing in a municipal pond, in
shorts, showing off their motor boats.

'It was good of Uncle to buy you a new boat,' says Jane.

'Yes,' replies Peter, 'and it was nice of Aunty to let you have
her old doll.' He looks a little incredulous in the facing picture.
'I hope you like it,' he adds.

As the blurb on the inside cover announces, '*Happy holiday*
embraces . . . the natural interests and activities of happy children', like flying kites in the hills, balancing on seaside donkeys,
leaping among the surf, whisking out on a motor boat – all the
interests, in short, that the dribbling, callipered, wheelchair-
bound pupils of the Roger Ascham could not do.

---

* William Murray, *Happy holiday*, Ladybird Key Words Reading Scheme, Book
7a, Wills & Hepworth, Ltd, Loughborough, 1964.

'It is fun here,' says Peter, picking up a crab, 'I always want to run and jump when I am on the sands.'

The preceding volumes seem to be devised for torture. *Play with us* – Oh, but not you, Wobble Legs. *Things we do* – Oops, things you can't. *Where We Go* – Not the same place as you Spags and Divvies, that's for sure. To ensure these cheerful messages were fully understood, teachers could buy 'flash cards' and make the cerebral palsy children chorus the words.

'I like Peter.'

I wish he'd die.

'I like Jane.'

Why doesn't she break her back?

'They like to play.'

Go do it on the train tracks.

And, accompanied by a painting of Peter and Jane flinging back and forth on a swing: 'Up they go. Up, up, up, they go.'

The Ladybird books are not entirely other-worldly. The series editor understood that the readership came from varied backgrounds and would have varied futures: towards the end of the volume with the swing painting there is a page of important, helpful information.

'Look, Jane, that is a Police car.'

'It says POLICE on it.'

In 3b, *Boys and girls* (no cripples, please), Peter and Jane are at it again, bounding into the air on a trampoline.

'Look at me, Jane. Look at me. Up I go. Up and up and up I go.'

Two pages later, even the pet rabbit jumps.

Cambridgeshire in the 1970s has a flavour of the 1870s. Because the family could not afford holidays for themselves, in the summer, from July until September, Judith did casual agricultural labour in the fields, planting in leeks, thrusting them into the soil under the scalding sun, being pernickety among the strawberries, gathering second-harvest potatoes in the leafy autumn.

'In them days, the only employment women without qualifications could get in the country around here was on the fields,' says Stuart's mother.

Some of Stuart's first memories are of these fields: 'sitting on the front of a tractor all day steering it', closely guarded by the nervous foreman 'what were doing about two mile an hour'.

They worked in rows. For potatoes (the most common crop) each woman took on one ridge of earth that stretched the length of the field, while the children rioted or (the unpopular ones) joined in. Toddlers were piled by the hedge. It was blank, exhausting work. One hour, two hours, four hours would go by and you'd have thought of nothing. Just emptiness, rows and rows of female emptiness, baking in the sun, picking spuds. It was quite pleasant, really.

The tedium of the day was broken by moments of gentle unexpectedness. Sometimes the machine that had gone ahead, shaking up the ridge to release the crop, would have sliced through a potato and its sheer face would glisten like honey beneath the clog of dirt. A weevil might scuttle between the sods. It was remarkable how few worms there were: so many potatoes, but no life. Farms prolific enough to require bussed-in teams of labourers have stillborn soil.

Stuart was five to ten years old during these holidays. When he could be caught and forced into labour, his job was loading: 'It was just . . . bosh! Trying to get the sack on the trailer with me hip and shoulder. Twisting me body to make it work. As soon as it left the ground I was . . . do-ing! Anything heavy, I've always had mad ways of doing things.'

When it was very hot Stuart's mother used to put a bottle of orange juice in the freezer the night before. The next morning they'd take the bottle with them, frozen solid, and by lunchtime it wouldn't even be cold. 'You'd do everything you could, throw it under the van to keep it cool, but it didn't very often work. When you're out on the field it's like being on a motorway.'

Paul tried doing the work for one day, collapsed and never went back.

Stuart's mother kept at it, every summer for ten years, with (once Stuart's half-sister and brother were born) up to four children in tow, each day picking up to three tons of spuds. Scoop, shake, into basket. Basket full. Trudge basket to huge container. Tip basket in. Back to row, scoop, shake.

'But they knew it was worth it, the kids,' says Stuart's mother. 'My £8 a day bought their pens for school, bits of uniforms, exercise books, extras. And it put food on the table. We ate a lot of stolen potatoes in them days.'

In November, when the children were back at school, Judith went on to Brussels sprouts.

'*Stu – you awake?*'

It was his brother Gavvy, whispering across the bedroom, half an hour after the last creak of the bed in his parents' room as his mother turned over into sleep position.

Stuart lay, eyes wide open, heart pounding.

'*Stu?* Can I come over?'

There was a double creak from Gavvy's bed: one (Stuart imagined) for rising up on elbow to listen for dangers, another for throwing legs from under blankets.

Night was exciting time in those days. In the last half-hour a dozen things had happened, just in the form of noises, to liven Stuart's imagination. The neighbours had returned home, back from a party: their car headlamps had swung across the window as they passed the church, then away as they rounded the cul-de-sac, then back across the window as they pulled up to their house, three doors to the left. Two doors had slammed.

'. . . told you not to fucking wear that skirt, you fucking . . .'

'Don't you *dare* have a go at me! I saw what you were up to with little Miss . . .'

Ten minutes later, next door, on the other side, the three-bedroom house, there was a scuff on the path, then a stumble, a giggle and a moment later the bang of a door. The father, one of the two sons, or the lodger? This family did not like the Shorters, and made it known. They said the Shorters had jumped the queue to get a four-bedroom house. They said a lot else besides, most of it unprintable. But the woman at the council had told Judith they were talking rubbish. If they could fit an illegal lodger in their house, which the council knew all about, then they didn't need an extra bedroom, did they? The two sons made up for it by pouncing on Stuart.

Then there'd been one of those chattering birds that sounded halfway between a woman being attacked and an owl with beak-ache. It had come from the churchyard, and made Stuart think of the gravestones, peacefully trotting on through life, day to day, minding their own business, and the yews, hanging over the bumpy corpses, bathed in moonlight.

'*Stu?*' Gavvy again.

'Come on, quick, yes,' Stuart breathed.

Gavvy clambered beneath the covers and filled up the room with stories about the rough and tumble of real school. Gavvy was the popular, easygoing joker of the class. 'Not cruel jokes, nothing like that,' insists Paul. 'He'd do Scotsman, Englishman, Irishman jokes, but never a cripple joke.'

Gavvy would leave school in a few years, at sixteen, and become a good workman in the press shop of the same car factory where Paul welded axles. If Gavvy had a subject, it was football. He loved the game. Mad about it.

'. . . and then Mark, you remember him,' said Gavvy, insinu-ating his arm around Stuart's waist and pressing hard against him, 'he was in the year above you? Ginger hair? Yeah, down the garage, he said, in Mr Carlyle's, what's now the biology teacher, his voice, fuck, ha ha, it was funny, he said, oh, fuck,

I can't say it, he said – you remember how Mr Carlyle has a fucking stupid lisp? – he said, "I want to exsh-pell this boy because he took out the . . ." – Ha ha! *Don't* be so nervous, Stu, Mum can't hear, it feels nice, doesn't it? – "I want to exsh-pell this boy because he took out the axsh-olotl to beyond the sh-cool boundary and ssh-*tamped* on it!"'

Stuart would roar with laughter. That nightmare revolting, deformed axolotl: it had sucked around a fishbowl in the biology-class window even when Stuart was a pupil there.

Gavvy had to cram a pillow in Stuart's mouth to stop him waking the whole village.

Next, a scrap:

'Yeah, so Adam tells Kev, "Do that again and I'll punch your gob in." I mean, he let him know, it wasn't like it was – anyway, then Wilbur – you know, in my year, big fucker? – he reckons he's hard, and he comes up and Adam just gives him one, fwaack, right as he's getting close, right in the dial, heard it across the park, like a fucking twig snapping . . .'

Gavvy's stories kept Stuart in touch with the fine and busy world of winning. He could smell the vigour on his brother's chest. Gavvy's arms were stiff with new muscles and excitement.

'What happened in your school?' Gavvy demanded.

Stuart tried to think. On the bus in to the Ascham he had seen a car by the side of the road with its bonnet dented and a woman standing on the verge, smoking. In fact, now that he considered it clearly, the woman wasn't really smoking, she was screaming. As the bus had gone by, he had spotted bodies in the grass, four at least, and the old wrinkled couple who lived by the golf course also. Arm in arm. Which made six. 'There was more in the ditch, too, I reckon, still in the pile, what was *two* articulated HGVs, one from Marks & Spencer's, the other from the . . . pet fish factory, plus a coach, *and* a bicycle, and they was all burning.'

Ruby had refused to stop the bus, of course. She'd screeched round the corner and away before you could say 'terrorist attack', but Stuart reckoned they had been the first on the scene. He'd spotted three helicopters – air ambulances – thumping over the horizon towards the carnage.

Gavvy hadn't heard about a road crash that bad in months.

'Yeah, and another thing . . .' said Stuart, as if it had only just occurred to him. He broke out of his brother's arms and turned to face the wall.

Gavvy laughed. He found Stuart a bit difficult at moments like this, when the boy suddenly went 'sensitive' on him. The very thing that attracted Gavvy – Stuart's undisguised, insistent vulnerability – also made him a bit of an embarrassment. 'Not another incident? At this rate there'll be nobody left in the whole world! Well? Aren't you going to tell me? What is it?'

'Nah. A friend. Remember the boy in the wheelchair what I told you about? What liked cars and told jokes, and I used to sit next to? What had what I've got? He died today.'

On the nights that Gavvy did not come over and press against him, Stuart lay awake listening to the lorries until one or two in the morning, imagining their lights cutting along the road, the gruff men in the cabs and the buffet of the airstream as they left him behind.

And this was when suddenly, aged eleven, Stuart ran away.

During the whole of the next five years, there was only one time when Judith and Paul recaptured Stuart once he'd got out.

It was 'an awful night, absolutely bloody awful. Horrend-ous,' Judith remembers. Snow and sleet stormed down. Drifts blocked roads, broke telephone cables. By the war memorial an oak cracked and exploded against the street, gouging a crater in the Tarmac. 'We'd been all round. Round and round and round, and when we came back we went an unusual way, because the tree was blocking the road, and we caught him in the headlights.'

'Get in!' shouted Judith. 'We've been up for two bloody hours looking for you!'

But, she says, 'he never ever told us why he used to run away. You'd ask him, *Why, Stuart?*'

'I don't want to live here.'

'Why? Is it the new baby? Is it because you want to be at normal school? Is it your real dad, living in Portsmouth?'

'I don't want to live here.'

'But what's the reason? There's got to be a reason, Stuart.'

'I want to go in care, I want to go into a children's home.'

20

'No!' shouts Stuart, grabbing the pages of the last chapter (he is catching up with me) from my desk. 'Don't you never learn?'

He storms around my study, kicks over a pile of books, waving fifteen sheets of typescript.

'What you on about, Alexander? You say . . . "*This is the next surprise: they are excellent.*" That's me school reports, you're talking about, what isn't excellent. "*It's no wonder Stuart didn't trust them.*" It's not them what I don't trust, Alexander, it's you. "*Nobody could connect the man now loping across the city with two suicide scars around his neck with . . .*" Did you *read* them reports?'

'Of course I read them reports.'

'And *was* they all good? *Was* they?'

He has now snatched the original school documents and is flapping these about like a flyswat.

'Not *all*.'

'Exactly!' There is glee in his voice. '"*Extremely disruptive*" . . . "*Very distractable*",' he exposes. 'And 'ere.' He gives the pages an extra stab with his finger. '"*He can be most uncoo . . . prara . . . tive and unpleasant to his classmates and adults.*" Why haven't you put those fucking bits in?'

'I di—'

'You don't get it, Alexander, do you?'

'Bec—'

'You haven't been *listening*, have you?'

'I bl—'

'You haven't done no "research".'

'Whe—'

'You can't even be bothered to fucking read a couple of school reports properly, can you?'

'Yo—'

'And now you're going to fucking make me out in this book like it was all good and then loads of things went wrong, that's –'

'Per—'

'Just talk, talk, talk with you, in'it? Yeah, you got the house, the education, the money, the fucking past what weren't full of abuse, you already got all that on me, and now you want me all tied up in explanations. That's what fucking people like you want, in'it? Because then it's all sorted, in'it? "Stuart? Done him. Stuart? Yeah, explained him." But you can't. *I* haven't had it that simple. Why should *you* get to put reasons on it when I've fucking lived it and still can't? These two scars?' He clenches his fists beside his throat and puts on a poncey voice, as if mimicking some faux swagger in my writing: 'These two fucking "suicide scars", as you call them, is these "suicide scars" simple? Is that, oh, he was good, then he was bad, and here are the reasons, one to fucking five? Tick them off, make them into more numbers, put them in a government speech, put them on the telly.'

Will the madman never stop? Waving his fists around near my grandmother's china, just as he ranted at me at the Home Office, clanging on dustbins, peering in letter boxes, pretending to be me looking for 'me simple fucking answers'. Now he's shrieking I haven't done my research! Three *years* of effort and a whole fucking *week* in the fucking university library reading Peter and Jane fucking *Ladybird* books, *Ladybird books!*

'Oh, for Christ's sake,' I suddenly explode. 'So what? So there are one or two bad comments in those reports. All children have their bad days. That's not interesting. When did you lose the good, that's what I want to find out. When did you become fucking useless? Look at you now, why couldn't you spend just ten minutes of your time, even when you were ten, without turning it into a fucking world war?'

'Alexander, it was *my* childhood,' Stuart spits, wrenching the study door open.

'*Was*,' I yell back. 'It's mine now.'

Stuart does not storm out of the house. A moment after going into the corridor I hear his heavy tread on the steps. He is clonking upstairs. Goodness knows why – there is nothing up there for him except the kitchen and the television. Perhaps he wants to test my telly out on the wall.

I sit back and listen to his slow progress: clonk, clonk, pause, clonk, clonk, pause. I imagine him hauling on the banister. When he was little, the effort of it regularly used to pull the handrail off the wall of his mother's house. Clonk, clonk, pause. The sound reverberates like someone banging on the central-heating pipe. Now I can hear him in the room above me: my housemate's office. He has a heavier tread on one side, I am surprised to notice. The left side? Because he is left-handed and his left side is stronger, like a prop? Or the right, because it falls to the ground with a greater thud? *Clonk*, clonk, *clonk*, clonk. He approaches the window.

I wish he'd throw himself out.

It would be messy and create a fuss, just when I want to finish writing this book, and to get to the window he would have to climb on my housemate's spare double bed, which is encrusted in Housemate's socks and underpants. In biography, most of the time, the real person is a nuisance. One wants them out of the way. If only they'd stop muddying the waters with inconsistencies, denials, forgetfulness and different interpretations of your language, you could extract their essence and be off down the publisher's. The heart of it is probably this: the subject fears that if you get what they are down on the page then you have debased them, so they flap about like aboriginals claiming photographs steal their soul. What, me? That's all there is to me? Fuck off! Biff! Take that!

I hear the squeak of the bed and start in my chair.

Then silence. I sit back again. Why would he want to jump? Because I've pinched his childhood? Because we've had a tiff? I *don't* think so.

The bed squeaks a second time.

But again, a long silence follows and I relax.

Then the rumble of the sash window shudders through the walls.

'STUART!'

There's a smash, something bursts; the bed sears halfway across the floor.

'STUART!'

'Alexander . . .'

'Stuart?'

'Alexander . . .'

I look round at the wreckage of glass. 'What?'

'You want to speak to your landlord about that window, you do. That might have chopped me fucking head off.'

'What a pity.'

I step across, crunching the fragments. The cords on this sash window are broken. Stuart had unlocked it, pushed the lower half up to look out at my balcony beneath, removed his hand, and promptly it had crashed back down again. Only one of the panes has shattered, but it's thrown glass splinters over the whole room.

Together we clear the nastier pieces out of Housemate's underwear. Stuart appears at a loss what to do with what he picks up, stuffs one or two big fragments in his pocket and piles

Stuart!

the rest in his right hand in the same way that he stores cigarette ash until it's formed a tepee. Then he clumps to the kitchen across the hall. 'Ooooh! It's disgusting in here. Don't you never wash up? This cooker – it needs throwing out. Aaauugh, the grill, what d'ya last cook on that? Dog food? Where's the bin? Alex*and*er, it's got mould on the *out*side, how'd you get fucking mould on the *out*side?' There is the sound of tinkling shards, then a pause as I imagine him peering closer. 'Is it the same as the stuff on the inside?

'It's a shame,' Stuart concludes. 'You could do something with this house. Put foreign students in it. Chinese ones. They're small.'

Downstairs again, reseated in my room, Stuart says, 'Sorry, Alexander, didn't mean to upset you, didn't mean to be rude.

You know – memories.' He puts down my mug and gives a spiral gesture with his hand that suggests a landscape of bafflement. 'It is hard for me sometimes.'

For the next half-hour, as happens only in the best moments, we sit in silence.

'Meant to tell you,' he remarks at last, forcing himself up and arranging his jacket and goods. 'I got a date for me hearing – it's only pleas and directions – about the incident in me flat. Remember, with the helicopter?'

Of course I remember. Forty police officers, knife fight, barricades . . .

'That's a point.' It's suddenly dawned on me – the little fact that's been niggling away at the back of my mind during the whole of this interview. 'Stuart, why are you here? Shouldn't you be in prison?'

The lobby of Cambridge Magistrates' Court part surrounds a huge, windowless, pale brick central block: these are the courtrooms, their entrances set out in an impressive, Orwellian line along one side. The crowd of accused slouching around in spivish suits is mostly young, male and lower class. Some have brought their families. A couple in a small recess are crying. Two women, just old enough to be out of gymslips, have prams. One group laugh and joke, and call out to each other as if they were just in the dining hall at school. Stuart thinks they might be part of the infamous Gypsy Smiths, cousins of his old mate Smithy. Every now and then there is a waft of alcohol and sweat.

Across the room a man in a baseball cap has slid so far down in his chair that his body pokes out parallel to the floor like a plank of wood. 'Fuckin' this, fuckin' that,' he grumbles. 'Fuckin' disgrace.'

'They don't look very upset to be here,' I remark.

'It's just the magistrates', in'it?' says Stuart absently. He has changed into a lime-green shirt and outsize tie, as if the brightness and scale of this propriety might hide a fraction of his offence. 'Fines, setting Crown Court dates, pleas and directions, which means, like, if you plead guilty or not, bound-overs, stupid things. Wait till they get to the Crown Court. That's the next step – when they get sent down.'

'How long before that happens?'

'Months. It can sometimes be so long after that you've forgotten what you've done. With any luck, I'll get time for a spring holiday in Wales.'

In, out, in, out. All day long: in, out, in, out. The pistons of the law.

The oldest people are the wardens. Every few minutes they receive bits of paper from an usher containing notes from the court, and shake their heads in disbelief. The solicitors, fresh and sober, march between courtrooms and the lobby in a self-absorbed manner. Stuart's one looks as if he hasn't started shaving yet.

What happened that night in the flat, as far as I can make out, is this:

One evening, in the local pub, Stuart called his next-door neighbour a poofter.

'Nah,' interrupts Stuart, 'I *didn't* call him a poofter.'

Sorry. Stuart didn't call his next-door neighbour a poofter.

Stuart nods. 'That's the whole point. He *thought* I'd called him a poofter but I didn't. He just sticks his head out his window and goes, "Who you calling a fucking butty boy, then?" Then he's come storming out, arms all in the way, eyes on fire.' Next-Door Neighbour is an army-loving man: the sort of lad who dreams of disembowelling disaffected members of the Saudi royal family with his teeth.

'And you hadn't said anything to him of the sort?

'Nah.'

'So what had you done?'

'Just asked his mate if he was a poofter.'

There are times when Stuart has the emotional acuity of a frog.

'But at the time,' Stuart protests, the mate 'just laughed and said, "Don't be stupid," and told me he suffered from premature ejaculation.' In fact, Stuart thought that this exchange improved everything wonderfully, because, as he readily admitted to the friend, 'I suffer from the same complaint meself. It is quite interesting, really.

'Did I tell you,' Stuart remarks to me as we're waiting in the magistrates' lobby, 'they're considering upping the charge to "attempted murder"?'

'On what grounds?'

'Because the fella says I tried to cut his head off.'

'Did you?'

'Yes, and if the bastard hadn't of moved I'd have got him, too.'

Stuart's solicitor, carrying a clipboard, breaks free of the flow of officials, strides across the floor and crouches on the floor in front of us.

Stuart agrees he is guilty of 'affray' ('I hold me hands up to that'), he denies everything and anything else, especially the charges of 'threats to kill' and 'attempted murder'.

'Yeah, because at the end of the day, he's got no marks on him, so obviously I didn't cut him. I might have fucking lost it and gone a bit mad and smashed me flat up and got all them Old Bill out of bed, but the fact that he ain't got no mark on him proves I didn't go overboard.'

Solicitor Boy taps his list.

'A couple of things I want to sort out before we go in. In one of the depositions, the police say they could smell smoking oil when they arrived at the scene. What was that?'

'Chip fat.'

'Ah, chip fat. Of course.' He taps some more.

'I saw a police officer outside the window. My head had already gone and I believe I had to burn the Devil out of me.

It was then that I put the chip pan on. I was intending to harm
myself and towards killing myself was going to pour the fat
over my head. Before I could harm myself with the chip pan
the electricity cut out. To self-harm I cut myself and started
drinking my own blood and locked the door.'

Another question concerns Stuart's bail conditions, which
require that he lives with his mother and stepfather, at the pub
they run in Midston. The police are goggle-eyed that Stuart
has got bail at all.

'But you want to change them so you don't have to live with
your parents all the time,' says Solicitor Boy, as if talking to
someone very spoilt.

'I can see why the prosecution's not happy about it,' agrees
Stuart. 'But, me being an alcoholic, it just don't seem sensible
to make me stay in a pub.'

Solicitor Boy makes another tick, taps the clipboard thoughtfully, then gets up and strides back to rejoin the stream of fellow
lawyers hurrying between doors, looking neither to right nor
left. Stuart and I wander across to the allocation board, then
into his assigned courtroom, which is not at all how I remember
the place from my one experience in the dock. The room in my
memory was a tawny, squeezed-up Tenniel drawing, and the
magistrate, high up, had hung over me like a cloud. 'Take your
hands out of your pockets, young man,' he had boomed.

This room is spacious and light. The sun glances in from
a spread of windows above and illuminates the considerate,
friendly woman presiding at the pale wood bench in front. We
are a few minutes early for Stuart's hearing, and are gestured
by an usher to the back row of the visitors' seats, where we
sit down and arrange our expressions into ones of respectful
attentiveness. At times like this, each display of politeness seems
like a reason to hope. The case before Stuart's is being finished
off. It concerns a portly man, 'widely respected in his community', who'd 'uncharacteristically' punched a total stranger
in the face in the toilets at Tesco's. He looks as though his usual

method would be to use a sherry bottle. He gets three months' community service.

Half an hour later we are back outside, Stuart undoing his tie as if shaking off an insect. The magistrate has agreed that his case is outside her domain, and has asked that it be referred to the Crown Court as a matter of urgency, given the dangers of keeping a knife-wielding sociopathic alcoholic confined to a public house.

'How long do you think you'll get?'

'Depends on the judge on the day. If he's had an argument with his missus, he could hand me a ten.'

One of the dealers caught in the Ruth and John raid had been expecting seven years. It was his second offence. A class-A drug. The judge was a known hard man. But on the morning of the sentencing, the judge didn't show up. He had to have a hip operation. A softie court recorder took over, and the dealer got away with a three. I know it's a trite observation, but it always shocks me: there is very little connection between law and justice.

'It's got to start at six,' Stuart reflects. 'Six plus. Me last two were for five, and I still haven't learnt me lesson, have I?'

Cambridge Magistrates' Court is a hundred feet above street level, a vertiginous building on top of the city centre multi-storey car park. The lift back to street level smells of urine and ash. It is ironic that Level D, where the homeless sleep, is in the same car park, four storeys further down: the greatest source of prison fodder efficiently connected to the institution set up to put them there by a lift. We step outside. There is a clutter of grubby types nearby: one begging next the telephone box, another entangled in blankets and beer cans against the wall, a third playing the penny whistle – all considerably trying to save the police and judiciary the bother of having to go the extra four floors lower, to Level D.

Stuart nods at the penny-whistle player.

'Funny, me and a mate was talking in the Man in the Moon

the other night about what become of all the people we used to know when we was in care. So many of them ended up on the streets. Matt Starr, he become a junkie, I seen him gouched out on a bench last Saturday; Ali Crompton, junkie, six months for shoplifting, gets beaten up by her bloke reglier; Timmy what's his name, Harris, dead, a car crash, and his brother Mike, but a different car crash, after a burglary; Julie Dover, selling herself, to pay for a habit. Eight out of ten of them are junkies, done bird, or dead. Two brothers have been charged with murder. One's already done two fours for GBH – he got a reduced to manslaughter for someone on the park. The other's done little bits of bird, and he got a six-year for stabbing his wife eighteen times.'

'Did you know which ones in care were going to pull through, sort themselves out, and which ones wouldn't? The man who stabbed his wife – did he, when you knew him, seem like the sort of man who'd end up doing that?'

'No, but that's what I keep saying to you. I never looked at things in that way. That weren't how I lived. Because you've lived such a different, fucking straightforward life, you're asking me to think like you'd think, and put perspectives on things. I can't do that. I can't even say I knew of any purpose I had in life meself.'

We walk on in silence, through the civic vulgarity of Lion Yard shopping centre, where 'Topple' died, past the *Big Issue* seller who's called Sean and injects in his stomach, and the Baker's Oven bakery and tearooms, on the roof of which 'Scouser' sleeps. This shop has good chocolate éclairs in its bins, which the homeless eat, although sometimes – if the manager's had a bad day, or one of the rough sleepers has been particularly untidy or abusive when rifling through – they are deliberately mixed with floor dust and glass.

'Put it this way,' I say, 'if you had to pick one thing only, one incident involving yourself that has made you become what you are, what would that be?'

'The day I discovered violence.'

He always says it like that.

'The day I discovered violence' – as if he had unearthed a great treasure.

21

'A lot of the madness now does stem back from when I was ten, eleven, twelve.'

The Discovery of Violence: Aged 10–12

'Stu Spag! Stu Spag! Stu Spag!'

'Wobble Foot!'

'Spaghetti Legs!'

Bobby and Johnny Grimes roaring out of the clouds, arms wide, balletic swoops across the street, shrieking like Stukas. Midston, 1979. Location: outside VG Stores.

'Divvy alert, nine o'clock right.'

'Looks like a bad 'un, Dad in nick 'un, has it up the bum 'un, spag on brain 'un, eliminate!'

'Bandy Boy!'

'Bendy Boy!'

'Skeeeeaaaaahhhh ... Divvy, *Paki*, divvy, *Paki*, divvy, *Paki* ...'

'Giiiimp-eee!'

'Nnnngguuuoooo ... *Vegy*bles, *vegy*bles, *vegy*bles ...'

One day Stuart, when he was older, would learn that he could speed up his legs by stabbing them. '"Live, legs, fucking live," I says to them. Key, pen, whatever I've got in me pocket at the time. Just wound them and hurt them, to make them go. "*Live*, legs, *live*."'

But on The Day He Discovered Violence they plodded.

'Get him! Pull his hair! Break his nose!' cried these ghastly *Lord of the Flies* children. 'Trip him! Kick him! Eat his eyes!'

Plod, plod, plod, went Stuart's legs. Yard after yard, minute by minute. Up Fore Street, North Street, Fenner's Green, the churchyard, Spense Road, the river, Castle Hill.

'What do you call a bloke who's got no arms or legs who is floating in the sea?'

'Bob!'

'What do you call a bloke with no arms and legs who sits in a bath of boiling hot Bovril?'

'STU!'

Plod, plod, plod, went Stuart's legs.

Outside the church gate, the Grimes' sister joined in and fluttered behind like a flag, throwing her polka-dot skirt as high as her shoulders with every skip.

Stuart battered through a hedge, down a path, across the park, the way behind bellowing with bloodlust.

'Three women, all up the duff, right?' whispered Bobby, trotting now, two steps behind. 'Buns in the oven? First one, she says, "I'm making this lovely pink sweater because I hope I'm gonna have a baby girl." Second one, she says, "I'm making this lovely blue sweater, because I hope I'm gonna have a little baby boy." But the third one, she holds up her sweater, and says, "Well, I hope I get a spastic, because I've fucked up these arms."'

'Stuuuuuaaarrrt . . . weee'rrrreee coming to kiiiii-llllll you,' whispered Johnny in his other ear. Soft and long and amorous.

Stepfather Paul was making tea when Stuart finally clattered into the kitchen.

Yet instead of giving sympathy, he also turned on the boy.

'He told me that if I didn't go out and stick up for meself, he'd fucking belt us one,' recalls Stuart.

'No,' protests Paul, 'I never would have said that. I never would have said I'd hit him myself.'

1980: Larry Holmes knocked out Muhammad Ali; Henbit won the Grand National on only three sound legs.

Stuart Shorter, four foot three in his nylon socks, opened the kitchen door, walked up the garden path and smashed his forehead into Bobby, the bigger bully's face.

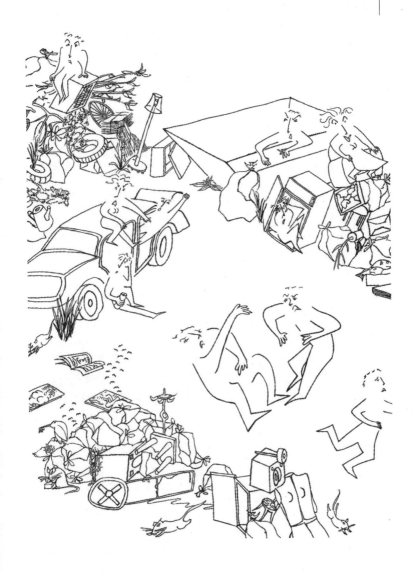

In Stuart's eyes, the whole of his life pivots on this incident. It was the unexpected moment at which he found some power, and the weakling became strong. In his 'murder story' like 'what Tom Clancy writes' the head-butting of Bobby is equivalent to the moment at which the timer on the anthrax bomb to serve up the president starts ticking down to zero, only Stuart's good character is not going to be saved. It is possible it still could be saved, if Stuart didn't have the luck of Job. But in this murder story the baddies have a few more tricks up their sleeves. Not the least of these is that Stuart is not sure, and never has been sure, whether or not he is one of the bad guys himself.

The next six months after his triumph over the Grimes boys were a feast of head-butts. 'Honestly, I got X-rayed a year ago and they said I had a hairline fracture in me skull what had been there since I was ten, twelve years old.'

'Doesn't it knock you out?' I ask. 'If I hit my head against someone it'd knock me out.'

'Yeah, cos that's the sort of bloke you are, in'it? Bang! You're on the floor and the other fella's fucking wondering if *he* hit you or bumped into a fly.'

'But it must hurt,' I reply stiffly.

'Not if you do it right. Chin down, look up. If you can get hold of the fella it helps, then push off and fucking whack back. Breaks his nose every time if you do it right. I've had me nose split open, bumps on me eye as big as an egg when somebody else has head-butted me.

'Yeah, alright,' he adds reflectively, 'sometimes you do get a bit of a headache afterwards, cos your brain do get mashed inside your bonce when you make contact, and the Discovery Channel says your skull isn't smooth inside like what you'd expect, where it's got these sharp ridges. But it only lasts an hour.'

In a fight, Stuart would tell his enemies to hit harder, or to kill him, or to use an iron bar since their fists were so feeble. When he was being kicked in the face, he'd call out: 'Is that the best you can do? What are you, a fucking girl?'

The Grimes brothers tried to restore their community standing. They arranged a rematch in the scrapyard and put the word about that Nutty Stu, the fella with all the fresh bumps on his head, was about to be crushed.

Children from all over the village were dotted about the heaps, sitting on old cars, in refrigerators, on discarded armchairs among the flies, when Stuart arrived. Nobody liked Spaggy Stu. Bobby and Johnny were standing in the middle, 'armed in steel toecapped boots' according to Stuart, cracking jokes. Mountainous stacks of garbage reared up on either side. Stuart was barefoot.

'Had to be, didn't I? Couldn't move in boots, could I? Too heavy for me legs.'

He walked straight up to Bobby and head-butted him.

Blood everywhere. Fight over.

What I admire about this triumph is its lack of gentlemanliness. Stuart didn't want honour or applause or to play by the rules. He had no intention of squaring up and indulging in fight foreplay. He wanted victory, so he took it. Those stupid Grimes boys didn't know that a fight does not need to have a beginning, only an end. Not just madness, but lawlessness makes people frightened.

Johnny ran away. So Stuart walked after him, across the metal-strewn scrapyard, past the silenced, now watchful children, over the twisting road, along the new-mown bowling green, right up to the Grimeses' front door, where Johnny had arrived minutes earlier, armed himself and 'was standing at the bottom of the stairs with an axe'.

'Well, do it! Go on, do it! Hit me with it!' Stuart coaxed.

Johnny's father phoned Stuart's mother up at that moment. 'He's a fuckin' nutter,' he says, 'he needs locking up, he's a danger to all our kids.'

'So, it was the children of Midston who began the process of messing you up?' I conclude.

'No. That was just kids being kids, bullying. Lots of kids get bullied and they come through it. They become responsible. But me – I decided to make out I was mad.'

Six months later Stuart realised he was no longer in control of his mind.

On the afternoon he discovered violence and head-butted Bobby, Stuart released or created (he can never decide which) an aspect of personality that for a period he toyed with at arm's length, like one of those fictional friends that imaginative children have. But then it grew too strong for him and became himself.

'Somebody who's educated could probably control it better, because they've got a stronger mind. The more I try and control it the worse it gets. There's no set pattern for my rage now. I don't even ever see it coming. I have these conversations with meself, where the more I try and calm myself often the worse I get. That's the bit I hate. I lie there fantasising, talking to myself, having mad conversations. I won't get out of bed for a couple of days, won't go out the house, won't undo the windows, won't answer the door, won't answer the phone. Then I start getting really paranoid. Well, I call it paranoid, but the doctors keep saying to me, that's not paranoid, it's anxiety. I beg to differ.'

By the time I got to know him, Stuart was trying to get a psychiatrist to say he was insane. If he could pin down his mental state with that label, there might be a drug that would bring him back to ordinariness.

Instead, Stuart's doctor diagnosed him with borderline personality disorder (BPD) – sometimes called 'Jekyll and Hyde syndrome'. BPD is not bona fide madness, but it has a death rate comparable to some forms of cancer. BPD is called 'borderline' not because it is less than a personality disorder, but for the opposite reason: because it is on the verge of madness. It exists in the shadow of lunacy.

By the 18th century, a few doctors were beginning to study the people in asylums, and discovered that some of these patients had, by no means, lost the powers of reason: they had a normal grasp of what was real and what wasn't, but they suffered terribly from emotional anguish through their impulsiveness, ragefulness, and a general difficulty in self-government caused others to suffer. They seemed to live in a borderland between outright insanity and normal behaviour and feeling.

These people, who were neither insane nor mentally healthy, continued to puzzle psychiatrists for the next one hundred years. It was in this 'borderland' that society and psychiatry came to place its criminals, alcoholics, suicidal people, emotionally unstable and behaviourally unpredictable people – to separate them off both from those with more clearly defined psychiatric illnesses at one border (those, for example, whose illness we have come to call schizophrenia and manic-depressive or 'bipolar' disorder) and from 'normal' people at the other border . . .

At first the students of Freud thought that the talking cure [psychoanalysis] would help all mentally ill people except those who were seriously psychotic. But over the years they found themselves dealing with some patients who were in the same 'borderland' described before: people who were not psychotic, but who did not respond to the talking cure in the way the therapists expected. Gradually, therapists began to define this 'borderline' group not so much by their symptoms as by the special problems that were underneath the symptoms, and by the effects these people had upon others. The symptoms of borderline patients are similar to those for which most people seek psychiatric help: depression, mood swings, the use and abuse of drugs and alcohol as a means of trying to feel better, obsessions, phobias, feelings of emptiness and loneliness . . . But, in addition, the borderline people showed great difficulties in controlling ragefulness.*

Two other symptoms of BPD are self-mutilation and inability to recall autobiographical memories.

* www.borderlinedisorders.com

There is one characteristic of BPD I have not seen in my reading about the subject, which makes the popular name of 'Jekyll and Hyde syndrome' particularly appropriate to Stuart. It is not just that Stuart's personality appears split between peace and rageousness, but that he first became unbalanced because he *discovered* his Hyde (just as Henry Jekyll did in Robert Louis Stevenson's novel), and for a while controlled it and relished the freedom from weakness that this violent side brought. Then he discovered also, as Henry Jekyll describes it, 'that I was slowly losing hold of my original and better self, and becoming slowly incorporated with my second and worse'.

'From the day I found violence,' says Stuart, 'I felt fifty times more strong. For once I felt normal, physically fucking normal, because I had this strength. And after you've been bullied and pushed about, and called spastic, is that you learn at a very early age that violence, and the fear of violence and madness, scare people, and people respect you a bit.'

If he deliberately got himself into rages, he found he could even 'get through the pain barrier' and no longer feel a thing in a fight. 'Yeah, violence and madness, people respect you a bit. Trouble is, as I got older I lost control and learnt it was the wrong type of respect.'

During Stuart's last two years at the Roger Ascham school for the disabled – up to, including and after the day on which he splattered Bobby's face – he oscillated increasingly out of control. If he did well in one subject one year, he set out to destroy it the next. In English:

I think he sometimes doesn't ~~bother~~ to think about his work enough.

Yet, in maths: 'Very pleasing work this year', 'tremendous

progress'. 'A likeable lad, although he and trouble are not
strangers!' writes the head teacher. Stuart was not a natural
delinquent, he believed. 'When he is good, he is very, very
good . . .'

The following year, in English, he 'tries hard'. His 'effort
has been inconsistent', but 'I have been particularly pleased
with his work on play-writing'. But now maths has collapsed:

SUBJECT

Arithmetic: It is such a pity that
Stuart' attitude to Maths is poor. He is
a distractive influence on the rest of the
class, and makes little effort to remedy
his mistakes.

There seemed, from the outside, even knowing about his
discovery of violence, to be no rhyme or reason to the boy.

In fact, there was an explanation for this erratic behaviour,
which is now recognised as symptomatic of a certain type of
distress.

Between these two pieces of paper, Stuart's last two reports
from the Roger Ascham school, his affectionate brother and his
babysitter had begun to rape him.

22

Spring turns to summer. Things do not change. Stuart is given a fresh car and 'wraps it through a roundabout'.

'Truly. The fucking trees was poking out me head.'

He finds a girlfriend. 'Walking back from the pub I was, and she 'twas on the other side,' he says blushingly, using oddly poetic speech. "Fancy a kiss, luv?" I says. And she says: "Yes, *please*!" Mad, in'it? Says she's been bang in love with me since she was a little 'un.'

'What? Through all the troubles? Homelessness? Prison? Care? Is she all right in the head?'

'Wondered that meself. Cor, big, healthy girl, if you know what I mean. She don't half wear me out.'

Mixing Viagra and Ecstasy, in proportions one to one and a half, he has discovered a cure for his premature ejaculation. It makes you 'fucking blow off the walls'.

A second car is abandoned on the A14. He and I and his new girlfriend, who turns out to be a psychiatric nurse, amble across the fields to try to jump-start it, but the engine is dead. For several weeks I pass this car-shaped piece of metal on my way to visit Stuart at his mother and stepfather's pub, where he continues to be under police curfew. It sits untouched in the lay-by as if the owner has just stepped into the bushes for a pee. Then one night vandals set fire to the seats. For a few weeks longer it clings on, blackened, lopsided, aching with burns. Then it is gone. Nothing left behind except three

smudges and a handful of windscreen safety glass, swept neatly
into a pile by the kerb.

Stuart is sometimes full of balm during these months: the plaintiff in the knife attack case has gone missing, the secondary witness is reluctant to testify, Stuart's solicitor has discovered an inconsistency in the prosecution statements. At other periods he is back on the smack, 'doing me nut in': two more witnesses have been found and his barrister has forgotten his name. He has been put on the temporary shortlist for a Crown Court appearance eight times, which means he must ring up the magistrates' office every night for two weeks to find out if tomorrow he will or will not get his day in front of the jury and be sent to prison for the rest of his life. Each time, the fortnight has passed without his case being picked, so he is taken off the shortlist and can relax for a month or two longer. The attempted murder claim has come up again. It looks again likely to be added to his charges.

Autumn approaches. 'If I wanted to find out where the homeless sleep and count them,' I ask Stuart one day, 'where would I go?'

'No use asking me. What might be the place one week isn't used next week because the police have come down heavy on it, or there's building works or someone's upset somebody else and it's fucking madness tonight where it used to be really peaceful yesterday.'

I have an idea for an article, I explain. The city council housing department has done a street count of the Cambridge homeless and found only nineteen rough sleepers. Everybody knows this is nonsense – the figure is a lie, a fudge or an ineptitude. But a lot of reward depends on it. Keep the street count low and central government provides grant money and plaudits; lose it into the twenties and thirties, and central government, which operates according to a sort of Soviet Union–cum–Lewis Carroll logic, withdraws funding and gets nasty.*

* The council's approach to homelessness has since improved. The housing department is now (2005) run effectively, energetically and with considerably more coordination of the various 'service providers' involved.

Cambridge, the homeless, hints of corruption: with that combination I'll be able to sell a newspaper article and make a few bob out of the homeless myself.

Except for one trouble: to do the research I have to do a street count myself. I need to know where the homeless sleep, especially the better hidden places, where the city council might not bother to look.

'Who else can I ask? I've tried the outreach workers. They'll lose their jobs. The hostel staff ditto. Everybody complains, nobody can afford to take part.' There is another reason Stuart doesn't feel able to help me personally: yesterday he tried to stab his stepfather and is feeling the worse for wear.

I have been to several of what are called 'agency meetings' between local-government representatives and charity staff, which follow a sickeningly predictable pattern: preceded by chin-jutting resolutions by disaffected staff 'to tell it as it is', concluded with angry walks back to the office muttering 'and *that's* when I almost said to her . . .' and filled up in between by an hour and a half of toadying.

It is no wonder the government doesn't know what it is about – their control of statutory funding for charities means charities have to toe the political line and no one reveals the truth. Altogether I am at a loss. How can I find out where the homeless sleep?

'Alexander, what are you like?' retorts Stuart. 'Think again.'

I think again and am left with the same answer.

'Ask somebody on the streets. Ask a homeless person.'

It is odd how, even in the depths of supposed concern, one forgets that these people are capable of usefulness.

It was at the courts in King's Lynn that Justice Jonathan Haworth (may the shame of it be inscribed forever upon his memory) directed the jury to convict Ruth and John. It is to the courts in King's Lynn that Stuart is finally to be taken to

trial. The date is fixed, his appearance checked, verified, vali-
dated, confirmed, checked again.

The same people who decided that Ruth and John were guilty
of 'knowingly allowing the supply of a heroin on the premises'
– despite Ruth and John arranging regular meetings with the
police (which the police usually did not attend), producing a
drugs policy that was sent to the police for approval (to which
the police never replied), banning people for even suspicious
conversations that might relate to drug purchases, and on a
number of occasions calling the police to get them to remove
suspected drug dealers from the premises (to which the police
usually responded four hours later, or, once or twice, so long
after the summons that the charity had closed for the day) –
these same sorts of King's Lynn people will also make up
Stuart's jury. It will be the same judge, too, awful in wig and
robes.

We take the train up together.

The lime-green shirt of Stuart's magistrates' court appearance has been replaced with a conservative deep blue item, three
sizes too large. His shoes, his smartest pair, are black Doc
Martens with the scuff marks drowned in polish. Because the
campaign's success in getting Ruth and John released so quickly
has been a mighty slap in Mr Justice Howarth's face, we wonder
if he might remember Stuart and decide to have him executed.

Yet Stuart is in good spirits. He is about to be convicted of
a ghastly, violent offence after two previous convictions for
ghastly violent offences, at a time when the Home Secretary, a
man who shops his own son to the police, swaggers about with
his baseball jargon policy of 'Three Strikes and You're Out'.
After the verdict, Stuart will have one last week of freedom
before sentencing. The term is likely to be fifteen years, possibly
longer. Yet he is treating the whole thing as if we're on a day
trip to north Norfolk to play in the penny arcades. How can
this high-strung, morbidly imaginative man remain sanguine?

The train jangles among the flat, black-rich fields of

Cambridgeshire and we talk about ramming cars into brick walls.

Did I know, he says, that the best stolen cars are 'rung'?

No. 'Rung', as in a missed telephone call? 'Wrung', as in what I did this morning to my towel after I'd dropped it in the bath?

'Nah, r-u-n-g, when the identity's changed. Like, you'd get a car what's a write-off, and go and nick another car what isn't, and turn the write-off into a new one,' explains Stuart with the confident air that this expels all misunderstanding.

'How can you turn the write-off into a new one?'

'Right, insurance companies have auctions of cars what have been written off, cos dealers can buy them to break down for spares?'

I nod.

'So you'd buy a smashed-up Ford Cosworth, go and nick a different car, change all the plates, change the numbers, give the nicked one a respray. If you know what you're doing, you can turn what looks an ultimate smashed-up never-driveable car again roadworthy.'

Clear as second-hand engine oil. Stuart's meaning is, I think, as follows: a) scrap dealers buy smashed-up, broken-down cars at insurance company auctions to use for spare parts; b) thieves can also buy these cars; c) to 'ring' a car (is 'ring' the present tense of 'rung'?) thieves steal a good car from the roadside, take all the distinguishing marks off it and attach the marks to the smashed-up car; d) because the smashed-up, broken-down car with no windscreen and only two tyres now has the good car's identifying marks, you can drive it again.

Immediately, as Bertie Wooster would say, I put my finger on the flaw in the argument.

'So, you've put all that effort in to turn a useless car with one set of numbers into another useless car with a different set of stolen numbers? Why not simply take the good car and change the numbers over to that one?'

'How can you ring the good one? It's fucked.'

'What? No! It's the other one that's fucked. The one you bought at auction.'

'No. *That's* the good car. It's the one you nicked that's not good because it's not legit, is it? Good don't mean *good* as in good quality. Good means good as in will the police bang you up if they catch you in it?'

What a classy misunderstanding. This is what I love about my friendship with Stuart: even the simplest words can spring surprises. It has turned out that we don't understand each other's use of 'good' and 'bad'.

For the next ten minutes I am lost in happy thoughts. The train rolls into Ely then rumbles off again, over the level crossing, under the grumpy eye of the Cathedral, alongside a canal lined with silvery willows.

It's not just 'good' and 'bad' either. I see, when I think about it, that our notion of the word 'car' is also different. If someone said to me, define a car, I'd find myself caught in a long physical description, cautiously philosophical, like Bitzer defining a horse for Mr Gradgrind in *Hard Times*: 'Automotive vehicle, modest in size, carrying up to eight passengers (seated), and wheels, minimum three, not confined to tracks.' To Stuart, the answer is contained in one fact: a car is its numbers. The 'bad' nicked car has been turned into a different, 'good' car because the engine numbers have been changed, usually done by substituting the engine portions that have 'bad' numbers impressed on them with similar portions from a smashed-up, auction-purchased legitimate 'good' car. The hulk of legitimate metal, though it has wheels and an engine and may even still putter along, has now ceased to be a car at all.

Revelation comes with these misunderstandings. Stuart's life and way of thinking momentarily exposed. Like a break in the hedgerow during the country lane part of a journey. For an instant you glimpse scenery you haven't seen before – fields of poppy and cornflower, trees gnarled in the shape of demons. Then it is gone again. You press on, exhilarated.

'What do you do with these rung cars, then?'

'Sell them. Use them for getaways. Depends.'

'How do you sell them? How do you advertise a rung (or is it "ringed") car?'

'Don't need to advertise. People just know. Posh people, cos they've got the money to buy them, don't they? Even people what have been brought up on a silver platter know about rung cars. They just hear about them on the estate, don't they?'

Stuart on top form – again. Posh people on council estates. People so posh they don't just get a silver spoon between their lips, they get carried around their four-bedroom semis on a silver salver like suckling pig.

The boy's a freak, surely.

No. He's not. People like Stuart – the lowest of the low on the streets, outcasts even among outcasts, the uneducated chaotic homeless, the real fuck-ups – people who've had their social and school training lopped off at twelve: they simply don't understand the way the big world works. They are as isolated from us normal, housed people as we are from them. If Stuart is a freak, then it is for opposite reasons: it is because he has had the superhuman strength not to be defeated by this isolation. It is because he has had the almost unbelievable social adroit-ness to be able to fit in smoothly with an educated, soft-skinned person like myself and *not* make me frightened half to death. If Stuart's a freak, I salute freaks.

'So,' I begin again, slowly, 'if I decided I want to ram-raid a place, where would I get a suitable car?'

'You'd just go and steal one.'

'By smashing in the driver's window and breaking the steering-wheel lock by twisting the wheel in opposite directions with my hands and feet.'

'Well done, Alexander,' says Stuart, giving me a look of Gradgrind approval. 'And if the street's too public to use a brick?'

'Then a "jiggler" key. These are ordinary keys, which have been blunted, so instead of fitting into just one car they fit into lots of cars.'

'Exactly. Not fit-fit, but almost fit. You only got to jiggle them a bit and it pops the lock. What if you haven't got a set of them?'

'A slide stick,' I reply smoothly. 'To make a slide stick, take a metal band from a pallet of bricks, cut down to eighteen inches, chop a big notch from one side and three smaller ones on the other. Slip into door panel.'

'Yes, mate.'

'But what if I wanted to get a car that's been rung?'

'You wouldn't get a car what's been rung to go and do a ram-raid with. What's the point? You just go and nick one, cos you'll just set fire to it or you'll burn the engine out and it might get smashed up.'

'I see. So, what next? I'm in the car, in the village, about to ram the . . .' I gesture at the window of our train carriage, imagining that it is the plate-glass shopfront that I'm about to accelerate into and behind it, among the Norfolk reeds and the River Ouse, lie bootloads of pinchable goodies. 'Do I go in front first?'

'No, rear first. You have to keep your head turned away from the window.'

'OK, rear first. Bkkoooowwww! I'm in the post office, boot in the rubble . . .'

'Alexander, what are you like? You wouldn't ram-raid a post office neither.'

Disappointed, I let go of my imaginary steering wheel. 'Why not? You did.'

'No, I told you before. That was a crowbar.'

'My mistake. What would you ram-raid then?'

'Electrical shops, warehouses, little places. There's no point in ram-raiding a fucking post office, because there's never no money in the tills at night and there's nothing else to steal, is there? Take it from me,' he says wistfully, 'gone are the days where a post office might get one big delivery a fortnight.'

An air of nasty stuffed-shirtery hangs over the cobbled squares of King's Lynn. As soon as the train clicks to a stop and the doors open, bundles of solicitors and barristers, displaced from Cambridge, clack down the terminus to the taxi rank. Behind them come the likely lads in shiny suits, surrounded by sallow girls and chain-smoking mums. They wander languidly to the bus stop. The lawyers will return in early afternoon, ciabatta in one hand, mobile in the other. Then the bus of likely lads will also reappear, but minus one or two of the members.

At the courthouse, Stuart's solicitor, the same pink-cheeked, pleasant boy we met in the last courtroom, takes him to a quiet hallway and whispers sternly.

From a distance, I watch Stuart frown, look shocked. My heart sinks. As Stuart's solicitor has often pointed out, it's a miracle that he has got bail at all, especially since his victim and principle witness are both still living in the area, alive and still stabbable. Now the judiciary must have come to its senses. They will snatch Stuart away on to remand and I will spend the rest of this book whispering to him in HMP visiting rooms while Alsations sniff my underwear for heroin wraps.

For a second, I have a sense of 'the System': a terrifying, clumsy, lumbering, inconstant, self-righteous, unself-critical, sloppy piece of state machinery. If it takes against you, you are never safe from it. If it can do what it did to Ruth and John, it can deliver the same outrage to anyone. It puts on a face of broad community concern. It wallows in baggy sanctimony, like American soldiers. It is always brutal in the details.

The police haven't given Stuart time even to put together a bag with his toothpaste and a change of clothes.

'Everything's changed,' Stuart acknowledges, returning at last.

I nod with resignation.

'What you looking so miserable about? We got the wrong idea. It's not the hearing today. It's just an affray charge, what the Old Bill want added, because of me threatening them on the night. They've still got to set a date for the proper trial. I'll have the summer, at least. It might be another six months yet.'

'What about the attempted murder?'

'Nah, that's been dropped. I ain't looking at life any more. It's six years again.'

'So you're not about to go to prison?'

'Course not. What are you on about? They can't go giving bail and taking it away just like that. Thought you'd know that by now, Alexander. This isn't Nazi Germany!'

We return in high spirits. Stuart banters with the woman in the station café and buys me a hot bacon and fried-egg sandwich – the first I've ever had – and a can of beer each, which we slurp on all the way back to Ely.

It is good, I tell myself, to step aside from Stuart once in a while. The homeless are not a real community. They are like a bunch of schoolkids, held together by proximity and pettiness and angst and the rules of tit-for-tat. Stuart's view of them is really no more than another view of Stuart. One needs to shuffle about among them to get a true view of homelessness. This is another advantage of my plan to investigate the claim that there are only nineteen people on the streets. It is not just an enjoyable desire to poke the city council in the eye but a love of truth that means I am now standing outside the city's drug-dealing public toilets at five minutes to midnight, waiting for a suicidal Glaswegian beggar who owns a £600 greyhound and claims to be an expert on Formula One sports car engines, in order that I can go around waking up all his fellow homeless psychopaths and say, 'Hello, I'm here to count you.'

I am covered in layers of thin clothes and have a tape recorder squashed into my pocket. I feel like a deep-sea diver putting on his suit – a social diver, I tell myself.

Another reason for my research is that Ruth and John's hearing against their conviction is due in two months. The campaign has been rumbling on since their release, but it is time to up the pace again.

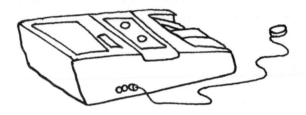

Jesus Green is bracketed by toilets. On the east side is a small car-park convenience, occupied by an old lady who cleans the floor and basins every day and wraps herself around one of the two lavatory bowls at night. On the west, a five-pissoir cottage, favoured by homosexuals, mentioned occasionally in indecency trials. Drug takers use the one I'm next to. It's neatly placed: across the river from the dole office, the Battered Women's Hostel, the Wintercomfort rough sleepers' day centre, the seventy-four-bed hostel on Victoria Road – it's the neighbour-hood dispensary. It's shaped like a cricket pavilion. In the other direction, across the moon-lit park and beeches, towards the glow of the city centre, are the spires of St John's and Jesus Colleges. I stand in the lamplight to one side, looking as idiotically harmless as possible and glancing occasionally in the direction of the amicable crowd around the loos. Different events are going on at each of the entrances. 'Women' is the hot spot. There are lots of ragged bundles shuffling near the entrance of that one, lots of laughter, cans being tossed around. 'Men', on the other side, is dingier, colder – a hint of squalor. It is for the younger ragamuffin. 'Wheelchair' is heavy duty. Every now and then someone emerges from this last cubicle and knits his way unsteadily down the ramp into the dark over the river. No time for a friendly 'Fuck this', 'Fuck that' – just straight off home.

Sam is five minutes late, ten minutes, fifteen minutes . . . then suddenly beside me. A thin, handsome man in his early twenties. 'I'm taking a big risk, doing this.' He indicates the bog moths outside 'Women'. 'If they find out, I'm for it. Police do a raid any time in the next two/three weeks they'll put two and two together and make fucking eight hundred.' He checks my £30 and asks for £10 more.

A scrappy fellow stumbles up and demands £3.

'Three pounds – it's just for *smack* – a bag costs a tenner,' sniffs Sam. 'That's all they think about, tenners. I'll bet you he's only got seven.' To the man: 'Got seven, have ya', mate?'

The other nods.

'This bloke's a journalist, mate. Counting the homeless.'

The man accepts this as a 'no' and clatters off across the footbridge.

'What percentage on the street take drugs?' I ask.

'Two-thirds. A lot of them become homeless because they're on it already. A lot of them start when they get homeless because of the cold. Someone says, "Here, have a toot of that. Warm you up." '

'A dealer?'

'No. Just friendship. Friendship gets you on the smack more than dealers do.'

And boredom keeps you there. 'That's the worst thing about the streets. It's so fucking boring. What else is there to do twenty-four/seven? Who will be your friend, tell you where the food and dossholes are, if you willna' associate with addicts? If you could get rid of the boredom of this life, a lot more people would give up drugs.'

It starts to drizzle. We squelch off across the park, stopping to check on the woman wrapped around the toilet bowl. 'That's your first one. Fucking tragic. The council wanna kick her out, but she's the only one who keeps this place clean. Cleans it spotless every morning.'

Nevertheless, it occurs to me a bit unkindly, bad luck if anyone who's caught short and has to sit there with a female tramp under their bottom. 'I have a friend who used to sleep in the toilets.'

'Ooh, aye? What's his name?'

'Stuart.'

'Never heard of him.'

'Psycho?'

Sam shakes his head.

'Knife Man Dan?'

'New one to me.'

'That mad bastard on Level D?'

Sam pauses a moment, then walks on. 'There's about fifty of them.'

It is while we're walking along Sidney Street that I spot the man himself, stalking ahead in the lamplit street, green puffa jacket, hands in pockets, the modern vision of Mr Hyde.

''Ere, mate,' Sam calls out.

But I cut him short – urgently – 'Shhh!'

We dart off down Green Street. 'That was your second,' protests Sam. 'He sleeps out.'

'No, I know about him. That's Stuart. He's got a tenancy.'

'I've seen him sleeping out.'

'Where?'

'Doorways and that.'

I feel annoyed. Almost jealous. Stuart should have told me. Why has he kept this a secret?

'You must be mistaken,' I say firmly. 'He's in a flat. Been there eighteen months, in Waterbeach. Away from Cambridge.'

Two incidents occurred that night that are important to record.

First, halfway down Green Street, Sam remembered that there was a sleeping spot in one of the buildings. We found the entrance in a dingy courtyard that smelt of vegetables. Inside was a brightly lit garage. Sam immediately began fiddling around the tables and boxes looking for 'mementos' and I found the next entrance, into the half-empty office block above. Here we found a computer and dozens of party things: balloons, streamers, colourful hats, all cast off and lifeless under the light from the street lamp outside. In the corner, three syringes and tinfoil. What happened next frightened me so much that my memory has already become confused about it. We heard a security guard. In the nick of time we slipped back to the stairwell, down towards the garage – and discovered we were locked in. The exit door had been bolted. Sam battered at it with his shoulder. The footsteps of the guard clicked down the steps. Sam wrenched the door handle, saw another door, grabbed at that – locked, too – started kicking it. The guard's footsteps now reached the landing. Click, click, click. One more turn and he'd have us.

When I think that I have now known Stuart for three years, met his parents, sister, social workers, been out with his friends, and studied and thought as hard as I can about his life, in detail, for two and a half of them, it seems astonishing that there have been only a handful of occasions when I have had a genuine sense of what it is be like to *be* Stuart. What's more, they are such apparently insignificant events: unexpected confusions about language, for example. This fright in the office block was another. Sam was terrified. He didn't know what to do. He cowered like a rat.

'We'll have to bluff it,' I said.

'Don't be fucking crazy.' He banged his hand against the door again. 'We'll get six months, minimum.'

We bluffed it. I walked in front, met, at the top of the stairs, the guard, who turned out to be nothing of the sort, just a businessman working late, and asked in my calmest tone if he would open the front door for us. He obliged without a hesitation.

It never for a second occurred to Sam that we might get

away with it. I have never felt before so strongly the fear of insignificance, and the power of a good accent.

In my recollection it was almost the middle of the day as we walked away, and the street full of people. But it wasn't. It was about 1 a.m. The town was empty. The pavement rang hollow. My memory has characterised my relief by filling it with crowds.

The second interesting incident took place half an hour later. Just as we were passing a large group of rough sleepers sprawled on the plastic seats at the bus station, they suddenly jumped up and started stumbling around, threatening to stab each other with hypodermic needles.

'Where's me fucking bike? Gimme me fucking bike!' shrieked a man with a scraggy beard.

'Stupid fucker!' This was Suze. I'd seen her before. She belongs to one of those weird families that are all homeless. Her father, her twin sister, her brother, her uncle: social nightmares, every one. Four foot six, wrapped in swathes of blanket, Suze danced about Whispy Beard as if there is nothing in the world to fear. 'I ain't got your frigging bike! What'd I want your frigging bike for?'

'It was 'ere a minute ago! Give it fucking back!'

'In me pocket? Up me fanny? How can I give it back? Where'd I put it?'

'Oh, fuck, this is all we need,' Sam kept saying. 'Oh, he's got a gun, he's got a gun, he's a *Yardie*.'

Yardie? But he's white.

There were eight in that bus shelter altogether. Overcome with a sudden sense of 'responsibility', Sam rushed into the fray and made it nine.

Not that Suze needed help. She'd got a can of lighter fuel out and was holding the nozzle up to her teeth.

'I'll burn your fucking face off!' She pushed her head forward, ready to spit the 'Yardie' over with lighter gas. With her other hand she flicked a cigarette lighter on and off, while a tall red-headed girl started pogo dancing, and a man with lots of scars ripped off his shirt and was busy trying to add to his collection of skin marks by getting in the way of anyone with anything sharp.

With an equally brutal shift of pace, in an instant it was over. The bus shelter was empty. The rag bundles were already half-way across the park, or through the shopping arcade, scuffing off in their separate ways.

Sam took me across the whole of the city on this night, and again on the next, and again, just to be sure I've got an unimpeachable average, on the third. We get on well. He claims his Gypsy family threw him out of Scotland after he moved in with a non-Gypsy girlfriend. 'She comes from a real posh family, laddie. Wheeee! You should see her mum's house. Worth a million!' He is a patient, gentle, intelligent man.

Thirty-one sleeping out.

We poke under bins, wander into graveyards, look under sheets of plywood in the builders' yards, run up and down the multi-storey car parks, tiptoe among the derelict changing rooms of the public swimming pool.

Thirty-one is over one and a half times what the city council is claiming.

Sam is a first-class guide. He has a strong theatrical sense, not just in the way he's constantly emphasising the poignancy of people's stories – shrewdly telling me lies on one or two or seventy-five occasions – but also in the way he sees himself. He is wrapped up in more defensive pretences than anyone I have ever met. He is a *guardian of his people*, a *man on the edge of being murdered*, a *selfless boyfriend*, an *exile because of his sense of honour*. Never is he just a tossed-out junkie. I suspect that his voice broadens an octave whenever he sees me.

I write the piece for the *Guardian*. It is published as a lead feature a month later.

I am a *Social Reformer*.

'Oh, right,' says Stuart, handing the article back to me.

Does this mean he dislikes it? I wonder, uneasily. He is not given to compliments about anything I've written.

I fold the pages back up and we return to what we had been doing before I first took them out of my folder, namely, waiting to see the Cambridge MP, Anne Campbell. After numerous delays and cancellations, Stuart's appointment has finally come through and we are sitting on an oak bench in a hushed, wainscoted corridor of City Hall.

Me, brimming with journalistic belligerence; Stuart, respectful.

Lower-middle-class vulgarity, the hallmark of British local politics, is stamped all over the place, from the industrial carpet tiles to the soft-drinks machines propped against the oak panelling and photographs of important figures in cheap business suits. Amid this, Stuart is a twenty-first-century David Wilkie painting: determined social outcast, beskinned with tattoos, going to face his ever-approachable New Labour MP with rough, manly honesty – a heart-warming portrait of *true* democracy.

His feet dangle from the bench, not quite touching the ground.

Ms Campbell's private assistant comes out bearing a shiny black folder.

'Mr Shorter and guest?' she snips.

We nod.

'I'm afraid you can't come in.'

We look boggled.

'Because Mr Shorter lives in Waterbeach, which means he is not from Anne's constituency – the protocol is quite particular about that. He must first go to his own MP.'

'But he has an important issue to discuss relating to "Anne's" constituency – it does not concern his own constituency.'

'All the same . . .'

'I am from Anne's constituency,' I pursue.

'Of course.'

'Then that's the answer: I wish to see Anne, taking Stuart as my guest.'

'For that you'd have to make a new appointment.'

'But we already have an appointment.'

'Not exactly. Mr Shorter has an appointment, with you as his guest. To make him your guest, you must remake the appointment.'

She excuses herself back to Ms Campbell, who comes out a moment later and ushers us in. It is a huge meeting hall, smelling of furniture polish, with large oil paintings on the walls and, at the far end, dazzled in sunlight, picture windows overlooking the market square.

Stuart, discomposed, sits nervously, folds his hands, and stumbles into speech at once.

'Right, not being funny, it's about the rough sleepers – the fellas what doss on the street? Right, well, like this year there isn't going to be an emergency winter shelter for them and I'm frightened because that means there's going to be more deaths.'

Ms Campbell gives a look as if she's eaten a pickled onion. She does not like deaths.

'Every year there's deaths. Sometimes more than one a month, and this year won't be no different, even worse, so I think there needs to be some emergency provision, and what scares me is I don't hear the council making no noises about that but they're just sitting and waiting for the bodies as far as I can see . . .'

She gives a second pickled onion.

'See, last year's shelter was brilliant. Everybody liked it. It weren't violent, not particularly, well, yeah, only once or twice, nothing much, and the staff and the customers got on mostly, it was in a sensible place. And this year, there's going to be more deaths than ever – that's what frightens me. Hypothermia, drug overdoses, especially those, you'll find, because . . .'

'Because . . . ?'

'Because there's been two new dog litters, of puppies, on the street.'

Christ to buggery! He's finally lost it.

Ms Campbell tilts her head to one side. Now she looks as if she's testing wines: Shiraz or Cabernet? Chateau Stuart: benefit scrounger or schizophrenic baby-killing drug psychotic? 'I'm not sure I follow,' she suggests.

'Right, not being funny, the homeless love their dogs. They fucking . . . sorry, excuse me French. What I'm saying is, a lot of them, like, they wouldn't give a . . . care if they never saw another human again. Pets is better than people to them. But the hostels don't fu . . . allow it – well, they only got two or three places what are for pets – and they get filled up every night as it is, reglier, which is why you'll find a lot of people with dogs sleeping out, even when there is non-dog places still available in the hostels. But now there's been two litters, loads more people are going to have dogs during winter, and it scares the fuck out of me cos . . .'

In short, unless the government stops their Singapore-style social fashioning and provides an emergency winter shelter *with* pet facility, more people than ever will sleep outside this winter, catch cold, take drugs and come unstuck.

Vintage Stuart. A vast conclusion exposed to have a tiny cause.

Ten breathless seconds between a dog and a bitch sometime in September dictates the course of a whole community's life and the period of its deaths.

Afterwards we do a post-mortem in a nearby pub. Stuart wonders if he was insulting. He thought perhaps Ms Campbell was annoyed. His point was not got across. He twice repeated himself foolishly; he said 'fuck'. I reassure him it is all untrue (except the last one). He made, as he always does, a profound and extremely effective impression. To stop his concerns becoming morbid, I distract him by pointing out an old, muttering alcoholic who is shuffling past the window with his trousers sagging.

'Terry Moore,' says Stuart. 'He's a good old boy.'

'Someone told me he'd once inherited a lot of money.'

'Thirty thousand quid. Some say it were £50 or £100,000. Old girl left it to him in her will, to help him get off the streets, and he just turned his back on his old mates, only hung about the people he looked up to and spent it all on champagne. So when he come back down again, his mates didn't want to know him any more. He was in McDonald's the other day, and I said to the waitress, cos she was about to call the police, "Look, just give him what he wants and he'll go." And he turned on me even though I was trying to help him! He's been in and out of the magistrates' court so many times. They must think: "Oh, no! Not him again! What can we fucking do with him this time?"'

This reminds me of the night I'd been going around with Sam and seen Stuart walking ahead.

'Tuesday? Oh, yeah, I remember! Sleep out? Don't be stupid! Well, nah, yeah, sometimes. Once, last week, when I missed the bus. Well, twice, actually. Not being funny, you don't suddenly become someone else when you come off the streets. Not frightening any more, is it? You've done it so much before, haven't you? Anyway, it's cheaper to sleep outside than get a taxi. Now, can we give it a rest?'

He takes a long drink of beer.

'Funny thing happened that night, though. I was going up to the hospital to fix me arm, what I showed you?' During one of his recent sudden depressions, he deliberately cut his bicep open, almost down to the bone, and the wound had become infected.

'Thing was, when I got there I saw that the A&E was really busy, so I went and sat down outside with me can of lager to wait till they'd calmed down. And a nurse went and called the police on me. I weren't making no noise or nothing. So the police came up in their car and CS-gassed me and arrested me.'

I am appalled, disbelieving. 'What were you doing? You must have provoked them in some way.'

'No. Just sitting outside, drinking. I puked up immediately because I got more of the CS in me gob than in me eyes. Then once it had kicked off I ripped open a can of beer and threatened to cut me throat open. When they got me down the police station, they ripped all me clothes off and, next morning, released me without charge. Mad, in'it?'

Mad? Frankly, it's unbelievable. 'You weren't swearing?'

'No.'

'Abusing the patients? Telling them to fuck off?'

'No. I'd gone in, saw it was really, really busy, then come outside to wait till it was quieter cos my case weren't urgent.'

'Not jacking up? Throwing beer cans at the ambulances? Defecating in the bushes?'

'Alexander! I was just sitting there minding me own.'

This event would keep me outraged for a decade if it had happened to me. It would be the centrepiece for every conversation I ever have for the rest of my life. But it is not serious to Stuart. Two days later he rang up the hospital to make another appointment.

In fact, I have heard another story by someone a little like Stuart (a street drinker, a man who lives in a hostel). He claims he'd had two ribs cracked when he was beaten up by 'security men' in the same place, just sitting by the outpatients' entrance, having a beer.

I tell Stuart about the fight I'd seen in the bus shelter and the gun.

'Really! What happened?'

'That's the thing – nothing happened.'

'That's what it's like with the chaotic,' Stuart agrees. 'It don't work like it does for the rest of the world. The minutes aren't connected together like it is for you people. Every day is like no day and, at the same time, it's a hundred different days.'

Suddenly, I feel annoyed and bang my hands together. 'I should have tried the council estates, too. I didn't look out there. I would have got much more! There must be dozens of rough sleepers out there too!'

'No, no, not on the housing estates,' Stuart replies gloomily. 'The people won't have it. That's where you're more prone to be attacked is on a housing estate than anywhere else. It's all clicky, in'it? Do you understand what I mean? All righteous people.'

He gets out his mobile phone. Last week, Stuart came round to my house in great annoyance. He had just called his son and got an answerphone message. 'It's rude,' he fumed, appalled. 'Really rude. Didn't think he was like that, cos, you know. I dunno. Listen to it! I was thinking he should go into business school! But, now, I dunno. It ain't right. Not at all. You know, really!'

I rang up and listened myself. A proper-sounding, fourteen-year-old boy's voice: 'If I don't know you, go away. I'm not in and I don't want to talk to you.'

'I'm really shocked to be honest,' muttered Stuart.

Since then he's had words with the boy about the importance of politeness.

Now, as we sit in the pub, Stuart takes a long drink of his Stella and rings again, deliberately at a time when he knows his son will be at school. Stuart listens, hangs up, dials a second time, his brow furrowed. Then he dials a third time and hands the mobile to me, beaming with paternal pride.

The young boy's crystal voice at the other end: 'I apologise for not being currently available. Be so kind as to leave your name and message.'

23

'*I say this quite openly, there's never been a day
gone by since my brother Gavvy has been dead that
I've missed him, because he was a monster, and I'm
so glad that it's all over. I was absolutely relieved
when they told me that they'd found him dead.*'

Karen, Stuart's half-sister

Sex:
Aged 12–15

The whole of Stuart's life after the age of twelve acquires a
sexual tinge. In his 'black mists' he is fuelled by his memories
of what his brother and babysitter – and, later, others – did to
him. His sexual relationships with women usually fail because
he finds intercourse 'dirty and disgusting'; his main topic of
conversation about prison is his hatred of sex offenders,
'bacons', 'pervs', 'nonces', 'kiddy-fiddlers' or, to use the Stuart
longhand, 'nasty fucking dirty scum cunts'. Several times he
deliberately lost his temper in jail because the warden mur-
mured something that associated Stuart with child molesters.
Then the riot squad had to grab their shields and clang along
the metal balconies, ram him down to solitary and 'ghost' him
the next day across country to yet another institution.

There are few details to be had from Stuart on exactly what
the babysitter and Gavvy did to him. Gavvy had been touching
him up since the age of nine or ten, 'but at first it was all like
loving. It wasn't horrible, if you know what I mean.' Then the
babysitter, six months older than Gavvy and full of hormones,
joined in. Stuart lost his last prop. His brother, who had previously held him with at least the pretence of a lover, now
penetrated him as prey.

As with the Unmentionable Crime Stuart can be asked about
it only in certain moods, and only on days at the end of an
untroubled week, when he has money to spend from the dole,
so there's a distraction to look forward to in the evening. Pick

the wrong day and the subject puts him into immediate depression; he drinks, cuts himself, and then injects citric acid.

In the last two years alone, my friend Stuart has on three occasions been sitting quietly alone in his flat when he has been suddenly overwhelmed by the resurrected agony of these memories, grabbed the nearest available implement and butchered himself.

His younger sister, Karen, is better controlled.

A slight, taut, attractive woman in her mid-twenties, dark hair pulled back into a ponytail, she has two young boys – Stuart's half-nephews. Like Stuart, she has a gift for unclouded imagery. She sits, precisely, knees together, on the edge of a bed in a guest room above her mother's pub during our interview. I loll opposite.

'It wasn't until four years ago that I finally told someone,' she begins, and immediately pauses to distract herself with a cigarette. 'But I don't want to talk about me.'

Karen's boyfriend knocks on the door. 'Stuart makes all the trouble for himself. He's just selfish, that's what I think,' he says, and leaves.

Karen's son runs in. She is friendly but a little cool with him. The boy grows bored and runs back downstairs.

'I think that Stuart's had a horrendous life,' she begins again. 'I think the reason Mum still pampers him like she does is because she feels guilty about it. I'd say 80 per cent of Stuart and everything he's done is down to what Gavvy and others did to him. He doesn't trust anybody. He's ever so feisty. If he gets caught in a topic he doesn't want to talk about, he can be sitting quiet one minute and he's off his head the next. I'm like that. I'm like two different people. I can go for months and months without thinking and then I'll have a week where I can't stop thinking about it. I shout, say nasty, horrible things. I used to sleep around with men, for attention. I took drugs, dabbled in them, really, for the same reason Stuart did, to forget about it, but then you come back to reality and you come back with a bang. Didn't ever stay in a relationship, wasn't interested. But since I've spoke about it, I've stuck with my boyfriend. I find days when I can't cope with it, and I don't want him even to cuddle me. And some days I need the affection, and I want the cuddles, and I want him to love me. That's me. One minute I'm as nice as pie, and next minute I'm a rattlesnake. In primary school, I was the same. I wanted people to notice me. I used to distract the whole class if I didn't think I was getting enough attention. I can remember my teacher saying, "It's all right, Karen, we can hear you." But when my son was born, I didn't want to be on my own with him. I didn't want people to think that I was doing to him what Gavvy did to me and Stuart, touching him. On a scale of anger, one to ten? I'm probably on four and Stuart's on eleven.'

We hear footsteps on the stairs. They reach the top, halt, suggest leaning forward, someone peering along to the closed door of our room, then creak down again. The sound of this interruption is, it occurs to me, similar to the sound her brother must have made when he came up to her bedroom to molest her. It is interesting that Karen's response even today is to freeze.

'Did Stuart know what Gavvy was doing to you?' I ask.

'That was my biggest reason why I didn't tell anybody, because of Stuart finding out. When I think about it now, the things Stuart said to me when I went to visit him in prison, he was almost asking me. I think Stuart had an idea. But I told you, I don't want to talk about myself. I've never ever been able to talk graphically about it. I was referred to group therapy, went three times and I couldn't handle it. I was normal compared to the others. Young girls, fifteen, sixteen, complete drug addicts. One girl kept trying to commit suicide, and I lost my temper in one of these therapy sessions because she hit a raw nerve, and I said, "Look, if you really wanted to commit suicide that bad why don't you tie a noose and hang yourself? You obviously don't want to be dead, else you would be by now." She'd tried to commit suicide over thirty times. I never went back after that. This counselling was on a Thursday between one and three, but I didn't always want to talk about it then. I don't want to talk about it every Thursday between one and three.'

It was four years ago, aged nineteen, when Gavvy was still alive, that Karen first revealed what he had done to her. Standing in a club one night she'd seen the babysitter (a grown man now) go up to one of her friends and rub against him with his hips.

'Get away from me, you fucking poof!'

'Yeah,' Karen joined in, 'you dirty queer!'

'Hmm*mm*,' he retorted, 'I don't know what you're smiling at. Your brothers liked it.'

Karen had run out of the club, and somehow in her burst of tears and seething all her secrets had come out too. 'And my boyfriend's gone absolutely fucking ballistic, dragged me to my mum's, kicking and fighting I was, and he sat me down and said, "Now tell her what he done to you." So I did.

'Actually, towards the last three months of his life Gavvy had been begging me to tell somebody. And I said to him, "Do you know what Dad and Stuart will do to you?" He said "I don't care." I said, "Do you know what they do to men like you in prison?" And he said, "I don't care, it's what I deserve." And I told him I'd told Mum. And he said, "She's got to tell Dad."

'The hardest thing is not just yourself, because if I'd said something it wouldn't have happened to the other kids Gavvy did it to. But when I was eight years old I was too frightened to tell anybody, and by the time I'd got to thirteen I didn't want to tell anybody because I was disgusted. He did it with a friend of mine. She was staying over, and I heard him come in the bedroom. And I heard his whisper, "Janey," and I heard him get in the bed with her, and then everything else after that

I blanked out. I don't remember, but I remember he got into bed with her, because I heard the squeak as he got in.

'Another night, Gavvy went upstairs to talk to this other girl. She was eight, nine, real fiery, said nasty evil things. She'd hit me, so Gavvy went up to sort her out. And I sat downstairs, but nothing anybody said was going in because I couldn't stop thinking about what I thought was going on upstairs. Gavvy come down and I went up about ten minutes later, and she had her nightdress on and her knickers were on the floor down the side of her bed. And I knew.'

One of the ironies of child abusers – or at least it was so with Gavvy – is that they so terrify and oppress their victims that they get a reputation for being especially good with the child: the only person in the house whom the child respects.

'Guilt is a large part of it,' agrees Karen. 'Gavvy, if he'd done something to me, he used to give me cigarettes or money. For years I felt like I shouldn't have taken the fags and money off him. But it was sort of a good thing for a bad thing. I do often feel like I encouraged it, because he knew he could buy me with fags or money.'

Karen was eighteen (Stuart was twenty-nine) when Gavvy went missing. His wife phoned Karen up.

'He's been drinking and he's gone off with some tablets, I don't know where he's fucking gone off. I've phoned the police and they're sending a police helicopter out.

'Karen,' she added, 'I know what he's done to you.'

'What? What are you talking about?'

And Gavvy's wife gave this astonishing reply: 'Karen, I know what he's done to you and I don't care. I don't hate you, Karen.'

The damage in Stuart's family is not just the number of people whose lives have been poisoned by one paedophile brother, but the corruption of their relationships with each other.

Three days later the police found Gavvy about half a mile from his house, dead, in the woods, 'and they said he really suffered, because of the tablets he took, and I'm glad he did. He hadn't had an excess amount of alcohol, but the tablets he took, coproximal, Anadin, they'd eaten his kidneys and his liver away before he died and he'd have been in absolute agony dying, and I'm glad. I'm glad he suffered.'

Stuart's character crumbled after the age of twelve.

He was studied by an expert on truancy, a former Cropwood Fellow of the Department of Criminology at Cambridge University, an easygoing, energetic man, widely considered one of the best practical educationalists in the county: Keith Laverack. Laverack's Cropwood thesis, 'Absconding from Kneesworth House', written while also still teaching at the school, investigated correlations between running away and build, height, weight, number of siblings, illegitimacy, previous taking and driving away offences, previous other offences, IQ, family structure, number of previous court appearances and reading age.

Mr Laverack made the first clever suggestion about Stuart's schooling in a decade: 'Listen to the boy.' Stuart is not spastic. He is not going to die before he's twenty and therefore does not need to be made ready for teenage years in a wheelchair. The boy says he wants to go to a normal school. Let him go.

Stuart went. He left the Roger Ascham and for six months joined a nearby comprehensive.

He got worse.

Laverack's inspired instruction had come too late. Stuart now used his great discovery, violence, in every new environment, as prisoners do in jail, to ward off all threats, real or fanciful. He and another thug in the making beat four boys to pulp behind the maths class, an incident that Stuart remembers with fondness. 'That worked in my favour a lot. People never called me spaggy legs again after that. The same people who used to be cruel were now cautious.'

'He seemed keen to establish himself as an aggressive and

worldly person since he had experiences of dealing with the police,' ventured the head teacher in his annual report, writing for a second wishfully in the past tense. 'He is quite proud of the fact that his natural father is "inside" and idolises the criminal experiences his father has had.' He boasted that his dad would 'sort out' everyone Stuart disliked. 'Many stories Stuart has written and scenes he has acted out have involved crime and prison.' After six months he was expelled.

Stuart was assigned a social worker – a careful, attentive woman who would drive out, attempt soothing conversations and then drive away again, having made not a jot of difference.

He was sent to an assessment centre. 'An immature lad, with slurred speech and an ungainly stance, 160 cm tall and weighing 45 kg, Stuart has a very poor relationship with his peers, being disliked by most ... Bedtime has proved to be particularly traumatic for him.'

The climax came in December 1981, Stuart aged thirteen. Stuart's mother was in the village, attending a parent-teacher meeting for her well-behaved son, Gavvy: a lively boy, very popular at school. No, not brilliant at maths. English? Well, no, but a thoughtful child, a good lad, a kind boy, even if he did seem recently to have found the Lord and say 'Hallelujah' a lot.

In the middle of this evening, Gavvy came running in, sweating, crying: 'Mum, quick, come home,' he shouted. 'Mum, Stuart's going mad.'

Judith coursed back. Already, in the hallway, neighbours at the house were trying to sort out the mayhem. Glasses shattered, plates splintered, table overthrown. Raging and stamping upstairs. Judith bound up. In Stuart's bedroom she found him. He stood weeping, beating his bloodied fist into the wardrobe. In his other hand, a knife. He went for her.

'I want to go into fucking care! I've asked enough, haven't I? If you don't put me in care I'll do those fucking babies! [Karen and Marcus] Put me into fucking care!'

'Why, Stuart, why?'

So Judith agreed. An hour later the police arrived and took Stuart away.

It would be ten years before Stuart revealed why he'd been so desperate to leave that night. Just before Gavvy had rushed off to get Judith, he and the babysitter had sodomised him with a milk bottle.

In my first version of this book (the one Stuart derided as 'bollocks boring') Stuart made almost no changes to his copy of the manuscript. The few written corrections he did suggest concerned this time, in care homes, after the age of twelve. They read as if he is highlighting spelling mistakes in library

books. *Exfeeled* ('Expelled') above a sentence about Elmfield

School. *not Expelled* ('Not expelled') next to Kneesworth

House. *not School Home* ('Not school home') for Water-

beach. *Remand Hostel* ('Remand hostel') beside Fitzwilliam Boys.

Stuart complains that he has been driven half to sleep by my awful sentences and lack of dramatic structure, but he hasn't put anything on the manuscript to help with that. It is as though only the labels of his past, not the evocations, can be fixed by writing anything down.

'His table manners,' noted the headmaster at Elmfield, 'are poor; throwing food and cutlery around and sometimes spoiling other people's dinner with salt or pepper . . . He dresses with reasonable care although he will often wear dirty underwear. This also reflects his personal hygiene, outwardly appearing clean but in reality, dirty.' When teachers questioned his disruptiveness, 'he would show no response and on most occasions would continue with his threatening behaviour. Then if staff felt it necessary to physically restrain him, Stuart would lose his self-control completely and lash out at any person or object near him. It has been noticed on a couple of occasions that Stuart's eyes were actually "rolling" and whenever questioned later his memory of the previous events has been very poor.'

'I used to go in such a state, just so I didn't feel nothing. Get yourself so fucking psyched out, so you couldn't feel it when they were jumping on you, pinning you down. You just keep struggling, whatever pain or position you're in, you still try and wiggle and get out. I've been tied up in blankets like as a straitjacket, just so they don't have to have so many staff holding me down. The police have come and handcuffed me in Knees-worth House and handcuffed me ankles, hands behind my back, then they used something like bootlace to get the two together, and then they tied a blanket up round me, on me chest, so I couldn't do nothing, then one just sat there and held me head. They always had to hold me head.' His head, he boasts with a toothy smile, 'is me strongest muscle'.

Stuart's old supporter Keith Laverack was now the principal at the next school, Midfield Assessment Centre. With Laverack came hope. Laverack had the intelligence to treat his pupils and their needs individually. He was the social services' 'Golden Boy'. Because of his height, the children affectionately nick-named him the 'Giraffe'.

'But not you, eh, Stuart?' I remark, becoming, as I period-ically do, rather sated with his misfortunes. 'You didn't like him any more than any other teacher who had tried to help you, did you?'

Stuart shrugs and remains silent.

'You know what makes it difficult for me? You don't like spaggy school: understandable. So you get out of it. Your brother was horrendous, so you then demand to be put in a children's home: understandable. What I don't get is that at the same time as wanting these things, you also turned against them and against your mother and your supporters, your parents, the teachers who were good to you. Then, to cap it all, when you are in care you repeatedly run away, *back home, to where your brother was*. Explain that if you can.'

Stuart has no explanation. 'Running away from institutions may represent a compensation for dependency cravings,' noted Keith Laverack in his thesis, 'obliquely revealed by the compulsive way absconders seek out further "trouble" and bring about inevitable re-commitment to institutional care.'

Stuart nods. Might be that, he thinks. Sounds a bit glib to Stuart. 'When you've been brought up in the System it's a very common thing that you're suspicious of everyone and their motives. When people get close, if you've been abused, you often set out just deliberately to wreck that relationship.'

'Oh, this bloody conspiratorial "System",' I say, frustrated. 'Linda, your Outreach Worker, she was part of The System, wasn't she? And you like her, don't you? Denis, he's part of The System, you told me these two people got you off the streets, saved your life. Wynn, your drugs counsellor – another System person.'

'That's not me point, Alexander.'

'Me, when I work at the Day Centre or Willow Walk Hostel, I'm part of The System, aren't I?' I pound on. 'Laverack, he got you out of the school you hated, didn't he? Another System man. Other teachers, I've seen it in the reports, they tried to make life better for you. System men and women, every one. Couldn't you see that? Couldn't you see any of the good? Distrust, yes, I understand, but why all this loathing before you'd even given the people a chance? In fact – no, *wait*, let me finish – your brother, your abuser, is just about the only character in this whole story who wasn't part of The System, isn't that the case? See, you ought to be thankful to The System, don't you think? The System's been the safest place for you. Why not try and be nice about it once in a while?'

A decade and a half after Stuart left Laverack's paternal care, the nationals broke the story:

Kids home
sex sicko
jailed for 18
years

Keith Laverack was convicted of eleven specimen counts of buggery and four of indecent assault against girls and boys.

Terrible crimes 'tip of iceberg'

His actual offences probably numbered thousands.

The 'Giraffe' lost interest when they had turned 14

The prosecutor compared him to Captain Hook, in *Peter Pan*: 'He is never more sinister than when he is at his most polite . . . The courtliness impresses even his victims, even his victims on the high seas, who note that he always says sorry when prodding them along the plank.'

I have now told Stuart many times that he should see the lawyer who has been fighting Cambridge County Council to get compensation for Laverack's victims. This lawyer is someone I know. A courageous, tireless man. He has had three group actions already, secured over a million pounds, and will soon be starting on a fourth.

Stuart shakes his head. He knows one person who gave evidence in a nonce trial to get compensation, and because of the memories he ended up 'cutting himself to pieces and hanging himself'. Also, Stuart finds it hard to be specific about what happened to him, because most of the time he was high on glue. 'One particular time, I'd been sniffing in a wood next to the school. Something horrible happened, but I don't know what. I don't know if it was with a member of staff or not. Sometimes when I used to glue-sniff, I used to see all the spunk over the bag, and you weren't sure if you was tripping or if it was real. Used to make me physically sick.' To some extent he holds himself responsible. 'When I used to get pinned down and they used to touch us up, well, one of the dirty cunts, he used to sit on me, right on me face with his bollocks on top of me gob. It's hard to say it, it's a horrible thing to admit, I made some of the abuse so easy for them because of my behaviour. They could justify bending me up or dragging me off somewhere quiet, to pin me down. Looking back, that's exactly how it feels, is that I created it to the extent that it happened. You've got this young violent little cunt who needs controlling.'

Stuart has, however, read the sneering remarks in certain papers about 'compensationitis' and how, when claimants start making money, it just brings scum out of the woodwork, making up stories, looking for easy cash. 'That can be so wrong,' he says quietly. 'Often, it's only because the victim's seen that other people have got through it, not all of them's hung themselves, that they get the courage to have a go. Them later claimants could be some of the most abused.'

Most of his life, he says, has been spent 'trying to block my experiences at these schools out. Every day, every day, it's like a big war what I'm always losing.'

The closest I have got to details is this: we were driving around the countryside together one day, and we passed the Midfield

School site where Laverack had been his headmaster; Stuart took me down the drive to have a look, and became momentarily confused by the building – a dull, extended, typical piece of nasty council work. It is now used as an old people's home.

'It's different – something's changed. I can't put my finger on it.'

Incidentally, I asked, 'How many times did you run away from here?'

'That's it, that's what's changed, it's only got one floor now. They must have knocked the old structure down and put this one up. I remember now, because I had to tie the sheets together to climb out of my bedroom, because it was on the next floor up. That day was the only time I ever run off twice in one day.'

'Why twice?'

'Because the police brought me back from Girton the first time. The police always brought you back here. That was one time it happened. That's why I ran off a second time.'

'Happened?'

'You know, in the office, after the police had gone.'

'What happened?'

In that chilling way that Stuart often manages to capture the essence of a thing, he says: 'I don't remember the face, only the movement.'

'Not Royston, Girton' he has written on his copy of the first, rejected manuscript of this book, beside the section on Kneesworth School. I had made another mistake in those pages. It was not from Royston but Girton the police brought him back to perform fellatio and be buggered.

24

'There's 365 days a year, all the different things what happen. For someone who's got a pea-brain like me, it's hard to keep anything.'

The Forgotten Years: Aged 0–10

'Going to write a book, are you? Thought so. As soon as I heard your voice, I said to myself, "He's going to write a book about Stuart." That boy has suffered. He deserves a book. You should write a book about me, too.'

Grandma Ellen and Little Bert live in Fen Ditton, on the edge of Cambridge, in a tiny prefab cube at the end of a line of paving slabs: a bungalow, an outsized sugar lump. 'Nan's small; she's always been small,' says Stuart. 'But she knows about me forgotten years.'

Grandma Ellen is sunk in an armchair peeping out over the middle rung of a Zimmer frame that she has parked in front of her. Her face is like a polished string purse. She has got so ancient that she's started to smooth out again.

'Hello, I'm Ellen, Stuart's grandmother. Ninety-three years old: pretty good, aren't I?'

She is the sort who'd be a boon in a war.

Little Bert is eight years younger. 'My toyboy,' she glows. 'Where's our tea?' Bert starts to roll into the room behind me. He reverses happily, renegotiates the door frame and rumbles off into the kitchen.

'So, what can you tell me about Stuart's ancestors?' I begin, lowering myself to fit on a chair opposite Grandma Ellen.

'Nothing,' she snaps.

Aha, then it is just as I suspected: he was brewed in a cauldron.

'*My* first memory is from 1912. Before the war, when I was at home with my mother in Buckinghamshire and she was took ill. We had a lavatory at the end of the garden, and I remember running down to it and looking through a hole in the wall, like this. I saw them through the hole coming to pick my mother up, in a cab and horse and they laid her on the back of it. It was the last time I ever saw her.'

Grandad Bert arrives back from the kitchen. He has attached a special tray of tea things to his Zimmer crossbar; they jiggle nervously as he wheels over the carpet strip. In the 1940s and 50s he was the herdsman in the neighbouring fields. Then he packed away his crook and goatskin cassock and became a bread slicer at a local bakery.

But, like Ellen, he can't say anything about Stuart's forebears. Bert grew up in a Welsh orphanage. His father was a merchant seaman and killed during the Great War. How? He doesn't know. Why? He doesn't know. Did his father die in the water, crossing the seas in a ship full of munitions and bandages, or on land? Bert hasn't been told.

He pours my tea. 'Milk?'

The only story Little Bert offers about his mother is that once he got a message from the orphanage that she had died. So he took three days off work and went to Swansea for the funeral, but as he walked up the road towards her house he found his mother lounging in the doorway with a bottle of beer, uproarious at the joke she'd just played on him, giggling at his bunch of flowers.

Stuart's ancestors belong, it appears, to the forgotten poor. Ellen and Bert were the first generation on his mother's side to step up from the unwritten classes. Anonymity presses in from all sides. Even to themselves Stuart's family is almost invisible.

I sip at my tea daintily. Manly glugs seem out of place.

'Biscuit?' suggests Bert.

When I look up again, Ellen is watching me. 'We haven't seen Stuart in years, you know.'

I do know.

'Lots of years.'

I nod, moving my head slowly and sympathetically. 'What's the point?' was Stuart's explanation to me. 'They're grand, me nan and grandad, but they'd want to know about what I've been doing and what could I tell them? They wouldn't understand.'

'His mother says it's because of the buses. They're not very convenient for coming out to us.'

'He says he would love to see you,' I offer, 'but life hasn't been easy for him recently.'

'I know, I know. That boy has suffered.'

The surfaces of Ellen and Bert's lounge are covered in photographs: their five children, sixteen grandchildren, twenty-seven great-grandchildren and two great-great-grandchildren. Panoramic shots of Midwest prairie, pleasant and inviting in this hot little room, are along the window ledge above Ellen's armchair. Their eldest daughter's American husband is in furniture retail. On the other window Judith, Paul and Karen have pushed forward to raise glasses around Ellen's head on her ninetieth birthday. Glance up during the adverts in *Weakest Link* and you can even see Stuart's rapist: Gavvy – heavy-eyed, hook-nosed – is marrying a buxom lady on top of the television. The mantelpiece basks below a school portrait in an oval mount of a fair, smiling boy: Stuart's son, the Little 'Un.

The only person missing in this mist of family pride is Stuart.

Bert bends down and struggles with a box in a side cupboard. 'They're some of him in here somewhere – just can't seem to get them out.'

'It's because you're so fat, dear,' remarks Ellen. Then, turning to me: 'We used to have wedding photographs of our daughter and Stuart's dad getting married. But one day Stuart come in and ripped them all to shreds. No, I don't remember what day it was. Or what set it off.'

Bert's box, now spilt across the floor, contains hundreds of snapshots. Stuart with half-long, half-shaven hair and broad shoulders. I don't recognise him. His sweater has a large hole exposing his bare arm. He is sitting – late teens – with his pretty, dark-haired girlfriend on a sofa, holding the Little 'Un. The second is another schoolboy: plump, shiny-eyed, do-gooder smile and fine, light brown hair brushed across his face in a sideways sweep. He looks exactly the same as his son above the mantelpiece; shirt collars out to his elbows.

A third, again from school days, is Ellen's favourite: Stuart wearing a glaring red sweater with an edge of pyjama top underneath, his hair unbrushed and dishevelled. He looks charming and not to be trusted. The other photographs I recognise as the man I know. Stuart in his late twenties: cropped hair; stubbled, ruminant jaw; shoulders weak, smile gone.

'And *I* know why he began to change,' pronounces Ellen, almost swankily. 'His brother *told* me. He came round one night special to let me know. No, can't tell you.' She shakes her head playfully. 'Promised I'd never tell. Three days later he committed suicide.'

After an hour, I get up to go.

'We've met as many famous names as posh people,' says Ellen as I say goodbye. She is eyeing me from behind her Zimmer again. 'When I was working as a barmaid, I saw the Prince of Wales there, which I didn't shake hands with. And I had an Egyptian who used to go shopping with me and I met his cousin, which I *did* shake hands with, and that was Omar Sharif.'

Bert has also touched the famous. When he was still at the bread-slicing factory, an elegant Indian boy used to come across from the university for temporary work during the holidays and raise Bert's cut loaves on to the packaging conveyor belt.

'And he was Rajiv Gandhi,' Bert reveals as he rolls me to the front door. 'Ever such a nice lad. He wrote a letter to a friend of mine a while back, which said, "And how is Little Bert?" After all these years! Something wrong with the post over there, though. It arrived six months after they, you know . . . *did* him.

'You never can tell, can you?' he adds, smiling proudly. 'Our families were down, then they come up, then up higher, but some come down again, like Stuart.'

The first decade of Stuart's life is easy to summarise. He does not remember it.

'I blew it out.'

' "Blew it out"? How can you blow your memory out? It's a faculty, Stuart, something you're born with, not a candle.'

'Me mum says it's a shame.'

I have a bad memory. I used to play a game on the train when I left home for the term to go to my school in Hampshire: I'd try to remember what my parents' garden looked like. Half an hour before I had been walking through this same garden, carrying my heavy suitcases, but it still took me ten or fifteen minutes to remember.

'I know the facts, but I don't got no pictures,' is the way Stuart describes it.

'How can you not have pictures? Everyone has to have a picture of what they're thinking about. I mean, if I say "car" it's because in my mind I have a picture of a thing on wheels.'

'Did you have pictures of your garden?'

'No, but that was the point. I couldn't remember. I was trying to remember.'

'Exactly. But you knew you had a garden, didn't you? If I'd turned up and said your mum and dad didn't have one, you'd have told me to fuck off, wouldn't you? That's a fact about it, in'it? That you got one?'

'Yes, but –'

'Like I said. No pictures.'

Even recent events escape him, such as the sleep-out.

'Two years ago? I can't *visually* remember the sleep-out. I know what happened.'

'Can you see the pavement? Do you remember where we were staying?'

'No.'

'What about something more dramatic? For example, the time you threw Sophie in the river. Can you picture that?'

'No. The only thing I know is the river. I know where it happened, but I've got no visual memory of it.'

One reason for this forgetfulness, he thinks, is drugs – legal ones.

'Cos that's exactly what a lot of the anti-psychotics I've had over the years are designed for, to stop you lying there, brooding, going over and over the same things. When I go on a really bad one, start smashing things up, cutting meself, it's because of all the thoughts that are still there, but there's no *reality* to them any more, there's no visual reality, it's just feelings within.'

Despite Stuart's insistence that his 'memories' are like a sequence of written facts projected across the back of his skull – and that even these may not be his own – he often talks about previous events as though he were studying a damaged photograph pixel by pixel. Parts of the image are missing entirely. Other parts are so clear that he will go over the smallest irrelevant detail, such as what colour shoes he was wearing or whether he waited ten or fifteen minutes at the pub before throwing the half-full ashtray at the whisky bottles.

Cycling back through Fen Ditton after visiting Stuart's grandparents, it strikes me how much of Stuart's life is based on forgetfulness. Is this a way to characterise the chaotic: they are people for whom forgetting has become more important than remembering?

Is this just a trite observation? Of course a chaotic person like Stuart wants to forget. He's been raped by his brother, raped by his teachers, bullied by school friends, told he's evil by the social services, spent eight years of his life with his nose stuck in a bag of Fix-a-fix, three more with his veins impaled on the end of a 5p syringe, tattooed FUCK in letters big enough for a road sign down his right arm and thinks the police are hiding cameras in his kitchen ventilation grate. Who wouldn't want to forget a life like that?

But as Stuart himself often points out, lots of people have had similar childhoods to his and still turn out decent citizens.

On the other hand, not all people who are chaotic became so after unpleasantness. A few come from extremely wealthy backgrounds, with kind parents, happy childhoods and genteel schooling. They have no apparent reason to be forgetful.

Even Stuart's ancestors are infected with memory blight. Ellen lost her mother before she knew her; Bert was rejected by his, then rejected her in turn; the paternal side are a bunch of tight-lipped Gypsies who refuse to supply information. And none of them write things down: the father's side, because they distrust the whole process, the mother's because they did not know how. It's hard to think of more ways in which a family can cut itself off from its own history.

It's pleasing that Stuart is their saviour. There's more written about Stuart in the papers, social service reports, police records, and recorded on videotape in television archives than about the rest of the family put together.

Stuart's childhood home is in the centre of Fen Ditton. Number 30 Church Lane: a condemned cottage without running water or mains drainage when he was born. Rupert Brooke sneers at the village in an especially doggerelish verse of 'The Old Vicarage, Grantchester':

> At Over they fling oaths at one,
> And worse than oaths at Trumpington,
> And *Ditton* girls are mean and dirty,
> And there's none in Harston under thirty.

In the 1930s, Stuart's other grandmother, the Gypsy one, a sharp-witted woman, dressed in a shawl, used to come to this village to sell matches door to door. Grandmother Ellen would bring her a cup of tea but never let her into the house. This Gypsy grandmother had ten children (including Stuart's father, Rex) and died young, whereupon her husband, a strict old stick who liked to belt his boys and girls, took to his bed and refused to get up again. Two months later he was dead, too. It was Rex whom the other children followed and imitated after that. They admired his contempt, his under-age drinking, his talent for fixing beaten-up old cars and his waddle. They used to march behind him like a line of young geese, imitating his distinctive, lilting walk. Then, after a few years, the boys (not the girls) discovered they could not escape the procession. They began to waddle the muscular dystrophy walk of their own accord.

In the 1960s, Rex strained his atrophying limbs across the fields from Cambridge to chat up Stuart's mother. He followed the river from the disreputable end of Chesterton Fen Road like Yeats's 'Second Coming', up to the paddock gate by the fourteenth-century church. When the mist buckles off the river in the early morning, Fen Ditton seems to rise from the vapour like a feudal island.

I think about knocking on the door of number 30. It would be interesting to see where Stuart slept. I could stand on the stairs that Stuart's brother leant over and cracked their dad, the unspeakable bully, across the head with a broom. A great moment.

But I don't knock. What would I say? 'My friend, a homeless thief, lived here, and I'm writing a book about him. Do you mind if I come in and spread myself around a bit?' If it had been Newton's old home or Bertrand Russell's or . . . but Stuart's? Suddenly conscious that I have just betrayed my friend, I get off my bike to do a drawing as a compromise.

Stuart is waiting on the steps of my front door when I get back.

'Your gran wants a visit,' I tell him, locking up my bike.

He extracts a tobacco pouch from his pocket. 'Me old nan used to make me laugh, because she used to love a fag, and if

Stuart's mother carrying Stuart. Gavvy scuffing behind.

she hadn't a fag, she'd roll tea leaves. Did she tell you much about me as a Little 'Un?' he asks politely, but without considerable interest. 'She'd know. She was old "old" even then.'

He pauses. 'I'm in court tomorrow. This time for real.'

How does he know that it's not another bluff? It has been a year since Stuart destroyed his flat and tried to burn himself alive. The magistrate said, because of Stuart's state of mind, that this matter should be resolved in 'weeks not months'. Since then, 3 per cent of Stuart's life has passed while he waits for the case to come to trial. Apart from when we took the train to King's Lynn together, Stuart has had one other appearance in Crown Court about the case, and that was also a false alarm: the witnesses didn't show. The Crown Prosecution Service had messed things up, contacted the witnesses too late, or sent the summoning letters to the wrong address. 'Look on the bright side,' the judge had said to the jury when he let them go without apology, half an hour in to a wasted day, 'at least you've got the afternoon off. It's nice and sunny out there. Have a sunbath.'

'But Stuart is adamant. I feel it in me bones this is the one.

Pray to God it's not Howarth.' ('Cambridge's answer to hanging Judge Jeffries' – *Private Eye*.)

Stuart has asked that the judge in his case not be Howarth. Please, Your Honour, not Howarth. No chance of fairness from Howarth. The next morning, Stuart and I go to the court together. It is Howarth.

For some reason I expect drum rolls and banners and flash photography. A man's life is at stake. A family's happiness, a Little 'Un's paternal influence, our friendship, my future as a writer, Stuart's role in biographical history – profound matters are up for question today. Perhaps the press have just rushed away for a moment, like the ornithologist who waits through hail and storm, sun and snow, to photograph a rare bird only for it to flash past when he is peeing behind a tree, or campaigners sleeping outside the Home Office hoping for three days and nights to see Jack Straw, and missing him because for five minutes they'd popped off to get radio batteries.

Before we push through the absent press corps and invisible banner-waving crowds, we wander twice around Market Square, saying, in effect, our goodbyes.

In the waiting room, I work myself up into a little rant. The last time I was in this dingy lobby with empty offices along one wall, which looks like a border crossing into an East European dictatorship, was when Ruth and John had just been jailed. As the sentence was read out, a homeless woman had stood up and clamoured, 'These people saved my life!' Then Ruth's son had shouted loud enough to rattle the cells, 'You bastard, you fool, you fuckwit!' Or words to that effect. Whereupon Judge Howarth promptly had him arrested and made to apologise. People said Howarth had been 'visibly shocked' at the vehemence of it all. He didn't know what he'd unleashed. And we'd showed him – got Ruth and John out in seven months. Then "The System" showed us. Two weeks ago the Appeal Court upheld the convictions. A clumsy, terrible, unjust moment in the history of law.

'Stuart Shorter!' The usher's call.

Inside the courtroom, the visitors' benches are almost empty. There are three reporters on the press seat. The police benches, set off to one side, are nearly full. I recognise a number of faces from the Ruth and John trial.

'All rise!' calls the usher, and Howarth-cum-Jeffries enters.

An hour later it is all over.

Howarth has thrown the case out.

He was, he said – we can hardly remember what he said – who cares what he said? – we are dancing! – it is beyond understanding – isn't the justice system delightful? – what a nice man that Howarth is, what a clever, fine, insightful man! – here, you, yes, you, sitting on the pavement there, here's a fiver from me and Stu! Take it, go get high! Make sure you get Howarth when they catch you!

Howarth said the case should have been dismissed months ago. He said that the police attempt to add and subtract charges in King's Lynn so long after the incident was against all good practice, and, in short, that the whole thing was a ragtag of mismanaged nonsense.

Howarth the Understanding! Howarth the poor man's friend!

I am even a little alarmed.

Are people like Stuart to wield knives and take on the police with impunity?

25

'Whooah! Alexander, you're a maniac! Can't see your fingers!'

I haven't heard Stuart knock. My landlord must have let him in. He's standing in the doorway of my study, legs curved as if he's just galloped here on an Arab steed (not capsized in the back of a Megarider bus), mouth agape, staring at me, typing.

Pleased with the compliment, I hit a familiar phrase and speed up a little more to show off. I imagine my hands blurring across the keyboard.

'Whooah!' Stuart cries again. 'You don't even look at the fucking screen! You just look at the keyboard!'

I stumble to a stop in a pile of spelling mistakes.

He has got that wrong, I say tetchily. A good typist (such as myself) never looks at his keyboard.

He flops into the armchair, beside the pink fan, dropping a thin sheaf of papers on the floor. 'Yeah, sorry', he nods, extracting a beer can from his pocket and drinking half the contents in one giant snatch. 'Aaaaahh!'

Outside, my Alexander Giraud rose, imported specially from Peter Beales in Norfolk, is sprouting pretty pink-red suspicions of petal. I have decided to experiment with artichokes and sweetcorn this season. Three sturdy plants of each are growing in a dustbin next to the larkspurs. Next door, I can hear the clink of glasses and rich laughter: the Professor of Theology is entertaining a visiting bishop in his garden.

The months since Stuart's acquittal have been mixed for

him. On the plus side is his girlfriend, the psychiatric nurse.
At last, with her and Viagra, sex is good again.

'You only need only one pill,' he reminds me. 'A mate of
mine said it worked even when you've been out on the piss,
though not very well. But the next day they'd gone shopping
and the trolley vibrating gave him an erection in the car park
what stayed on him for twelve hours.'

Another mate in Swansea says he knows someone who might
be able to sell Stuart two or three proper tablets (not Internet
rip-offs; not herbal), and there's a rumour that there will be a
large stolen batch available at the Cambridge Strawberry Fair
music festival, £10–15 a pill. Stuart knows for certain that his
stepfather has some put away somewhere in the pub flat, but
he can't think how to bring the subject up.

'What do I say? "Oooh, Dad, will you sell us your hard-on
pills?"'

He worries that it'll do more damage to their relationship
than the attempted stabbing.

On the minus side is Stuart's muscular dystrophy. Because
of his record, the doctors still refuse to prescribe him proper
painkillers – all he has to get him through the wrenches of his
dying muscles is Nurofen. He remembers now a reason why he
used to take so much heroin: it is one of Nature's best painkillers. Also on the bad side: his new girlfriend. The relationship
is tainted by ambivalence. Her night-time energies remind him
of the pin-down measures that the paedophiles in care inflicted.
Her tenderness suggests someone about to eat a meal. Stuart
begins to brood and feel resentful; he wonders if their affair
might end in violence. Val is not as close to the homeless world
as Sophie was, she is not a hostel worker. Homelessness is not
her 'kick'. But one still has to wonder *why* she wants to be with
a man like Stuart – a man so like one of her patients.

So, all in all, the conclusion of his trial – the long anxiety,
months of speculation, constant repetition of familiar facts in new
interpretative guises, 3 a.m. nightmares that it might all come

out worse than ever conceived in the quiet rationality of day – is akin to finishing a manuscript: obsessive rearranging of details, restructuring, dreaming for a few minutes of fantastic success, fretting for the rest of the day about abject failure. Result: when the trial/manuscript is over it's not joy and liberation as people expect. Tension gone, ennui, loss of purpose and a herd of difficulties rush in to fill the gap. The day after his celebration party, Stuart fell promptly into a tedious gloom and said he was going to leave Cambridge altogether. His mind was made up. He was off to Wales to bore them with his problems there.

To be honest, at the moment, none of this particularly interests me. What matters is the pages he's dropped at the edge of my round rug. I know what they are. The first two chapters of my latest version of my attempt at his life: backwards, present tense, 'Tom Clancy' style. He nudges them with his foot. He's started from the beginning again.

'Yeah, I read 'em.'

Ever gracious, our Stuart.

He's read 'em, but he's still not happy. There are bits he likes. My description of his diary, for example:

> Pages stiff with Tipp-Ex . . . indicate appointments made too far ahead, subsequently cancelled, because events take place with startling swiftness in Stuart's life and he can never be certain that, though happy and full of plans on Monday, he won't be in prison, or in hospital, by Friday.

'That's me – you got me there, Alexander,' he laughs. He is also pleased by my account of his furniture:

> There is a single bed in the corner, a chest of drawers, a desk – sparse, cheap furniture, bought with the help of a government loan . . . A 1950s veneer side cabinet, with bottles and pill cases on top, is against the inside wall, and in the corner a big-screen TV standing on an Argos antique-style support.
>
> Stuart likes his TV. He has thrown it at the wall twice and it still works.

'That's good, that. I like that. "Thrown it at the wall twice."
It was three times, actually.'

The thing he objects to is that my sentences don't make sense. I frown.

'They begin on one thing and go to something totally different,' he explains.

'A completely un*related* subject?'

'Yeah.'

I am perplexed. First the way I type, and now every line of what I type. 'You've got to have got that wrong. I don't *ever* do that.' To put it bluntly, I am offended.

'Yes. All the time. Like, at the beginning of a paragraph. It's confusing.'

Stuart squeezes down and picks through the pages. 'Look – there! That bit!' He taps his finger just under the chapter number triumphantly. 'See what I mean!'

5

Homelessness – it's not about not having a home. It's about something being seriously fucking wrong.

2 Laurel Lane: Aged 29

'I put meself on the streets this last time,' Stuart says firmly. 'Just come out of prison: robbery, a post office. Done four and a half years out of the five-stretch because

I hardly know whether to guffaw or beat him over the head. 'That's an *epigraph*, you silly duffer.'

He's been reading it as the first line, and thinks the fact that it is removed from the body of the text is just an accident, and considers me an idiot.

Stuart shakes his head suspiciously. 'Epi-*what*? You sure? Looks fucking funny to me.'

I grab a book from my shelf: *Adventures with Insects* – but it doesn't have epigraphs. There aren't any in *The Official Theory Test for Drivers of Large Vehicles* either. But *Mauve* has them! Stuart's favourite! Good old *Mauve*, biting back at last! I bang through the chapter heads. 'See, *epigraph*. There, *epigraph*. Another one, *here*. There, again, *epi*graph. Don't you ever even *look* at a book?'

In the end I glance up and see that he has started to laugh again. 'Never seen you that angry before, Alexander. It's quite funny, really. Yeah, that's me only objection, your sentences don't make sense. Otherwise, you done well. Yeah, I'm proud of you, Alexander.'

'How about – I mean for the title now – think about it for a moment once I've said it, Stuart, because I think it has a nice ring to it, I mean, it'll make people perk up when they read it, and think "I wonder what this is about?", which is what we want, after all, so don't just dismiss it out of hand . . .'

'Get on with it, Alexander.'

'*Stuart Shorter: Stabbing my Stepfather*. You've got to admit, it has shock value.'

Stuart shakes his head emphatically. 'Definitely not. Me and him are getting on really well at the moment. He's had enough of me stabbing him in real life without me doing it on the front of a book as well.

'Something with "madness" in the title, I reckon,' he proffers. '*Living with Madness*.'

'Too bleak. *Life and Deaths on Level D*.'

'That's cheerful?'

'I can't bear books called "Madness",' I admit, determined

to cure him of this weakness. 'They're such types. Like books with "Daddy" in the title, which drone on about how the author's father was too busy with his prize dahlias to notice them during their youth. I know: *Stuart Shorter: Lock Him Up!*'

Warming to the theme I sip my coffee and stick my feet on the table. 'Then we could have a sequel: *Keep Him Locked Up!*'

Stuart laughs once more. He has a good, dirty laugh, like Sid James, except it's a short burst rather than a continued lewdness. I have decided to put his drinking (an unusual thing for him to do in my room) down to tension, though heaven knows why at this time, when he says he's happy and 'getting it all together' and just about to go out to his little sister's house to try on some shirts. To his delight, he's to be best man at her wedding later this month.

Encouraged that he is starting to relax at last I get carried away. 'What about *The Ten Best Solitary Confinement Cells of Great Britain* or *How to Screw Your Life Up in Three Easy Lessons*? I know: *Knives I Have Known.*'

Why I Dangle Me Little 'Un Out of Me Kitchen Window – I manage to stop myself in time before I say that one.

'Nah, don't like any of them. Let me think about it. I'll write some down for when we next meet, OK?'

Out comes the squashy diary and we decide on next Wednesday. 'I'll tell you what, I wanted to ask if I could borrow £20.'

'Of course you can.'

'I'll pay you back.'

'Of course you will.' He always does.

'It's just I need . . .'

'No need to explain, Stuart. You borrow money off me when you need it. I borrow money off you when I need it. What's the fuss about?'

'Thanks. Appreciated.'

I hand over the cash and he stands up to go through his usual departing ritual of returning the odds and ends of cigarette papers and tobacco and diary into his pocket, together with the items that have spilt on to the armchair seat during his stay, then in goes the opened beer can, too, into the other pocket.

I offer to give him a lift.

'Yes, if you don't mind. Thanks. Feeling a bit weak today. Not too much trouble?'

'Depends where you need to go.'

He knows full well I'd drive him to Edinburgh if he asked. This is not just friendship speaking, but the fact that I now own his old car with the sticky blobs, which he has sold to me for £275, plus alloy wheels, a £25 discount on what he was planning to raise.

'Only into town. The King's Street Run.' A pub.

Going outside, Stuart grapples down the steps through my buddleia, edges into the car and drops the last few inches with a bounce.

'You know, Alexander, I don't know meself how I got to be like this,' he remarks as we drive beside the river, then cross the bridge past the Wintercomfort Day Centre where, at that Ruth and John campaign meeting, years ago, Stuart first encountered his 'middle-class people'. 'It's too easy to blame, in'it? Sometimes, I think I'm the child of the Devil. Honestly, I do believe that. I've invited the Devil in, and now I can't get him out. I've tried burning him out and cutting him out and he don't take no notice. Why should he? He doesn't want to be homeless. He's got me. Little, skinny, violent me.'

We drive by the public toilets where Keith Laverack was once caught soliciting, at just about the time when he was headmaster of Stuart's old school. Stupid man, he tried it on with an undercover policeman. Not that that stopped the council employing him as an overseer of young boys.

'Do you think,' I ask, not knowing quite how to phrase the question at first, 'do you think – is your unpleasant lifestyle due to something particular about you?'

Stuart juts out his jaw to consider the idea. 'I don't know. It's something I'm quite philosophical about. Some people have grown up, have learnt to cope and accept and have been very successful, and led a very, in brackets, normal competitive life. And then I've met so many people who've led the same sort of lifestyle as I have and had the same sort of childhood and experiences and they're torn to pieces.'

'So, if you had to change one thing, just one thing to make it right, what would it be?'

'Same answer. Don't know. Changing one thing? How much is one thing? Change me brother – does that change me getting rageous? The muscular dystrophy? That don't change the nonces, the System, do it? It's such a mess. Not being funny, change one and you got to change them all. Be easier just to change me.'

We reach the pub down a couple of backstreets and I pull over as near to the door as possible.

I turn to face him, rather hoping that he'll suddenly remember that his sister has invited me to the wedding too. I'd like to see him got up in shirt and tails like a penguin, tattoos poking out beyond the cuff links. But if she has asked him to invite me, he's forgotten about it.

'You know,' I remark as he prepares to haul himself back on to the pavement, 'we have come to the end of this book, and there's still one question left.'

'What's that, mate?'

'Can't you guess?'

'No, mate,' he says, squeezing around on the seat to pick up the infernal Rizlas that have dropped out of his pocket once again. I love that word, 'mate'. Stuart uses it with me very rarely.

'What's your date of birth?'

'Right,' he says, cheerfully, as if our hundreds of hours of conversation are about to start at the beginning again. 'Right. I'm Stuart Clive Shorter, born 19th of the 9th, 1968 . . .'

'So you're thirty-three, aren't you?'

'I'm thirty-three. Getting older, as they say. I lead a very controversial, unpleasant life.'

Stuart and Gavvy

EPILOGUE

Stuart's body was blasted fifty feet through the air when the
11.15 London to King's Lynn train hit him, just outside his
home village of Waterbeach. His corpse spun across the upland
tracks and crashed down among the scrub and discarded crisp
packets in the cess alongside the line. A hundred yards further
on, the train engine and its two carriages finally came to a stop
in the midnight summer air.

For a moment, I believe, there was a stillness. A shocking
realisation by all things – beetles, dormice, the spiders spinning
their webs in the moonlight, even the hot metal of the tracks
and the wind in the trees – that Death had just shrieked past
like a stinking black eagle and made off with a remarkable man.
Only the passengers in the train carriages did not know what
had happened. The light from their windows fell in yellow
stripes and lit up a hint of fields.

Then came the crunch of gravel as the Balfour Beatty workman who'd been checking signals nearby walked along the
embankment, curious to understand why this train – known as
the 'graveyard' service, because it was the last one of the night
– had come to an unscheduled stop. He discovered Stuart's
shoe lying by one of the rails. Poking his torch beam among the
brushwood, he spotted what was left of the man.

Stuart's trousers had split open and slipped to his ankles.
His forehead was caved in. Out of an old-fashioned sense of
politeness, the Balfour Beatty workman covered the body with

his coat and then did what everyone has always done in matters concerning Stuart: he called the police.

Of course everyone thought it must have been suicide. There was a bitter, pessimistic satisfaction in thinking that his life had been melodramatic and tragic to its last split second. But in fact there was no good specific reason to believe that it was.

In the afternoon before his death Stuart had been at his sister's house, happily trying on the shirts for her wedding, and he'd told his mother that he thought at last his life was 'coming together'.

The major injury, to the left side of his forehead, also argued against suicide. It suggested that he had been walking right to left when the train hit him, which meant that he had been heading home, in the direction of his flat. The coroner's rather heartless contribution to the debate was to observe as well that Stuart had not been 'splattered' when he died. The coroner had seen train suicide cases before and in general they were 'splattered'. Some people, for example, simply kneel between the tracks and watch their death pound up the line to hit them. They are the sort that are 'splattered'.

Sitting immediately below the coroner as he kept repeating this appalling word, Judith did not appear to flinch.

Stuart's mother is another hero of this story. Throughout the horrors, Judith has kept her head up, remained loyal and protective, even when that has meant tearing herself into two contradictory positions, such as over the urge to defend and love both her eldest son and Stuart – the predator and the prey. To me, this explains why a sort of glaze comes over her when, during interviews, the conversation gets deeply into the subject of Stuart's misfortunes. Where else, except in vagueness, can a person hide from thirty years of failed justifications and untenable arguments?

Some discussion was also occasioned by the fact that Stuart's hands were lifted to shoulder height, suggesting, perhaps, someone about to push something away – a 150-ton train, in other words. This gesture, the coroner seemed to think, might have been preserved from the moment Stuart had been hit, undisturbed by his entire flight through the air and crash landing.

'He had raised his arms, like this?' asked the coroner, putting up his own hands, pulsing them back and forth and looking up with a grimace. 'Perhaps to protect himself?'

'Yes,' agreed the train driver, who repeated the gesture, except that his arms were still and his expression almost blank. He recollected that just before the collision Stuart had looked up and caught his eye.

The jury returned an open verdict: neither suicide nor accident, but unfathomable.

The homeless and the addicts came to Stuart's funeral, even though it was held in Midston, which is ten miles out of Cambridge, and a number of the more befuddled ones got scattered about in villages elsewhere because they'd got into the wrong buses.

After the service, a crowd gathered by the grave. It is not a pauper's grave. It is the sort of grave that ordinary people dream of: under the boughs of a horse chestnut, in the company of yews and flocks of rooks, in a Norman churchyard. Beyond the aged wall that borders this blissful cemetery the hills and copses rise like waves. Stuart had made himself a popular figure during the last three years of his life – and the homeless and the addicts paid their respects by throwing on to the coffin lid the things they said he'd need for the journey ahead: a packet of Rizlas and a pouch of tobacco containing some cannabis.

It is to these good friends of Stuart's that the last scene of this book must go. They stayed behind long after the rest of us mourners had left the cemetery. From the nearby primary school they pinched a bench and dragged it to the graveside, then they opened up a full crate of beer and had a party. There was dancing and singing and speeches. One of them took off his T-shirt and passed it round; all the celebrants scrawled farewell messages on it then laid it across the mound. There was a ghetto blaster playing Stuart's favourite punk music from the 1970s.

Over the road, Judith could hear this primordial fiesta from her bedroom until late in the night; it must have kept dozens of her neighbours in despair of ever getting to sleep. But they all knew Stuart and had followed him and his exploits from birth. So no one complained.

The next morning, before the vicar could spot her, she crept up to the grave and removed the cans and needles.

ACKNOWLEDGEMENTS

My deepest and most important thanks are to Dido Davies. She has read the manuscript of this book a thousand times and agonized over every aspect, from the overall structure to the nuance of each word. Without her inventiveness, humour, encouragement and our endless boozy battles on my balcony in Cambridge – come rain, sun or snow – I would not have got past the first pages.

How many other people there are! To Stuart's mother, Judith, I owe thanks for Stuart himself. To her daughter, Karen, Stuart's half-sister: I understand Stuart's pride in you. Both Karen and Judith allowed me to interview them extensively about often difficult subjects. Their information has been essential to the book. To Stuart's grandparents, I am grateful for much of the material in Chapter 24. My mother, Joan Brady, has been marvellous with professional literary advice, delightful enthusiasm and a gift of a laptop computer.

Ruth Wyner's defiance, relentlessness and refusal ever to be knocked down have been an inspiration. Gordon Bell, the kind, subtle manager of Willow Walk hostel for the homeless, has given me a great insight into homelessness (as also have, of course, the many residents – the friendly, the fascinating and the not so friendly – who live at Willow Walk, and the other staff I worked with during the time I was writing *Stuart*.) John Brock was nearly destroyed by the judicial attack on both his reputation and his belief in fairness, and from him I got my greatest and most eloquent sense of impotence and fury that injustice inspires. Andrew Grove, the unstoppable lawyer who has done so much to get compensation for children who, like Stuart, were abused in 'special' schools around Cambridge – he deserves applause just for what he does. Austen Davies: I am forever in his debt for his legacy of £10,000 that enabled me to take time off work to run the Campaign to Free Ruth and John, and then to start work on this book, four years ago.

Havovi Ankelsaria, Linda Bendall, Sarah Burbidge, James Cormick, Xanthe Dennis (aged 13), for picking up my spelling mistakes, Denis Hayes, Cathy Hembry, Catherine Hurley, Jenny Mace, Graeme Mitchison, Catrin Oliver, Rodney Palmer – all read the manuscript and made valuable suggestions. (Catrin read it twice.) I am also grateful to Wynn Turley, QEST, and Anabel and Andrew Turtle for their help with information and advice.

In 2003, The Arts Council awarded me a Writers Award for the first three chapters of *Stuart*. This startling recognition (and £7000) did more than almost anything else to boost my confidence in the last year of writing and helped me to secure my agent, Peter Straus, who is responsible both for the subtitle, *a life backwards*, and for capturing the attention of my calm, shrewd editor at Fourth Estate, Nicholas Pearson. I am also grateful for the support of Mitzi Angel. Julian Humphries arranged the cover and Vera Brice designed the elegant page layout.

Both the Society of Authors Contingency Fund and the Author's Foundation have provided valuable encouragement, in the form of hardship grants of £500 and £1000. I am particularly indebted to the excellent Cambridgeshire Collection at Cambridge Central Public Library for research material, and to Cambridge University Library for providing a pleasant place to work when my own study became too sickeningly familiar.

The people who were involved in the Campaign Committee to release John and Ruth enabled me in different ways to understand that a book about Stuart was important: Louise Brock, David Brandon, Jim and Angela Brown, Julie Crocker (the invaluable Campaign secretary), John Hipkin, Michelle Howard, Sarah Jones, Rodney Keen, Hilary Johnys, Sharon Khazna, Bob Lucas, Andria Efthimiou-Mordaunt, David Mckay, Pat McCafferty, Nicky Padfield, Drew Park, Colin Shaw.

Diana Allan and Curtis Brown: it was while staying at their house in Cortona that I realised how to do Chapter 11, which had been causing me endless trouble. My landlord Dr Simon Norton was ceaselessly tolerant about my always-late rent and my messy habits; Robin Sarin has been a constant support. Clare Sproston did splendid work typing up many of my initial interviews with Stuart.

Finally, and with my love, Flora Dennis: from Milford-on-Sea to Florence to Springfield, Illinois (where we sorted out the chronological difficulties of Chapter 3) she has filled my time away from the manuscript with excitement and happiness.

Grateful acknowledgement is made for the use of the following:

'Three questioned following robbery' (29 June, 1993) and 'Bubblegum king stuck behind bars' (24 September, 1993), both from the *Peterborough Evening Telegraph*.

A short passage from *From the Inside: Dispatches from a Women's Prison*, by Ruth Wyner, published by Aurum Press, 2003.

'Liquor trouble at jail', published in *The Times*, 23 December, 1993.

'Jailed man told: Illness no excuse for crime' (January 2nd, 1973) and the portion of the final edition headline 'FREED' (11 July, 2000), both from the *Cambridge Evening News*.

'Charity pair are freed to appeal over heroin case', published in *The Daily Telegraph*, 12 July, 2000.

'Punk does a bunk to join Mullah's army', by Fiona Wyton, published in *The People Magazine*, 3 December, 1989.

4th Estate Matchbook Classics

In the mid-twentieth century, the matchbox industry was booming. Matchboxes became the host of tiny canvases which displayed a range of ideas: foxes skipping through Polish forests, celebrations of Russia's space race successes, orchards coming into blossom. Such micro-masterpieces serve as the inspiration for the new 4th Estate Matchbook Classics series. The ten books – novels, memoirs and one very unusual biography – are some of the best loved and most admired that 4th Estate has published, each of them as unique as the matchbox that inspired its cover.